Autodesk Fusion 360

Black Book

(V 2.0.6508) Part 1

By
Gaurav Verma
Matt Weber
(CADCAMCAE Works)

ISBN # 978-1-988722-70-2

DEDICATION

To teachers, who make it possible to disseminate knowledge
to enlighten the young and curious minds
of our future generations

To students, who are the future of the world

THANKS

To my friends and colleagues

To my family for their love and support

Table of Contents

Part 1

Chapter 1: Starting with Autodesk Fusion 360

Chapter 2 : Sketching

Chapter 6 : Solid Editing

Chapter 7 : Assembly Design

Chapter 8 : Importing Files and Inspection

Chapter 9 : Surface Modeling

Part 2

Chapter 12 : Sculpting

Chapter 13 : Sculpting-2

Chapter 14 : Mesh Design

Chapter 20 : Introduction to Simulation in Fusion 360

Chapter 21 : Simulation Studies in Fusion 360

Chapter 22 : Sheetmetal Design

Preface

Autodesk Fusion 360 is a product of Autodesk Inc. Fusion 360 is the first of its kind software which combine 3D CAD, CAM, and CAE tool in single package. It connects your entire product development process in a single cloud-based platform that works on both Mac and PC. In CAD environment, you can create the model with parametric designing and dimensioning. The CAD environment is equally applicable for assembly design. The CAE environment facilitates to analysis the model under real-world load conditions. Once the model is as per your requirement then generate the NC program using the CAM environment.

The **Autodesk Fusion 360 Black Book** (V 2.0.6508) is third edition of our series on Autodesk Fusion 360. The book is updated on Autodesk Fusion 360 Ultimate, Student V 2.0.6508. With lots of features and thorough review, we present a book to help professionals as well as beginners in creating some of the most complex solid models. The book follows a step by step methodology. In this book, we have tried to give real-world examples with real challenges in designing. We have tried to reduce the gap between educational use of Autodesk Fusion 360 and industrial use of Autodesk Fusion 360. This edition of book, includes latest topics on Sketching, 3D Part Designing, Assembly Design, Rendering & Animation, Sculpting, Mesh Design, CAM, Simulation, Sheetmetal, 3D printing, 3D PDFs, and many other topics. The book covers almost all the information required by a learner to master the Autodesk Fusion 360. The book starts with sketching and ends at advanced topics like Manufacturing, Simulation, and Animation. Some of the salient features of this book are :

In-Depth explanation of concepts

Every new topic of this book starts with the explanation of the basic concepts. In this way, the user becomes capable of relating the things with real world.

Topics Covered

Every chapter starts with a list of topics being covered in that chapter. In this way, the user can easy find the topic of his/her interest easily.

Instruction through illustration

The instructions to perform any action are provided by maximum number of illustrations so that the user can perform the actions discussed in the book easily and effectively. There are about **1930** small and large illustrations that make the learning process effective.

Tutorial point of view

At the end of concept's explanation, the tutorial make the understanding of users firm and long lasting. Almost each chapter of the book has tutorials that are real world projects. Moreover most of the tools in this book are discussed in the form of tutorials.

Project

Free projects and exercises are provided to students for practicing.

For Faculty

If you are a faculty member, then you can ask for video tutorials on any of the topic, exercise, tutorial, or concept.

Formatting Conventions Used in the Text

All the key terms like name of button, tool, drop-down etc. are kept bold.

Free Resources

Link to the resources used in this book are provided to the users via email. To get the resources, mail us at **cadcamcaeworks@gmail.com** with your contact information. With your contact record with us, you will be provided latest updates and informations regarding various technologies. The format to write us mail for resources is as follows:

Subject of E-mail as **Application for resources of _____ book**.
Also, given your information like
Name:
Course pursuing/Profession:
E-mail ID:

Note: We respect your privacy and value it. If you do not want to give your personal informations then you can ask for resources without giving your information.

About Authors

The author of this book, Gaurav Verma, has authored and assisted in more than 16 titles in CAD/CAM/CAE which are already available in market. He has authored **AutoCAD Electrical Black Books** which are available in both **English** and **Russian** language. He has also authored books on various modules of Creo Parametric and SolidWorks. He has provided consultant services to many industries in US, Greece, Canada, and UK. He has assisted in preparing many Government aided skill development programs. He has been speaker for Autodesk University, Russia 2014. He has assisted in preparing AutoCAD Electrical course for Autodesk Design Academy. He has worked on Sheetmetal, Forging, Machining, and Casting designs in Design and Development departments of various manufacturing firms.

If you have any query/doubt in any CAD/CAM/CAE package, then you can contact the authors by writing at cadcamcaeworks@gmail.com

For Any query or suggestion

If you have any query or suggestion, please let us know by mailing us on *cadcamcaeworks@gmail.com*. Your valuable constructive suggestions will be incorporated in our books.

Chapter 1

Starting with Autodesk Fusion 360

Topics Covered

The major topics covered in this chapter are:

- *Overview of Autodesk Fusion 360*
- *Installing Autodesk Fusion 360 (Educational)*
- *Starting Autodesk Fusion 360*
- *File Menu*
- *User Account drop-down*
- *Data Panel*
- *Simulation Browser*

OVERVIEW OF AUTODESK FUSION 360

Autodesk Fusion 360 is an Autodesk product designed to be a powerful 3D Modeling software package with an integrated, parametric, feature based CAM module built into the software. Autodesk Fusion 360 is the first of its kind 3D CAD, CAM, and CAE tool. It connects your entire product development process in a single cloud-based platform that works on both Mac and PC; refer to Figure-1.

Figure-1. Overview

It combines mechanical design, collaboration, simulation, and machining in a single software. The tools in Fusion 360 enable rapid and easy exploration of design ideas with an integrated concept to production toolset. This software needs a good network connection to work in collaboration with other team members.

This software is much affordable than any other software offered by Autodesk. To use this software, one need to pay the monthly subscription of Fusion 360. You can work offline in this software and later save the file on Autodesk Server. User can access this software from anywhere with an internet connection. The user is able to open the saved file and also able to share files with anyone from anywhere as long as he/she has the software and good internet connection. Also, the pricing of this software is cost effective so anyone can use it for manufacturing of tools and parts. Autodesk Fusion 360 is build to work in multi body manner: both parts and assemblies build in a single file. The procedure to install the software is given next.

INSTALLING AUTODESK FUSION 360 (STUDENT)

• Connect your PC with the internet connection and then log on to **http://www.autodesk.com/products/fusion-360/students-teachers-educators** as shown in Figure-2.

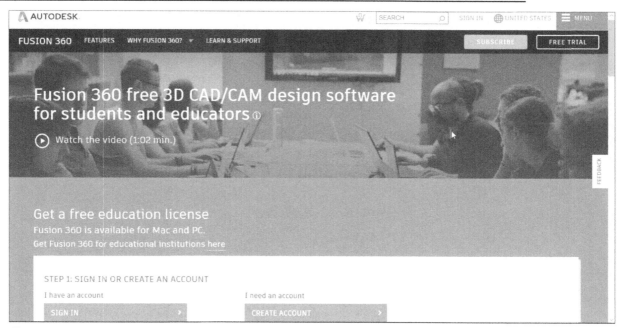

Figure-2. Autodesk Website

- Click on the **Create Account** button and on next page, select your Country and Education role. In **Education role** drop-down, you need to select **Student** (There is free subscription for students with license term of 3 years) as shown in Figure-3.

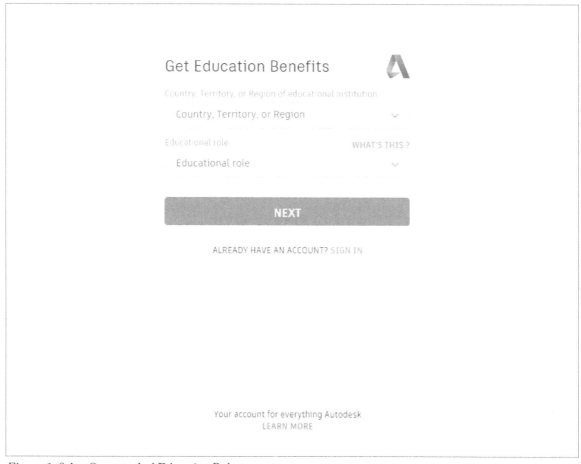

Figure-3. Select Country And Education Role

- After filling the details, click on **NEXT** button. The next page of this website opens. In this page, you need to fill your personal details and then click on **Create Account** as shown in Figure-4.

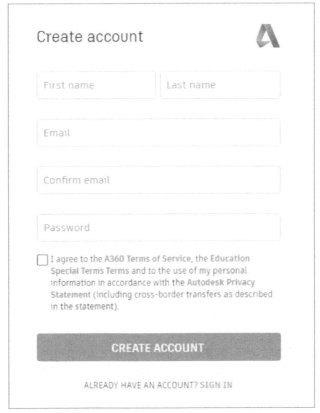

Figure-4. Creating account

- After creating account, you need to verify your E-mail address by login into your E-mail account. After verifying E-mail address, you need to give your **Education details**.
- After completion of these processes, you need to sign-in your Autodesk Account and search the **Autodesk Fusion 360 software**.
- Download the **Autodesk Fusion 360 software**.
- Open the download setup file and follow the instructions as per the setup instruction.
- The software will be installed in a couple of minutes.

STARTING AUTODESK FUSION 360

- To start **Autodesk Fusion 360** from **Start** menu, click on the **Start** button in the **Taskbar** at the bottom left corner and then select Autodesk Fusion 360 option from the **Autodesk** folder. Select the Autodesk Fusion 360 icon; refer to Figure-5.

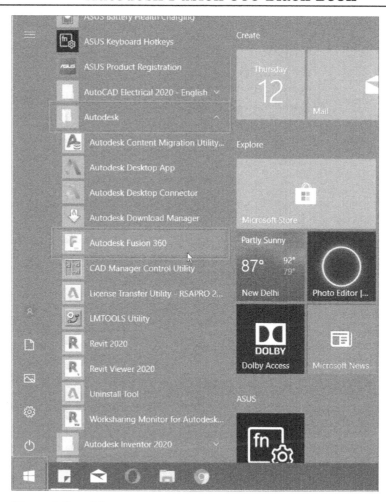

Figure-5. Start Menu

- While installing the software, if you have selected the check box to create a desktop icon then you can double-click on that icon to run the software.
- If you have not selected the check box to create the desktop icon and want to create the icon on desktop now in Windows 7, then right-click on the **Autodesk Fusion 360** icon in the **Start** menu and select the **Send To-> Desktop(Create icon)** option from the shortcut menu displayed. If you are using Windows 8 or later then drag the Autodesk Fusion 360 icon from **Start** menu to Desktop.

After clicking on the icon, the Autodesk Fusion 360 software window will be displayed; refer to Figure-6.

Figure-6. Autodesk Fusion 360 Application Window

STARTING A NEW DOCUMENT

*   Click on the **File** drop-down and select the **New Design** tool as shown in Figure-7. A new document will open.

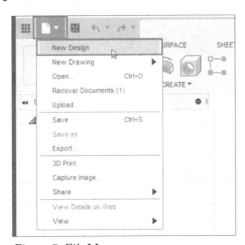

Figure-7. File Menu

*   Select the desired workspace from the **Workspace** drop-down; refer to Figure-8.

Figure-8. Workspace Drop Down

- There are six buttons available in **Workspace** drop-down in Educational version; **DESIGN, RENDER, ANIMATION, SIMULATION, MANUFACTURE,** and **DRAWING.**

- The **DESIGN** button is used to create solid, surface and sheet metal designs.

- The **RENDER** button is used to activate workspace for rendering realistic model for presentation.

- The **ANIMATION** button is used to activate workspace for creating automatic or manual exploded views as well as direct control over unique animation of parts and assemblies.

- The **SIMULATION** button is used to perform Engineering Analyses.

- The **MANUFACTURE** button is used to generate G-codes for manufacturing process like turning, milling, drilling cutting, probing, and so on.

- The **DRAWING** button is used for generating drawings from model and animation.

If you are working on Professional version of software then another workspace **GENERATIVE DESIGN** is also available using which you can generate different iterations of designs based on specified limits and goals.

You will learn more about these work-spaces later in this book.

FILE MENU

The options in the **File** menu are used to manage files and related parameters. Various tools of **File** menu are discussed next.

Creating New Drawing

The tools in **New Drawing** drop-down are used to initialize a new drawing from animation or design; refer to Figure-9. The methods to use these tools will be discussed later in the book.

Figure-9. New Drawing

Opening File

The **Open** tool is used to open files earlier saved in cloud or local drive. You can also use this tool to import supported files of other software. The procedure to use this tool is given next.

- Click on the **Open** tool from the **File** menu or press **CTRL+O** from keyboard. The **Open** dialog box will be displayed; refer to Figure-10. Note that we are working in online mode of Autodesk Fusion.

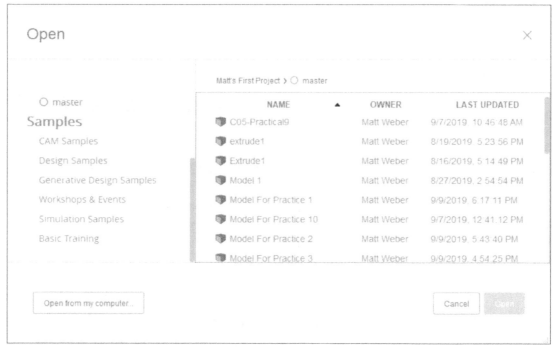

Figure-10. Open dialog box

- By default, files saved on cloud are displayed in the dialog box. Select the desired file and click on the **Open** button. The file will open in Autodesk Fusion.
- If you want to open a file stored in local drive then click on the **Open from my computer** button. The **Open** dialog box will be displayed; refer to Figure-11.

Figure-11. Open dialog box

- Select the desired file and click on the **Open** button. The file will be displayed in the application window. If you have selected file of different format from native format then the **Job Status** dialog box will be displaying notifying you the status of file import; refer to Figure-12.

Figure-12. Job Status dialog box

- Once the status of import is complete then click on the **Open** button from the **Action** column in the dialog box. The model will be displayed; refer to Figure-13 (Creo Parametric file imported in Fusion 360).

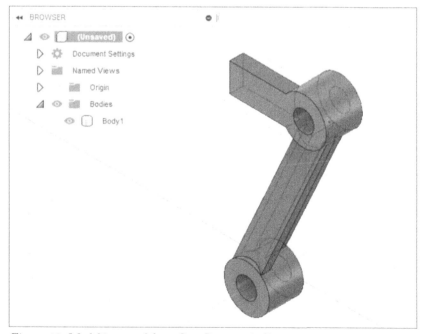

Figure-13. Model imported from Creo Parametric file

Recovering Documents

The **Recover Documents** tool is used to recover unsaved file versions which are created when software closes unexpectedly; refer to Figure-14. Note that there is an auto save feature in Autodesk Fusion which saves versions of file at a specific time intervals. If software has created the auto save version of your file then only you will be able to recover the file. By default, this time interval is 5 minutes and it can be changed in **Preferences** dialog box which will be discussed later. The procedure to use this tool is given next.

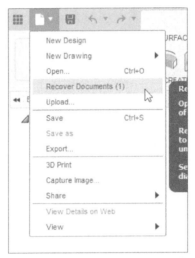

Figure-14. Recover Documents tool

- Click on the **Recover Documents** tool from the **File** menu. The **File Recovery** dialog box will be displayed where you need to select auto save version of your file; refer to Figure-15.

Figure-15. File Recover dialog Box

- Click on the file version that you want to be recovered and click on the **Open** button from the displayed menu. The file version will open in **Autodesk Fusion 360**. If the opened version is as desired then save it otherwise close it and open the other version from the **File Recovery** dialog box.

Upload

The **Upload** tool is used to upload files on cloud. The procedure to use this tool is discussed next.

- Click on **Upload** button from the **File** menu. The **Upload** dialog box will be displayed; refer to Figure-16. Click on the **Select Files** button or Drag & Drop the files to be uploaded in the **Drag and Drop Here** area of the dialog box.

- If you want to change the location where files will be uploaded then click on the **Change Location** button and select the desired location from the **Change Location** dialog box; refer to Figure-17. After selecting desired location, click on the **Select** button. You will return to **Upload** dialog box with updated location. Note that you can also create new folders and new locations by using the options in **Change Location** dialog box which will be discussed later in this book.

- Click on the **Select** button to upload files and select multiple files while holding the **CTRL** key from the **Open** dialog box displayed; refer to Figure-18. Click on the **Open** button from the dialog box to upload files. Or, drag the files in the dialog box and drop them. The options in the **Upload** dialog box will be updated; refer to Figure-19.

- If you have select a .PRT file of NX or Creo then select the **.PRT files are not assembly files** check box to explicitly tell software that these files PRT files are not connected to any assembly.

- After specifying the desired parameters, click on **Upload** button from **Upload** dialog box. Files will be uploaded and status will be displayed in **Job Status** dialog box.

Figure-16. Upload dialog box

Figure-17. Change Location dialog box

Figure-18. Open dialog box for file upload

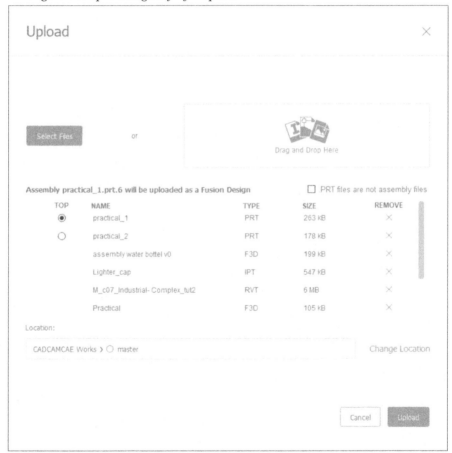

Figure-19. Updated Upload dialog box

Save

The **Save** tool is used to save the current file on cloud. You can press **CTRL+S** key from keyboard to save file. The procedure to save file is given next.

- Click on the **Save** tool from **File** menu or select the **Save** button from **Application bar** as shown in Figure-20. The **Save** dialog box will be displayed asking you to specify the **Name** and **Location** of your file; refer to Figure-21.

Figure-20. Save tool

Figure-21. Save dialog Box

- Specify the desired name in the **Name** edit box.
- Click on the down arrow next to **Location** edit box in the dialog box if you want to select a different location on cloud. A list of locations created for/by you in Autodesk Cloud will be displayed; refer to Figure-22.

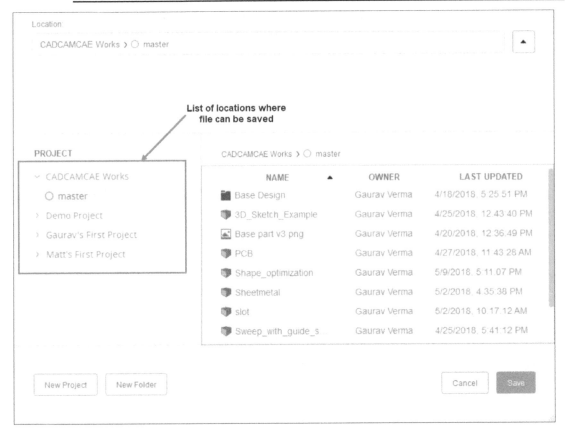

Figure-22. Locations to save files

- By default, Demo Project is added in the Project list. To add a new project, click on the **New Project** button at the bottom left corner of the dialog box. You will be asked to specify name of the new project; refer to Figure-23.

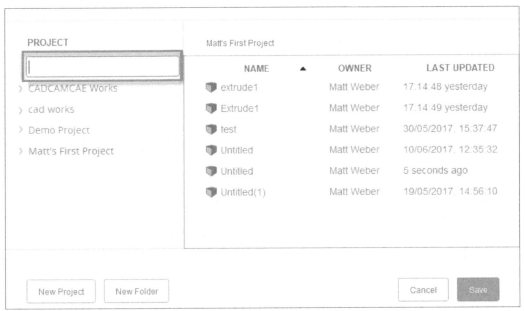

Figure-23. Specifying Project Name

- Specify desired name for the project in displayed edit box and click anywhere in blank area of the dialog box. The new location will be created. Select this new location to save the file; refer to Figure-24.

Figure-24. Location selected for saving file

- If you want to create folder in the project with desired name then click on the **New Folder** button from the dialog box. You will be asked to specify the name of the folder. Specify the name of folder and click in blank area of the dialog box.
- To save your file in the folder, double-click on folder name to enter the folder and then click on the **Save** button. The file will be saved at specified location.

Note that when next time you will use **Save** tool after making changes then the **Add Version Description** dialog box will be displayed asking you to specify description for this new version of same file; refer to Figure-25. Type any short description about what has changed in this version and click on the **OK** button. You will notice that file name has changed from xxxxx v0 to xxxxx v1 which describes that this is the version 1 of same file. These versions can be accessed by **Data Panel** which will be discussed later.

Figure-25. Add Version Description dialog box

Save As

Using the **Save As** tool, you can save the file with different name at different location. The procedure to use this tool is discussed next.

- Click on **Save As** tool from **File** menu; refer to Figure-26. The **Save As** dialog box will be displayed as shown in Figure-27.

Figure-26. Save as tool

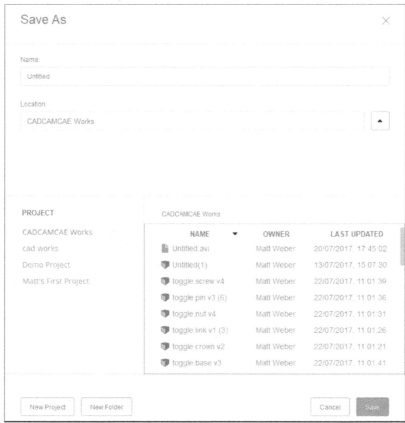

Figure-27. Save As dialog Box

- Specify desired name and location for the file, and click on the **Save** button. The options in this dialog box are same as discussed in **Save** dialog box.

Export

The **Export** tool is used to export the file in different formats. The procedure to use this tool is given next.

- Click on the **Export** tool from the **File** menu; refer to Figure-28. The **Export** dialog box will be displayed; refer to Figure-29.

Figure-28. Export tool

• In the **Type** drop-down, there are various options to specify export format; **F3D**, **IGES**, **SAT**, **SMT**, **STEP**, **IPT**, **DWG**, **DXF**, and so on. Select the desired format from the drop-down. Note that for some file formats, a cloud conversion will be required and take some time. You will be able to see progress of conversion in **Job Status** dialog box.

Figure-29. Export dialog box

• Specify the desired name and location for the file. Note that you can save the files only in the local drive by using this dialog box.
• Click on the **Export** button from the dialog box to save the file.

3D Print

The **3D Print** tool is used to prepare and send current model for 3D printing. This tool convert the selected body to mesh body and sends the output to 3D-Print Utility or converts it to **STL** format. The procedure to use this tool is given next.

• Click on the **3D Print** tool from the **File** menu or click on the **3D Print** tool from the **Make** panel in the **Tools** tab of the **Toolbar**; refer to Figure-30. The **3D PRINT** dialog box will be displayed; refer to Figure-31.

Figure-30. 3D Print

Figure-31. 3D PRINT dialog box

- By default, the **Selection** button is active in this dialog box and you are prompted to select model to be 3D printed. Click on the model to be 3D Printed.
- Now, select the **Preview Mesh** check box to see the number of triangles forming in the selected body when it converts to mesh.

If you don't know why preview in display then you need to know full name of standard file format used for 3D printing. STL format is used as standard for 3D printing which abbreviates **Standard Triangle Language**. So, your model will be broken into very small triangles and then these triangles will be arranged in the shape of your model in layers.

- Select the desired level of resolution for printing in **Refinement** drop-down menu. There are four resolution in this drop-down. If you select the **High**, **Low**, and **Medium** command then the **Surface deviation, Normal deviation**, **Maximum Edge Length**, and **Aspect Ratio** parameters in the **Refinement Options** section will be adjusted automatically. (Click on the arrow before **Refinement Options** node to expand the section.) If you want to adjust these parameters manually then you need to select the **Custom** option in **Refinement** drop-down; refer to Figure-32. Note that your 3D printing machine should be able to print the model as set resolution. A higher resolution will take more time and power in 3D Printer. Unnecessarily high refinement should be avoided in 3D printing.

Figure-32. Refinement Options

Now, for the technical stuff :

The **Surface Deviation** is difference between real surface of model and triangulated tessellation of model. In simple language, it drives the number of triangles to be generated along the surfaces/faces in mesh; refer to Figure-33. The value specified in **Surface Deviation** edit box will be taken as maximum deviation allowed, the software will process the deviation lower than specified value but it will not go higher.

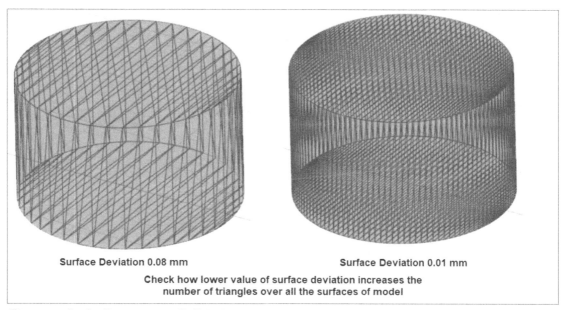

Surface Deviation 0.08 mm   Surface Deviation 0.01 mm

**Check how lower value of surface deviation increases the
number of triangles over all the surfaces of model**

Figure-33. Surface Deviation in 3D Printing

The **Normal Deviation** is gap between two normals of consecutive triangles in tessellation. In simple words, a lower value of normal deviation will increase the number of triangles perpendicular to the edges of model in a given region; refer to Figure-34.

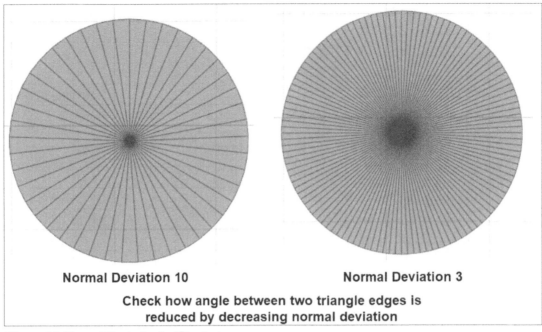

Normal Deviation 10   **Normal Deviation 3**

**Check how angle between two triangle edges is
reduced by decreasing normal deviation**

Figure-34. Normal Deviation in 3D printing

The **Maximum Edge Length** is used to define the maximum length of triangle edges. If you decrease the maximum edge length then more triangles of smaller edge length will be created in best possible orientations; refer to Figure-35.

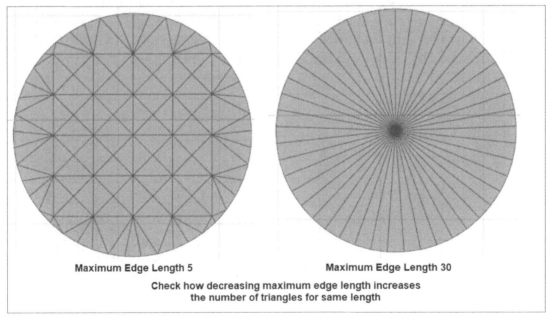

Maximum Edge Length 5   **Maximum Edge Length 30**

**Check how decreasing maximum edge length increases
the number of triangles for same length**

Figure-35. Maximum Edge Length in 3D Printing

The **Aspect Ratio** defines the ratio of number of triangles along width and height of the model; refer to Figure-36. (If you have irregular shape model then don't bother finding aspect ratio, you computer know better!!)

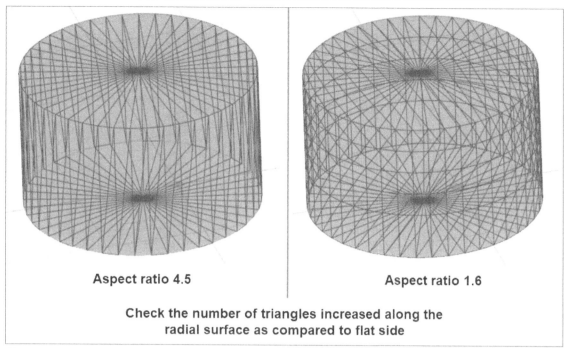

Aspect ratio 4.5   Aspect ratio 1.6

Check the number of triangles increased along the radial surface as compared to flat side

Figure-36. Aspect ratio in 3D printing

- Select the **Send to 3D Print Utility** check box in **Output** section to further edit the model in 3D printing utility. Select desired 3D Printing utility in **Print Utility** drop-down; refer to Figure-37. Note that 3D printing utilities are not installed automatically during Fusion 360 installation. On selecting the utility in **Print Utility** drop-down, an option to download and install the utility will be displayed in the dialog box. Download and install the desired utility.

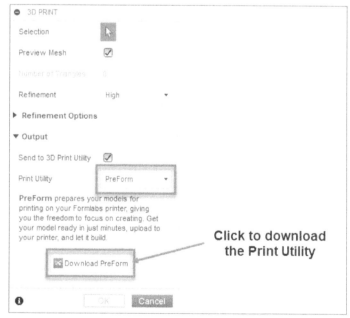

Figure-37. Option To Download Print Utility

- Clear the **Send To 3D Print Utility** check box if you want to save the project file in **STL** format so that you can open this file later in any 3D Printing software.
- In our case, we have selected **PreForm** option from the **Print Utility** drop-down (Needless to say, we have installed it already). Click on the **OK** button from the dialog box. The **PreForm** application window will be displayed; refer to Figure-38.

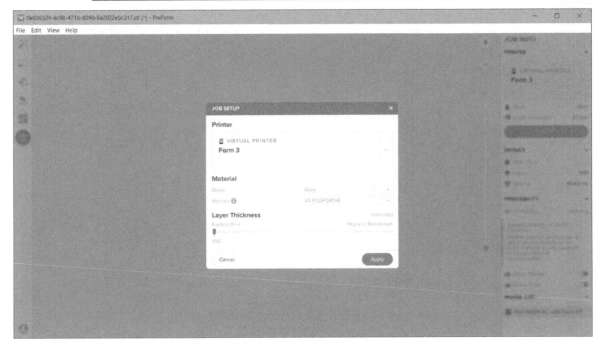

Figure-38. PreForm Window

The tools of this application are discussed next.

PREFORM

Click on the **Apply** button from the **JOB SETUP** dialog box to enter the print utility, we will come back to these options later. On clicking **Apply** button, the model will be displayed in PreForm application window; refer to Figure-39.

Figure-39. Interface of PreForm

Orienting the Model

There are two ways to orient a model in Preform, using **Orientation** tool from **Toolbar** or by using **Manipulator** displayed on the model. We will discuss both the ways here.

Orienting Model Using Manipulator

Click on the **Circle** handle in **Manipulators** for direction in which you want to rotate the model for orientation and drag the handle; refer to Figure-40. Note that software will automatically place the flat face of model on the bed of virtual machine.

If you want to move the model at some other location then click on the **Move** handle in **Manipulators** and drag it to desired location; refer to Figure-41.

Note that the **Manipulators** are displayed on model only when the model is selected. If the **Manipulators** are not displayed by default in your case or it is hidden then select the **Show Manipulators** option from the **View** menu; refer to Figure-42.

Figure-40. Orienting model using Manipulator

Figure-41. Move handle in Manipulator

Figure-42. Show Manipulators option

Orienting Using Orientation Tool

- Click on the **Orientation** tool ↺ from the **Toolbar** at the left in application window. The **ORIENTATION** toolbox will be displayed; refer to Figure-43.

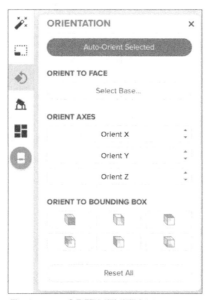

Figure-43. ORIENTATION toolbox

- Click on the **Auto-Orient Selected** button to automatically orient the selected model on bed. (Note: this option was clumsy while writing this book and could not generate a proper orientation so we do not recommend this tool.)
- Click on the **Select Base** button to define the face which will be placed flat on the bed. After selecting this button, click on the face to be used as base of model; refer to Figure-44. The model will be automatically oriented to bed. Click on the **Done** button from the information box displayed in top-left corner. (This is the most used and recommended method to orient the part.)

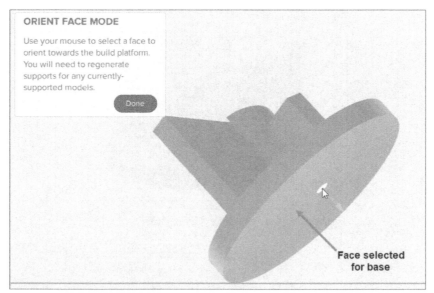

Figure-44. Selecting face for base

- You can use the spinners in **ORIENT AXES** area of the dialog box to define orientation angles for model. (These options are generally used to tweak the orientation; refer to Figure-45. You can also use handles in Manipulators to tweak the orientation.)

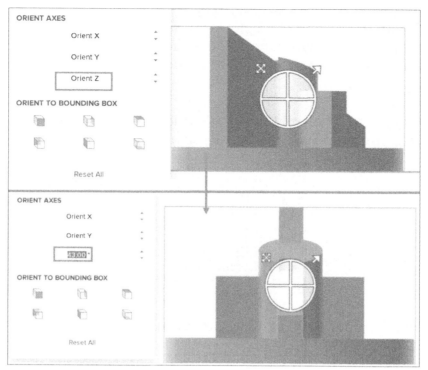

Figure-45. Tweaking the orientation of model

- The buttons in **ORIENT TO BOUNDING BOX** area of toolbox are used to orient the model along respective faces of the bounding box. (Bounding box is an imaginary cuboid which defines maximum length, width, and height occupied by the model.)
- At any time, you find that you have messed up the orientation then you can move back to original orientation by click on the Reset All button at the bottom in the toolbox.

Note that there are two sides of bed for 3D printing machine called FRONT and MIXER SIDE; refer to Figure-46. The front is the side from where you will be extracting the 3D printing model so this is the side of machine where you will be standing while controlling the machine. The Mixer side is the one where material cartridge of 3D printer will be located.

Figure-46. Sides of machine bed

Changing View

You can use the **Up**, **Down**, **Left**, **Right**, and **Home** buttons at the top-right corner of application window to switch between different views; refer to Figure-47. To dynamically change the view, right-click in modeling area, hold the button, and drag the cursor.

To zoom in and zoom out, click on the **+** and **-** buttons respectively which are available the **View Switch** buttons or you can scroll up and scroll down with mouse.

Figure-47. View Switch buttons

The shortcut keys for changing views are given next.

Up View	CTRL + Up key
Down View	CTRL + Down key
Left View	CTRL + Left key
Right View	CTRL + Right key
Home View	F
Zoom in	+ or Scroll up
Zoom out	- or Scroll down
Pan	SHIFT + Right-click drag
Dynamic View change	Right-click drag

Scaling Model

To scale up or scale down the model, click on the **Size** handle in **Manipulators**, hold the button and then drag in desired direction to scale up or scale down; refer to Figure-48.

Figure-48. Size handle

OR

- Click on the **Size** button from the **Toolbar** at the left in application window. The **SIZE** toolbox will be displayed; refer to Figure-49.

Figure-49. SIZE toolbox

- Specify the desired scale value in the **Scale** edit box of toolbox or you can use the spinner to change its value.
- You can also use **X**, **Y**, or **Z** spinners to change the scale of model. Note that size of model will increase or decrease uniformly in all direction so it does not matter whether you use **Scale**, **X**, **Y**, or **Z** spinner.
- Click on the **Reset** button if you want to revert back to original scale. Close the toolbox after making desired changes.

JOB INFO Settings

The options in the **JOB INFO** area are used to set parameters related to printer. You can also check the warnings and details related to 3D printing process. Various tools and options are discussed next.

Selecting and Adding Printers

- Click on the **Edit** button from the **JOB INFO** area at the right in the dialog box. The **JOB SETUP** dialog box will be displayed; refer to Figure-50.

Figure-50. JOB SETUP dialog box

- Click in the **Select Printer** box of **Printer** area in the dialog box to select desired printer. The **PRINTER LIST** dialog box will be displayed; refer to Figure-51.

Figure-51. PRINTER LIST dialog box

- Select the desired printer from the list and click on the **Select** button from the **PRINTER DETAILS** dialog box displayed.
- If you want to add a new printer in the list of **PRINTER LIST** dialog box, click on the **+Add** button from the dialog box. The **ADD PRINTER** dialog box will be displayed; refer to Figure-52. Specify the IP address of network printer in the IP address input boxes and click on the **Connect** button. The printer will be added in the list.

Figure-52. ADD PRINTER dialog box

- If you have selected a 3D printer which has options to select different types of materials then options to select material will be activated in the **Material** area of the dialog box; refer to Figure-53. Select the desired resin and version of resins from the respective drop-downs in the dialog box.

Figure-53. Material options

- Move the layer thickness slider to desired size for increasing print speed or resolution.
- Click on the **Apply** button to set the parameters.

Job Details

Various details of the printing job will be displayed in the **DETAILS** rollout of the **JOB INFO** area like estimated printing time, number of layers in 3D printed model, and total volume of material used in 3D printing.

PRINTABILITY Options

There are three options in the **PRINTABILITY** rollout of **JOB INFO** area; **Printability**, **Show Minima**, and **Show Cups**. The **Printability** icon defines whether the model is good for printing, there are warnings for 3D printing, or there are errors stopping from 3D printing like in Figure-54 a warning is displayed telling you that you need to elevate the model and add some supports for proper extraction.

Figure-54. Warning for 3D printing

- Select the **Show Minima** radio button to display the unsupported areas of model if the model is not oriented correctly; refer to Figure-55.

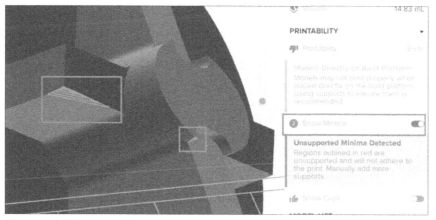

Figure-55. Unsupported minima areas of model

- Select the **Show Cups** radio button from the **PRINTABILITY** rollout to display areas on model that can trap air while 3D printing. Most of the time cups are generated when there are holes/cuts perpendicular to base plane.

Adding Supports

The Supports tool in the Toolbar is used to add supports to the 3d printing object. Supports are used when the model is unstable or extraction of 3d printed model from base plate can cause damage to the model. The procedure to add supports is given next.

- Click on the **Supports** tool from the **Toolbar** or press **C** from keyboard. The **SUPPORTS** toolbox will be displayed; refer to Figure-56.

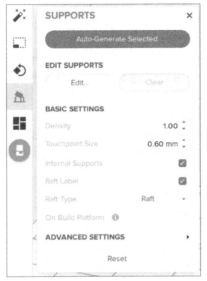

Figure-56. SUPPORTS toolbox

- Click on the **Auto-Generate Selected** button to automatically generate support features for the selected model; refer to Figure-57. Note that using this button, only positions of support elements are decided. It does not automatically decides the shape and size of support elements. So, you should click on this button after you have specified the parameters for supports in the toolbox.

Figure-57. Applying supports

- Set the desired density and touch point size in respective edit boxes in the toolbox. Density is the thickness of support base and touch point size is the thickness of upper section of support where it touches the model.
- Select the **Internal Supports** check box if you want to create internal supports whose start point and end point are on the model; refer to Figure-58.

Figure-58. Internal supports created

- Select the **Raft Label** check box if you want to 3D printing name of file on the support raft.
- Select the **Mini-Rafts** option from the **Raft Type** drop-down if you want to minirafts for supports; refer to Figure-59.

Figure-59. Raft types for supports

- Select the **On Build Platform** check box if you want to place the base of model on bed of machine directly; refer to Figure-60.

Figure-60. Model placed on build platform

- Specify the desired parameters in the **ADVANCED SETTINGS** rollout of the toolbox if needed.

Creating Layout for Multiple Part Printing

- Click on the **Layout** tool from the **Toolbar**. The **LAYOUT** toolbox will be displayed; refer to Figure-61.

Figure-61. LAYOUT toolbox

- Set the desired parameters like space between two instances of the model, raft overlap, rotation lock, and number of duplicate copies of model to be created on same bed.
- After setting desired parameters, click on the **Create** button. The copies of model will be created on the bed. Note that every time you click on the **Create** button, new copies of the model are created so it is better to set the duplicate count value carefully and then click on the **Create** button; refer to Figure-62.

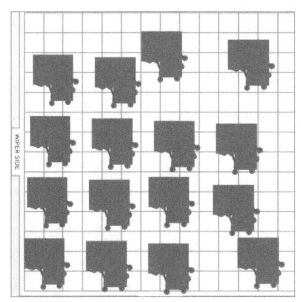

Figure-62. Duplicate copies of model

- Click on the **Layout All** button to arrange the copies of model in such a way that maximum number of copies can be accommodated on the bed; refer to Figure-63. Note that after using this tool, you might be able to add more copies of the model on bed.

Figure-63. After using Layout All tool

• Click on the **X** button at top-right corner to exit the toolbox.

Printing

Now, we are ready to start 3D printing of model layout. If you have printer connected with your system then click on the **Start a print** button from the **Toolbar**. The **PRINT** dialog box will be displayed; refer to Figure-64. Click in the Job Name edit box and specify desired name for print job. If you have 3D Printer connected then it will be displayed in the Printer list. You need to select the printer from the list. If your printer is connected to a network on FORMLABS then you need to specify account information or log in to your FORMLABS account. After setting desired parameters, click on the **Upload Job** button. The file will be uploaded on formlabs account for printing.

Figure-64. PRINT dialog box

After performing desired operations, click on the **Quit PreForm** tool from the **File** menu in the application window to exit the PreForm application.

Capture Image

The **Capture Image** tool is used to capture the image of model in current state. The procedure is discussed next.

- Click on the **Capture Image** tool from **File** menu; refer to Figure-65. The **Image Options** dialog box will be displayed.

Figure-65. Capture Image Tool

- Select the desired option from the drop-down in **Image Resolution** area to define size of image. All the other parameters of **Image Resolution** area will be defined automatically.
- If you want to set image resolution other than the standard one then select the **Custom** option from the drop-down and define the parameters. By default, you are asked to specify size in pixels but you can also define the image size in inches by selecting the **Inches** option from the drop-down next to **Width** edit box. Now, you will be able to define pixel density in the **Resolution** edit box manually. Clear the **Lock Aspect Ratio** check box to specify values of height and width individually.
- Select **Transparent Background** check box for setting the background of the image to be transparent.
- Select the **Enable Anti-aliasing** check box to smooth jagged lines or textures by blending the color of an edge with the color of pixels around it.
- After setting desired parameters, click on the **OK** button from **Image Options** dialog box. The **Save As** dialog box will be displayed; refer to Figure-66.

Figure-66. Save As dialog box for image capturing

- Select the desired format from the **Type** drop-down for image. There are three formats available: PNG, JPG, and TIFF.
- Set the other parameters as discussed earlier and click on the **Save** button to save the image.

Share

The **Share** tools are used to share the file or project on various portals. Click on the **Share** tool from **File** menu. Four options will be displayed in **Share** cascading menu; refer to Figure-67.

Figure-67. Share Cascading Menu

Launch Screencast Recorder

The **Launch Screencast Recorder** tool is used to record Autodesk Fusion 360 commands and entire product development process into the shareable videos. The procedure to use this tool is discussed next.

- Click on **Launch Screencast Recorder** tool from **Share** cascading Menu.
- On selecting this tool, you will redirected to the **Autodesk** Website through which you can download **Autodesk Screencast Recorder** for Windows or Mac OS; refer to Figure-68.

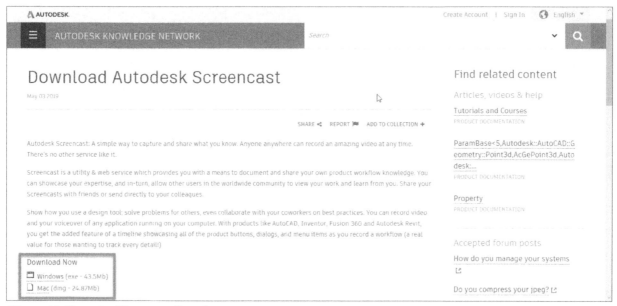

Figure-68. Download Screencast Recorder

- While installing this application, select the check box **Create a Desktop icon** to create the icon of this application on the Desktop.
- After finishing the installation, double-click on the **Screencast Recorder** icon. The Screencast application will be displayed; refer to Figure-69.

Figure-69. Autodesk Screencast Recorder

- Click on **More** button and select a region on which you want to record a video from **Select a program** drop-down; refer to Figure-70.

Figure-70. Select a program drop-down

- Select check boxes for **Microphone** and **Capture Keyboard Events** from the expanded dialog box to record voice and keyboard strokes while recording screencast.
- Note that if dimensions for recording are different from application window size then cross button will be displayed in the expanded dialog box; refer to Figure-71.

Figure-71. Mismatch in recording
dimension and application size

- Click on the cross button to automatically resize the application according to recording dimensions.
- Switch on the **Record** button and start recording. Once you have completed the recording, click on the **Stop** button from **Screencast** application window. The **Screencast Recording Preview** dialog box will be displayed; refer to Figure-72.

Figure-72. Screencast Recording Preview dialog box

- If you want to edit the audio and video of recording then click on the **Edit Audio/ Video** button from the bottom of preview window. The time bar for recording will be displayed as shown in Figure-73.

Figure-73. Updated options in timebar

- Move the time seeker at desired location and click on the **Set green marker on playhead** button to set start point for editing video/audio. Now, move the time seeker to position upto which you want to edit the video/audio and click on the **Set red marker on playhead** button; refer to Figure-74.

Figure-74. Marks created for editing

- Click on the **Re-record Audio** button if you want to re-record the audio for section between green and red markers.
- Click on the **Insert Silence** button if you want to mute the audio for given section.
- If you want to delete the selected section then click on the **Delete Selection** button from the bottom of application window.
- After performing desired editing, click on the **Finish Editing** button.
- Click on the **Save and Upload** button to save and upload the video on Autodesk Knowledge Network. The **Screencast** dialog box will be displayed; refer to Figure-75.

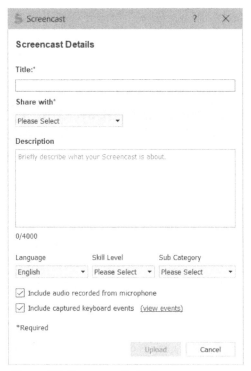

Figure-75. Screencast dialog box

- Set the desired title, description, and other parameters in the dialog box, and then click on the **Upload** button to upload video on AKN.

Share Public Link

The **Public Link** tool is used to share the project link with anyone. The procedure to use this tool is discussed next.

- Click on **Public Link** tool of **Share** cascading menu from **File** Menu.
- On selecting this tool, the **Share Public Link** dialog box will be displayed, refer to Figure-76.
- Click on the toggle buttons to activate or de-activate respective functions.
- After activating the sharing function, copy the link from **Copy** box and share the link via E-mail or other method with anyone. Set the **Allow item to be downloaded** toggle button to allow downloading of file.

- Activate the **Require a password to access the public link** option and specify the desired password in the edit box displayed below it to secure your link with a password.

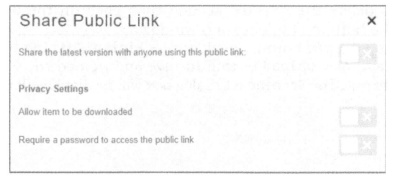

Figure-76. Share Public Link dialog box

Share To Autodesk Gallery

The **Autodesk Gallery** tool is used to share the file online to the gallery of Autodesk where the file is accessible to everyone registered with the gallery. The procedure to use this tool is given next.

- Click on **Autodesk Gallery** tool from **Share** cascading menu. The **SHARE TO FUSION 360 GALLERY** dialog box will be displayed; refer to Figure-77.
- Click on the **NEW PROJECT** button from the dialog box. The options will be displayed as shown in Figure-78.

Figure-77. Share To Autodesk Gallery Dialog Box

Figure-78. Screen Capture Of 3D Model

- Scroll down in the dialog box and specify the information as required.
- Once all the desired information is specified, click on the **Publish** button. **Your project has been successfully shared** message will be displayed.
- Click on the **Go and take a look!** button to check your model in gallery.

Publish to GrabCad

Autodesk Fusion 360 allows you to publish your model directly to **GrabCad** portal. The procedure to use this tool is given next.

- Click on **GrabCad** tool from **Share** cascading menu. The **PUBLISH TO GRABCAD** dialog box will be displayed; refer to Figure-79.
- Login to GrabCAD platform with your GrabCAD account details to upload or share the project. If you do not have an account on GrabCAD then you can create the account by clicking on **Sign Up** button at the bottom in dialog box and following the instructions.
- Once you have login to your account, the dialog box will be displayed as shown in Figure-80.

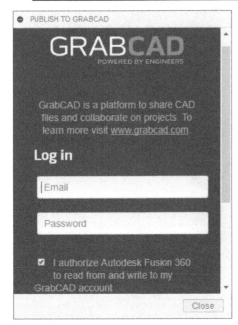

Figure-79. Publish To GrabCAD Dialog Box

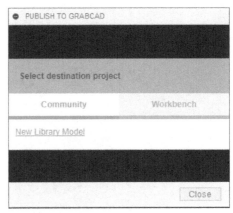

Figure-80. Select Destination Project

- Click on the **New Library Model** link button if you want to save model in community. If you want to share model in a workbench project then click on the **Workbench** tab in the dialog box and then click on the **New Workbench Project** link button. Based on your selection, the respective information will be displayed in the dialog box; refer to Figure-81.

Figure-81. New Library Model Details

- Set the desired parameters and click on the **Create model** button. In the next page, click on the **Publish Here** button. Your model will be uploaded to Grabcad.

View details On Web

The **View Details On Web** tool is used to display the details of current file on Autodesk cloud in web browser. You can use this option only after you have saved your file on Autodesk cloud.

Figure-82. View Details On Web option

View

The **View** tool is used to show and hide various elements of Fusion 360 application window.

- Click on the **View** tool from **File** menu. The **View** cascading menu will be displayed; refer to Figure-83.

Figure-83. View cascading menu

Various tools in this cascading menu are given next.

Hide ViewCube

The **Hide ViewCube** tool is used to hide the **ViewCube.** If the **ViewCube** is already hidden then **Show ViewCube** tool will be displayed in place of it. On again selecting this tool, **View Cube** will be displayed. You can also show/hide **ViewCube** by pressing the **CTRL+ALT+V** keys.

Hide Browser

The **Hide Browser** tool is used to hide the **Browser** from the current screen. If the **Browser** is already hidden then **Show Browser** tool will be displayed in place of it. This tool can also be activated by pressing **CTRL+ALT+B** together.

Hide Comments

The **Hide Comments** tool is used to show and hide the **Comments** from Fusion 360 software. If the **Comment** is already hidden then **Show Comment** tool will be displayed in place of it. This tool can also be used by pressing **CTRL+ALT+A** together.

Show Text Commands

The **Show Text Commands** tool is used to show **Text Commands Bar**. If the **Text Commands Bar** is already displayed then **Hide Text Commands** tool will be displayed in place of it. This tool can also be activated by pressing **CTRL+ALT+C** together.

Hide Navigation Bar

The **Hide Navigation Bar** tool is used to hide the **Navigation bar**. If the **Navigation Bar** is already hidden then **Show Navigation Bar** tool will be displayed in place of it. This tool can also be activated by pressing **CTRL+ALT+N** together.

Show Data Panel

The **Show Data Panel** tool is used to show the **Data Panel**. If the **Data Panel** is already showing then **Hide Data Panel** tool will be displayed in place of it. This tool can also be activated by pressing **CTRL+ALT+P** together.

Reset To Default Layout

The **Reset To Default Layout** tool is used to reset user interface to default settings. This tool can also be used by pressing **CTRL+ALT+R** together.

Scripts and Add-Ins

The **Scripts and Add-Ins** tool is used to run and manage **Scripts** and **Add-Ins** in Autodesk Fusion 360. The procedure to use this tool is discussed next.

*   Click on **Scripts and Add-Ins** tool from **ADD-INS** drop-down in **TOOLS** tab. The **Scripts and Add-Ins** dialog box will displayed; refer to Figure-84.

Figure-84. Scripts And Add-Ins

There are two tabs in this dialog box; **Scripts** and **Add-ins**. Select the **Script** tab to run Python scripts in Autodesk Fusion. Select the **Add-Ins** tab to run the third party applications inside Autodesk Fusion 360.

Creating Script and Add-Ins

*   To create a script or Add-Ins, click on the **Create** button from **Scripts and Add-Ins** dialog box. The **Create New Script or Add-Ins** dialog box will be displayed; refer to Figure-85.

Figure-85. Creating New Script

*   Select **Script** radio button to create a script or select the **Add-In** radio button to create an Add-In.
*   Select the desired radio button from the **Programming Language** area to define the language in which you will be writing script/Add-in codes.

- Set the other parameters as required and click on the **Create** button. A new script/ Add-in will be added in the dialog box.
- Select the newly created script/Add-in and click on the **Edit** button. If the script/ Add-in is coded in **Python** then an information box will be displayed asking you to download and install VS Code. Download & install the application and once installation is complete, codes will be displayed in application when you edit; refer to Figure-86. If you have opted for any other language then system will ask you for respective Programming software to display codes. If you like coding then you can check **Learning Python, 5th Edition by Mark Lutz** as reference book for Python programming.
- Click on the **Run** button from the **Scripts and Add-Ins** dialog box to run selected script.
- If you want to debug a script/Add-in then select it from the **Scripts and Add-Ins** dialog box and click on the **Debug** button in **Run** drop-down; refer to Figure-86. Programming interface will be displayed based on language of selected script/ Add-In.

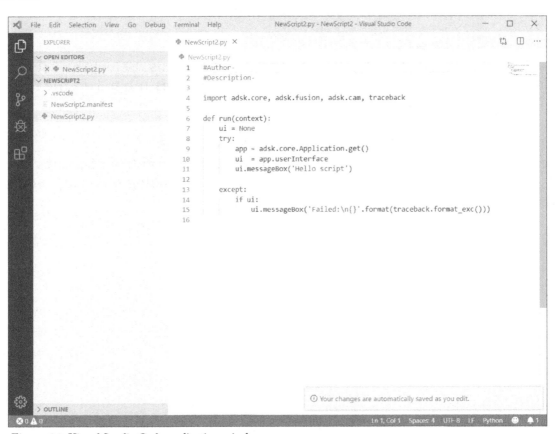

Figure-86. Visual Studio Code application window

Fusion 360 App Store

The **Fusion 360 App Store** tool in **File** menu is used to download and install third party Apps in Autodesk Fusion. On clicking this tool, a webpage is displayed in your default web browser; refer to Figure-87.

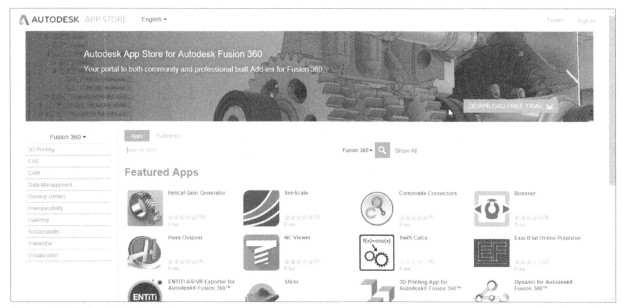

Figure-87. Fusion 360 Store Webpage

- Login to your Autodesk account after clicking **Sign In** button at the top right in the web page.
- Select the desired app, set the operating system option and click on the **Download** button from web page; refer to Figure-88. The software will start downloading.

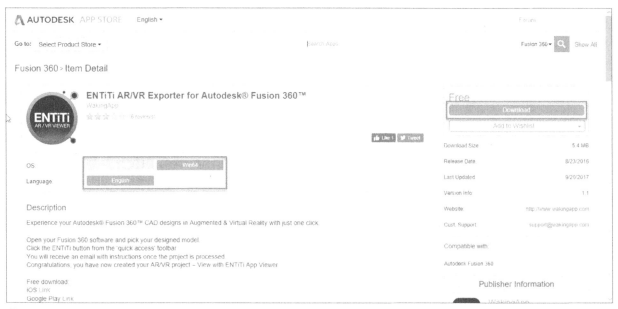

Figure-88. Downloading App

- Once download, double-click on the setup file to install it and follow the instructions as displayed during installation.
- Once the app is installed, you can access it from **Add-Ins** tab of **Scripts and Add-Ins** dialog box; refer to Figure-89.

Figure-89. Installed App

UNDO AND REDO BUTTON

The **Undo** tool is used to revert back to condition before performing most recent action. The procedure to use this tool is discussed next.

*   Click on **Undo** tool in **Application bar** or press **CTRL+Z** keys; refer to Figure-90.
*   You can't undo some actions, like clicking commands on the **File** tab or saving a file.

Figure-90. Undo And Redo Button

*   The **Redo** tool is used to redo an action reverted by Undo tool. To use this tool, select the **Redo** button in **Application bar** or press **CTRL+Y** keys.
*   The **Redo** button activates only after you have undone an action.

USER ACCOUNT DROP-DOWN

The tool in **User Account** drop-down are used to manage user account details and preferences for Autodesk Fusion 360; refer to Figure-91. The tools in this drop-down are discussed next.

Figure-91. User Account drop down

Preferences

The **Preferences** tool is used to set the preferences for various functions of the software like you can set units, material libraries, display options, and so on. The procedure to use this tool is given next.

- Click on **Preferences** tool from **User Account** drop-down; refer to Figure-91. The **Preferences** dialog box will be displayed where you can specify various parameters for application; refer to Figure-92.

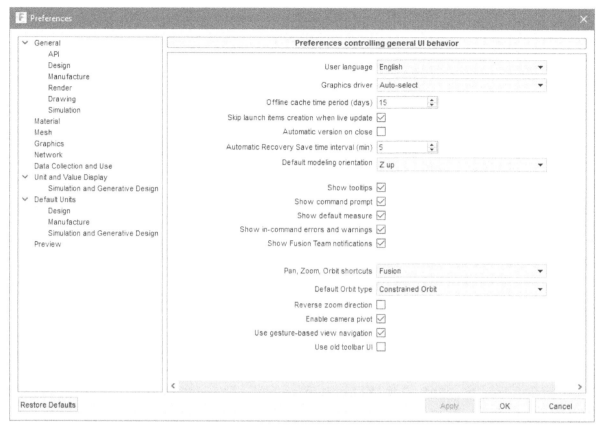

Figure-92. Preferences Dialog Box

General

In **General** node, you can specify the preferences for language, graphics, mouse functioning, default workspace, and so on. Click on the **General** node at the left in the dialog box to display general options. Various important options are discussed next.

- Click on the **User language** drop-down and select the desired language for Autodesk Fusion interface.
- Click on the **Graphics driver** drop-down to select the graphics driver to be used by Autodesk Fusion.
- **Offline cache time period (days)** edit box/spinner is used to specify the number of days up to which your documents can be in the cache memory of Autodesk Fusion before you go back to online mode of Autodesk Fusion. If you specify high value then more local memory will be used by Autodesk Fusion to save temporary copy of your documents. If you specify a low value here then system will prompt you soon to go back online. The maximum number of days specified here can be 360 and minimum number of days can be 7.
- Whenever Autodesk Fusion is updated, launch icons are created automatically in various locations. Select the **Skip launch items creation when live update** check box to skip creating new launch icons.
- Select the **Automatic version on close** check box to automatically save the newer version of file when you close Autodesk Fusion.

- Specify the desired time in minute after which a recovery copy of your model will be created automatically in the **Automatic Recovery Save time interval** edit box.
- Click on the **Default modeling orientation** drop-down and select the desired direction option to define default orientation of model. In most of the CAD software, Z axis upward is the default orientation of model. To set the common orientation, select the **Z up** option from the drop-down.
- Select the **Show tooltips**, **Show command prompt**, **Show default measure**, **Show in-command errors and warnings**, and **Show Fusion Team notifications** check boxes to display respective interface elements.
- Select the desired software style from the **Pan, Zoom, Orbit shortcuts** drop-down to define which software style for shortcuts of pan, zoom and orbit should be used. If you are switching from Alias, Inventor, Solidworks, or Tinkercad to Autodesk Fusion then you can select respective option from the drop-down to use familiar shortcuts.
- Select the desired option from the **Default Orbit type** drop-down to define the default orbit type for rotating model view. There are two options available for orbit, **Constrained Orbit** and **Free Orbit**.
- Select the **Reverse zoom direction** check box to reverse the zoom direction of mouse scroll and other zoom methods.
- Select the **Enable camera pivot** check box to display camera pivot point used as center for orbiting.

Note that by default the pivot point is placed on center of mass point of model but if you want to change the position of pivot point then right-click in blank area of canvas and select the **Set Orbit Center** option. The green point will get attached to cursor and you will be asked to define the location of orbit point. Click at desired location to place the orbit center.

- Select the **Use old toolbar UI** check box if you want to display toolbar in older style. Note that this check box will not be available for long so you should get familiar with new style soon.

API Options
- Click on the **API** option under **General** node in the left of the dialog box and set the desired parameters to define default location and language of scripts/Add-Ins.

Design Options
- Click on the **Design** option under **General** node in the left of the dialog box to set the parameters related to model creation. The options in the dialog box will be displayed as shown in Figure-93.
- Select the **Active Component Visibility** check box to display only currently active component and hide rest of the components.
- Select the **Capture Design History** option from **Design History** drop-down if you want to keep detail of every operation you perform on the model in model history. If you want to save space or want to hide operation details while sharing file then create the model after selecting **Do not capture Design History** option from the **Design History** drop-down. Note that changes made in most of the options will be applied only after you have restarted Autodesk Fusion.
- Select the **Animate Joint Preview** check box if you want to check small animation of how joint will work. The animation can give you clues about degrees of freedom which are constrained by selected joint.

- Select the **Allow 3D sketching on lines and splines** check box if you want to create lines and splines which are not confined to single plane.

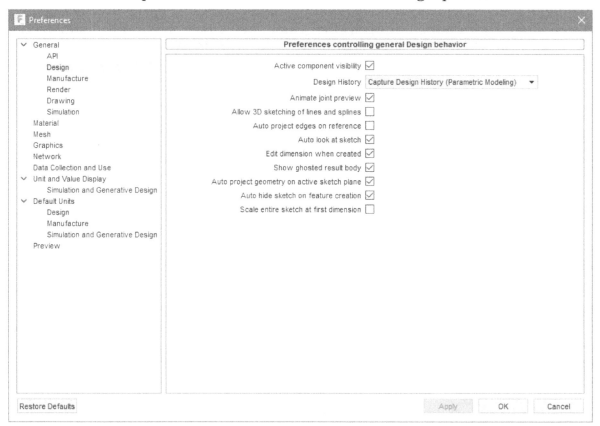

Figure-93. Design Page

- Select the **Auto project edges on reference** check box if you want to automatically project edges of model when they are used as reference for dimensioning or constraining of other sketch elements. Refer to Figure-94.

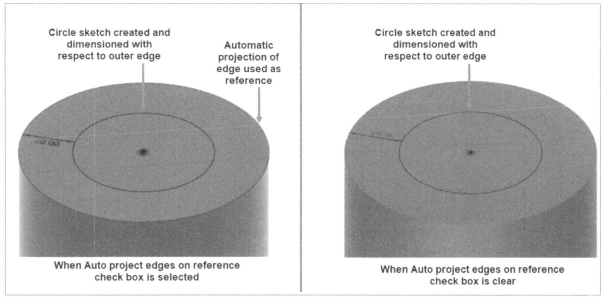

Figure-94. Use of Auto project edges on reference check box

- Select the **Auto look at sketch** check box to automatically make sketching plane parallel to screen.
- Select the **Edit dimension when created** check box if you want to edit the values of dimensions when you are applying dimensions to objects.

- Selecting the **Show ghosted result body** check box will create a ghost image of model before a sculpting operation is performed on it. Note that the ghost image will be displayed until you are in sculpt mode; refer to Figure-95. When you exit the model after making changes then the ghost image will not be displayed.

Figure-95. On selecting Show ghosted result body check box

- Select the **Auto project geometry on active sketch plane** check box if you want to project geometry on the sketching plane by default.
- Select the **Auto hide sketch on feature creation** check box to automatically hide the sketch after it has been used to create a feature.
- Select the **Scale entire sketch at first dimension** check box to automatically fit the sketch objects in view area with reduced dimensions after you specify first dimension of the sketch; refer to Figure-96. Note that all the other objects reduce in same ratio as the first dimension reduces it respective entity.

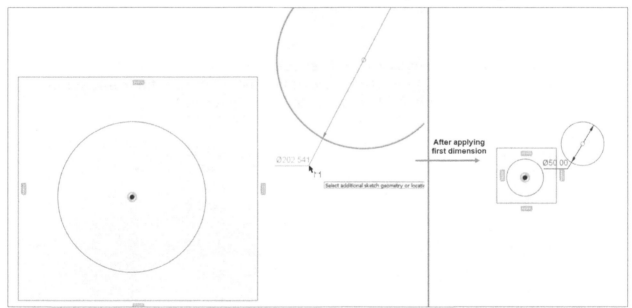

Figure-96. When scale entire sketch at first dimension check box is selected

- Similarly, set the other options as required on different nodes of the dialog box. We will work with options in this dialog box during rest of the book whenever a change in application settings is required.
- After setting the parameters, click on the **OK** button from the dialog box and restart Autodesk Fusion if needed.

Autodesk Account

The **Autodesk Account** tool in **User Account** drop-down is used to manage your Autodesk account profile in default web browser.

My Profile

The **My Profile** tool in **User Account** drop-down is used to manage your project data stored on cloud via web browser.

Switch Team

The options in Switch Team are used to switch between various teams working on different projects. Note that this options is usable only in subscribed versions of software. You can not use this option in free or educational versions.

Work Offline/Online

The **Work Offline/Online** toggle button is displayed on clicking **Job Status** button at the left of **User Account** drop-down; refer to Figure-97. Click on this button to toggle between offline and online mode of Autodesk Fusion.

Figure-97. Work Offline Online

Extensions

Click on the **Extensions** button to display the list of current available extensions for adding more functionality to Autodesk Fusion; refer to Figure-98. If you want to use these extensions then click on the **Add to Cart** button and then click on the **Buy Pack** button.

Figure-98. Extensions dialog box

HELP DROP-DOWN

When you face any problem working with Autodesk Fusion 360, the tools in **Help** drop-down can be useful; refer to Figure-99. Tools in the drop-down are given next.

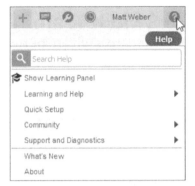

Figure-99. Help Drop Down

Search Help Box

When you are facing any problem regarding tools and terms in the software, then you need to type keywords for your problem in **Search Box** and press **ENTER** to find a suitable solution to your problems; refer to Figure-100.

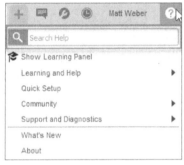

Figure-100. Search Box

Learning And Help

The tools in the **Learning and Help** cascading menu are used to display video tutorials, help files, and fusion 360 api related content in web browser; refer to Figure-101. On clicking the **Start Here** button in the **Learning and Help** cascading menu of **Help** menu, the website of Autodesk Fusion 360 will be displayed; refer to Figure-102.

Figure-101. Learning and Help

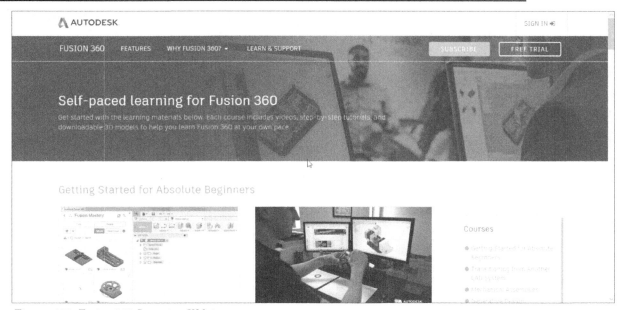

Figure-102. Fusion 360 Learning Website

Similarly, you can use **Learning and Tutorials** and **Fusion 360 API** tools to learn about Fusion 360 interface, design methodology, and APIs.

Quick Setup

When you are new to Autodesk Fusion 360 then this tool will help you to understand this software terminology and basic settings.

- Click on **Quick Setup** tool from **Help** menu. The **QUICK SETUP** dialog box will be displayed; refer to Figure-103.
- Set the desired unit in the **Default Units** drop-down.
- The navigation functions of mouse can be set as per Autodesk Inventor, SolidWorks or Alias software by selecting respective option from the **CAD Experience** drop-down.

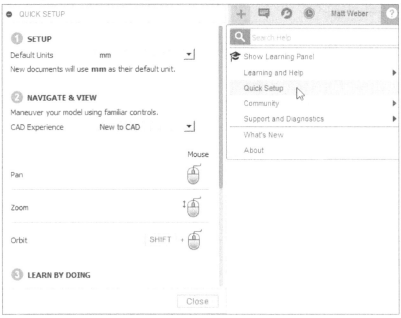

Figure-103. Quick Setup

- If you are new to CAD then you can select the **New to Cad** option in **Cad Experience** drop-down. The mouse will function as per Autodesk Fusion 360.

Similarly, you can use **Community Forum, Ideastation, Gallery, Roadmap, Blog** tool to get help from Autodesk Fusion 360 users or provide feedback.

Support and Diagnostics

When you are having a problem in Fusion 360 and want **Technical support** team to look at software problem data, then you can create the log files and send it to the support team of Autodesk.

- To create log files, select **Diagnostic Log Files** tool under the **Support and Diagnostics** cascading menu in **Help** drop-down. The **Diagnostic Log Files** dialog box will be displayed; refer to Figure-104.

Figure-104. Diagnostic Log Files

- Click on **Open File Location** button and select the log file which you want to send to technical support team for the solution of problem.

Similarly, you can use **Graphics Diagnostic**, **Clear user cache data**, and other tools from **Help** drop-down in Autodesk Fusion 360.

DATA PANEL

The **Data** panel is used to manage the Autodesk Fusion 360 projects. The projects you save in cloud are shown in the **Data** panel. You can easily access the saved project files from anywhere and anytime with the help of internet access.

To show or hide the **Data** panel, click on the **Show Data Panel** or **Hide Data Panel** button ▦ at upper left corner of the Fusion 360 window; refer to Figure-105. A box will be displayed with files of current project. In this box, there are two sections; **Data** and **People**.

In **Data** section, the files which you have saved earlier in current project will be displayed. You can open any file by double-clicking on it.

In **People** section, the information of users will be displayed who have access the files of current project; refer to Figure-106.

Figure-105. Data Panel

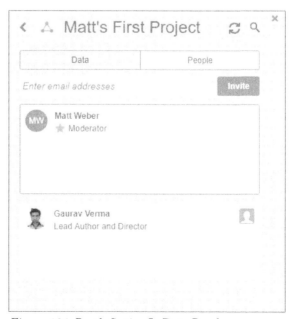

Figure-106. People Section In Data Panel

Cloud Account of User

To open the cloud account of user, you need to click on the arrow button (**Leave Data Details** button) at the top left corner of the **Data** panel. On selecting this button, details of user's cloud storage will be displayed; refer to Figure-107.

• Click on the down arrow next to **ALL PROJECTS** option in the dialog box and select the desired filter; refer to Figure-108.
• Double-click on the desired project to check its files.
• In **SAMPLES** section, you can check sample projects provided by Autodesk. To open any one of these samples projects double-click on the respective link.

Figure-107. Leave Data Details

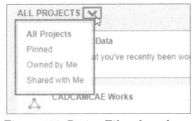

Figure-108. Project Filter drop-down

BROWSER

The **BROWSER** presents an organized view of your design steps in a tree like structure on the left of the Fusion 360 screen; refer to Figure-51. When you select a feature or component in the **BROWSER**, it is also highlighted in the graphics window.

Figure-109. Browser

- Click on the **Eye** button to toggle the visibility of respective object.
- If you select any object in **BROWSER** then it is highlighted in blue color which indicates that the respective object is active for various operations.
- To change the units of the design or sketch, select the **Change Active Units** button as highlighted in the above figure. The **CHANGE ACTIVE UNITS** dialog box will be displayed. Select the desired unit and click on the **OK** button.

NAVIGATION BAR

The **Navigation Bar** is available at the bottom of graphics window of Fusion 360. It provide access of navigation commands for design. To start a navigation command, click on any tool from the **Navigation Bar**; refer to Figure-110.

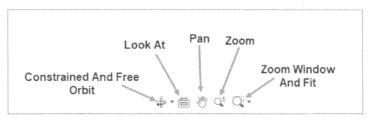

Figure-110. Navigation Bar

There are various tool in **Navigation Bar** to navigate the model which are discussed next.

- **Orbit**- The **Orbit** tools are used for rotating the current model. There are two types of orbit tools i.e. **Free Orbit** and **Constrained Orbit**. **Free Orbit** is used to rotate the design view freely and **Constrained Orbit** is used to rotate the view in constrained motion relative to current origin point. The **Constrained Orbit** tool is displayed on clicking down arrow next to **Free Orbit** tool. After selecting this tool, click at desired location on model and drag the cursor to rotate model view. You can do the same function by using **SHIFT** + Middle Mouse Button dragging.

- **Look At**- This tool is used to view the selected face parallel to screen. To use this tool, select the desired face of model, and then click on the **Look At** tool from **Navigation Bar**.

- **Pan**- It is used to move the design parallel to the screen. You can do the same function by middle mouse button drag.

- **Zoom-** It is used to increase or decrease the magnification of the current view. After selecting this tool, click on the model, hold, and drag mouse upward/downward to zoom in/out. You can do the same function by rolling the mouse wheel up/down.

- **Zoom Window** and **Fit - Zoom Window** tools is used for magnification of selected area. **Fit** tool is used to position the entire design on the screen. You can do the same function as **Fit** tool does by pressing **F6** from keyboard.

DISPLAY BAR

The tools of **Display Bar** are used to visualize the design in different viewports; refer to Figure-111.

Figure-111. Display Bar

Display Settings

The options in the **Display Setting** flyout are used to enable or disable various commands related to **Visual Style**, **Visibility of objects**, **Camera settings**, and so on; refer to Figure-112.

Figure-112. Display Settings flyout

- Select the desired visual style of 3D model from the **Visual Style** cascading menu. Various styles available are Shaded, Shaded with Hidden Edges, Shaded with Visible Edges only, Wireframe, Wireframe with Hidden Edges, Wireframe with Visible Edges only. (You can open a sample file of 3D model and check the effects of different visual styles.)
- The **Face Groups** check box available in the **Mesh Display** cascading menu is used to used to display or hide mesh group faces. You will learn more about this option while working on mesh.

- Select the desired option from the **Environment** cascading menu to define color scheme of the canvas.
- Select the desired check boxes for effects that you want to added in display style from the **Effects** cascading menu. Similarly, you can display or hide objects from the **Object Visibility** cascading menu.
- The options in **Camera** cascading menu are used to change the display to Orthographic, Perspective, or Perspective with Ortho Faces.
- Click on the **Ground Plane Offset** tool from the **Display Settings** flyout. The **GROUND PLANE OFFSET** dialog box will be displayed; refer to Figure-113. Clear the Adaptive check box and set the desired offset value if you want to change the location of ground plane. Note that position of ground plane is generally changed for rendering which will be discussed later.

Figure-113. GROUND PLANE OFFSET dialog box

- If you want to run Autodesk Fusion 360 in full screen then press **CTRL+SHIFT+F** from keyboard.

Grids and Snaps

- The **Grid and Snaps** flyout is used to activate or deactivate various options like **Layout Grid**, **Layout Grid Lock**, **Snap to Grid**, and so on. You can also define the size of grid and snapping increments by using **Grid Settings** and **Set Increments** tools in this flyout.

Viewports

- The options in **Viewports** flyout are used to switch between four viewports and single viewport in the Fusion 360 screen. Click on the **Multiple Views** option from the **Viewports** flyout to display the current model in different views in four viewports. You can click in each of the viewport and reorient the model. If you want to set these views to synchronous again then select the **Synchronize Views** check box from **Viewports** flyout. If you want to move back to single viewport then select the **Single View** tool in **Viewports** flyout. By pressing **SHIFT+!** keys, you can toggle between single viewport and multiple viewports modes.

ViewCube

The **ViewCube** tool is used to rotate the view of model to access different faces of model. Click at desired location on model and drag the **ViewCube** to perform a free orbit. There are six faces in **ViewCube**; **Top, Bottom, Front, Back, Right,** and **Left** to access different orientations of model. To access the standard orthographic and isometric views, click on the faces and corners of the cube; refer to Figure-54. Right-click on the **ViewCube** to access options related to perspective mode and other view modes.

Figure-114. ViewCube

Mouse Functions

You can use the mouse shortcuts to zoom in/out, pan the view, and orbit the view; refer Figure-115.

* Scroll the Middle Mouse Button downward/upward to zoom in or zoom out, respectively. Note that this function can be reversed by using options in **Preference** dialog box.
* Click and hold the Middle Mouse Button to pan the view.
* Use the **Shift** + Middle Mouse Button to orbit the view.
* Press the left mouse button select any object or tool.
* Press right mouse button (right-click) to access shortcut menus in the software.

Figure-115. Mouse shourtcut keys

Timeline

The **Timeline** bar is very useful for saving time while editing. It records the design feature in chronological order; refer to Figure-56. Note that the **Capture Design History (Parametric Modeling)** option must be active in the **Design** node of **Preferences** dialog box to access **Timeline** bar.

Figure-116. Timeline

If you want to edit any feature of model, then double-click on the respective feature from **Timeline** bar. The respective dialog box/interface element will be displayed. Make the desired changes and apply the parameters. The final design will be generated automatically with the applied changes; refer to Figure-117.

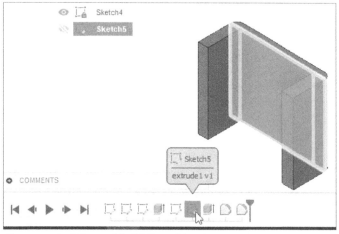

Figure-117. Editing Model From Timeline

CUSTOMIZING TOOLBAR AND MARKING MENU

In Autodesk Fusion 360, you add or remove any tool in the displaying panels of **Toolbar**. You can also add or remove tool from right-click marking menu. These operations are discussed next.

Adding Tools to Panel

- Click on the **Three dot** button next to tool to be added in the panel from the drop-down of **Toolbar**. The shortcut menu to customize toolbar will be displayed; refer to Figure-118.

Figure-118. Shortcut menu for tool customization

- Select the **Pin to Toolbar** check box from the shortcut menu. The tool will be added in the panel.

Assigning Shortcut Key

- Click on the **Change Keyboard Shortcut** option from the shortcut menu as shown in Figure-118. The **Change Keyboard Shortcut** dialog box will be displayed; refer to Figure-119.

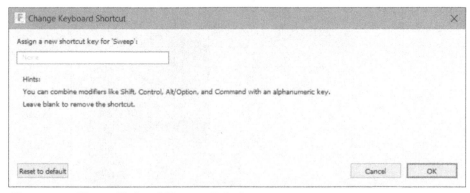

Figure-119. Change Keyboard Shortcut dialog box

- Use the desired combine modifier like **SHIFT**, **CTRL**, or **ALT** and then press the desired alphanumeric key to create a shortcut button.
- If you want to remove shortcut key then user Backspace to delete shortcut key from edit box. Click on the **OK** button from the dialog box to apply the settings.

Adding or Removing tool from Shortcut menu/Marking menu

- Select the **Pin to Shortcuts** check box from the shortcut menu for tool that you want to add in right-click shortcut menu/marking menu; refer to Figure-120.

Figure-120. Adding tool to shortcut menu

- Clear the **Pin to Shortcuts** check box from the shortcut menu for tool that you want to remove from right-click shortcut menu/marking menu.

Note that the shortcut menu is Workspace specific so what you find in shortcut menu for **DESIGN** workspace will be different from **MANUFACTURE** workspace and so on.

Removing Tool from Panel in Toolbar

To remove a tool from panel in **Toolbar**, select the tool and drag it to canvas; refer to Figure-121.

Figure-121. Removing tool from panel

Similarly, you can change position of tool by dragging it within the panel.

Resetting Panel and Toolbar Customization

Right-click on any of the tool in **Toolbar**. A shortcut menu will be displayed as shown in Figure-122.

Click on the **Reset Panel Customization** option to reset current panel to original state. Note that this options will be available only when you have added or removed a tool from the panel.

Click on the **Reset All Toolbar Customization** option from the shortcut menu if you want to reset the complete toolbar including all the panels to its original state.

Figure-122. Shortcut menu for Resetting Toolbar

Self Assessment

Q1.   ....is used to manage the fusion 360 project.

Q2. Which tool is used to share the files to GrabCad?

Q3. The...............button is used for producing CNC codes.

Q4. Which of the following workspace is not available in Autodesk Fusion 360 application?

a.   Patch Workspace
b.   Model Workspace
c.   Assemble Workspace
d.   Drawing Workspace

Q5. Discuss the use of **Save** tool with example.

Q6. Discuss the process of exporting a project in computer with example.

Q7. Discuss the use of **3D Print** tool with example.

Q8. Which tool is used to generate **Toolpaths** for model?

Q9. How to reset the default layout?

Q10. Explain the process of creating **Script** with example.

Q11. Mark the following statements as True or False:

   a. Autodesk Fusion 360 software can be used to perform CAD operations.
   b. Autodesk Fusion 360 software can be used to perform CAM operations.
   c. Autodesk Fusion 360 software can be used to perform CAE operations.
   d. Autodesk Fusion 360 software can be used to perform PLM operations.
   e. Autodesk Fusion 360 software can be used to perform direct 3D printing on 3D Printer.

Q12. Which of the following tool is used to create a new part model in Autodesk Fusion?

a. New Design
b. New Drawing->From Animation
c. New Drawing->From Design
d. New Drawing->New Drawing Template

Q13. Which of the following workspace is not available in educational version of Autodesk Fusion 360?

a. Animation
b. Manufacturing
c. Generative Design
d. Simulation

Q14. Which of the following tool is used to save the file in local drive in Autodesk Fusion 360?

a. Save
b. Save As
c. Export
d. Upload

Q15. STL format is used as standard for 3D printing which abbreviates Standard Triangle Language. (T/F)

Q16. Which parameter of an STL file can decrease the angular distance between two edges of triangle as shown in next figure (from left to right)?

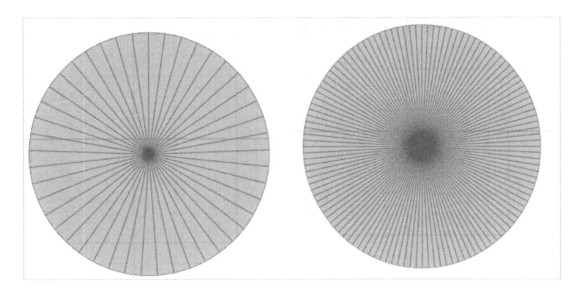

a. Surface Deviation
b. Normal Deviation
c. Aspect Ratio
d. Maximum Edge Length

FOR STUDENT NOTES

FOR STUDENT NOTES

Chapter 2

Sketching

Topics Covered

The major topics covered in this chapter are:

- *Starting Sketch*
- *Sketch Creation Tools*
- *Sketch Editing Tools*
- *Sketch Palette*
- *Constraints*
- *Sketching Practical and Practice*

INTRODUCTION

In Engineering, sketches are based on dimensions of real world objects. These sketches work as building blocks for various 3D operations. In this chapter, we will be working with sketch entities like; line, circle, arc, polygon, ellipse and so on to create base feature for various 3D operations. Note that the sketching environment is the base of 3D Models so you should be proficient in sketching.

There is no separate workspace for Sketching and tools to create sketches are available in **Design** workspace. So, we will be working in **Design** workspace in this chapter. We will learn about various tools of toolbar used in sketching and 3D Sketching.

STARTING SKETCH

- To start a new sketch, click on the **Create Sketch** tool from **CREATE** drop-down in **SOLID** tab of **Toolbar**; refer to Figure-1. The three primary planes will be displayed on canvas screen; refer to Figure-2.

Figure-1. Create Sketch tool

Figure-2. Select sketch plane

- Click on the desired plane from the canvas screen. The selected plane will become parallel to the screen and act as current sketching plane. Also, the tools to create sketch will be displayed in **SKETCH** contextual tab in the **Toolbar**; refer to Figure-3. Now, we are ready to draw sketch on the selected plane.

Figure-3. Sketching mode

First, we will start with the sketch creation tools and later, we will discuss the other tools.

SKETCH CREATION TOOLS

There are various tools in **CREATE** drop-down for creating sketch entities. These tools are discussed next.

Line

In Autodesk Fusion 360, the **Line** tool is used to create a line or arc. The procedure to use this tool is discussed next.

- Click on **Line** tool of **CREATE** drop-down from **Toolbar**; refer to Figure-4. You can also press **L** key to select the **Line** tool. You will be asked to specify start point of the line.

Figure-4. Line

- Click at desired location to specify start point and move the cursor away from selected point in desired direction in which you want to create the line. **Angle** and **Length** edit boxes will be displayed with the preview of line.
- Enter the desired value of length in the **Length** edit box. Press **TAB** key to toggle to **Angle** edit box; refer to Figure-5.

Figure-5. Making of line

- If you are making a freestyle line then click on the screen at desired location without specifying any value in **Length** and **Angle** edit boxes. Press **ESC** after specifying end points to exit the tool.
- To create a line for construction purpose, click on the **Construction** button from **SKETCH PALETTE** displayed at the right in the application window after activating **Line** tool; refer to Figure-6. (You will learn more about **SKETCH PALETTE** later in this chapter.) You can also right-click on the line after creating it and then click on **Normal/Construction** button from **Marking menu** to do the same; refer to Figure-7.

Figure-6. Construction button in SKETCH PALETTE

Figure-7. Marking menu

Marking menu

It is the radical display of most frequently used tool and tools related to selected entities. This menu also provide a quick access to the tools of the toolbar. This menu is the fastest way to activate the tool. To access this menu, right-click anywhere on the screen within the graphics window. To select any tool of this menu, move the cursor towards the tool and the tool will be highlighted. Click on it to activate the tool.

Creating Arc using Line Tool

You can create an arc using the **Line** tool which has one of its end point shared to another entity. In simple words, the starting point of arc created by Line tool will lie on end point of another line or arc. The procedure to create arc is given next.

- Click on the end point of a line or curve to define start point of arc, hold the LMB (Left - Mouse Button), and drag to the point where you want to specify the end point of arc; refer to Figure-8.

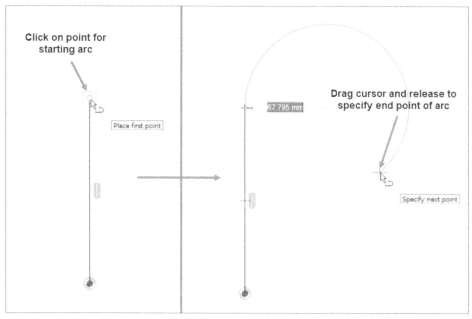

Figure-8. Creating line arc

Rectangle

The tools in **Rectangle** cascading menu are used to create rectangles. There are three tools in **Rectangle** cascading menu; **2-Point Rectangle**, **3-Point Rectangle**, and **Center Rectangle**; refer to Figure-9.

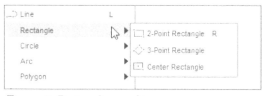

Figure-9. Rectangle cascading menu

You can also activate the **Rectangle** tool by pressing **R** key while in **Sketch** mode. The procedures to use these tools are discussed next.

2-Point Rectangle

- Click on the **2-Point Rectangle** tool of the **Rectangle** cascading menu from **CREATE** drop-down in **SKETCH** contextual tab. You will be asked to specify the first point.
- Click on the sketch canvas to specify first point of rectangle. You will be asked to specify the other corner point; refer to Figure-10.

Figure-10. Creation of 2-point rectangle

- Specify the length and width of rectangle in the dynamic input boxes. To switch between the length dynamic input box and width dynamic input box, press **TAB** key.
- After specifying the parameters, press **ENTER** to create the rectangle. To exit the tool, press **ESC** key.
- If you want to create a freestyle rectangle then click on the screen to select the first corner point and other diagonal corner point of the rectangle on the sketch canvas.
- To add dimensions, right-click on the line of rectangle and click on **Sketch Dimension** tool in **Sketch** drop-down from the **Marking menu**. You can also activate the **Dimension** tool by pressing **d** from keyboard after selecting the line. You will learn more about dimensioning later in this chapter.

3-Point Rectangle

- Click on the **3-Point Rectangle** tool of **Rectangle** cascading menu from **CREATE** drop-down. You will be asked to specify location of first corner point of rectangle.
- Click at the desired location to specify first corner point of the rectangle on the sketch canvas; refer to Figure-11.

Figure-11. Creation of 3-point retangle

- Next, click to specify the second corner point (end point of base line of rectangle) on the canvas or specify the dimension in dimension box.
- Next, click to specify the third point of the rectangle to define the length of rectangle and complete the rectangle creation.

Center rectangle

- Click on the **Center Rectangle** tool of the **Rectangle** cascading menu from **CREATE** drop-down. You will be asked to specify center point of the rectangle.
- Click on the canvas to specify the center point of the rectangle; refer to Figure-12. You will be asked to specify corner point of rectangle.

Figure-12. Creation of center rectangle

- Enter the dimension for rectangle in the edit boxes and press **ENTER** to create the rectangle.
- If you want to create freestyle rectangle then click on the screen to select the center point and corner point of rectangle.

Note that you can switch between different types of rectangles from the **Rectangle** section of **SKETCH PALETTE** after activating the **Rectangle** tool.

Circle

There are five tools in **Circle** cascading menu to create circles; **Center Diameter Circle**, **2-Point Circle**, **3-Point Circle**, **2-Tangent Circle**, and **3-Tangent Circle**; refer to Figure-13.

Figure-13. Circle cascading menu

The shortcut key to use the **Center Diameter Circle** tool is by pressing **C** key from keyboard. The tools to create circle are discussed next.

Center Diameter Circle

The **Center Diameter Circle** tool is used to create circle specifying center location and diameter value. The procedure to use this tool is given next.

- Click on the **Center Diameter Circle** tool from **Circle** cascading menu in the **CREATE** drop-down of **SKETCH** contextual tab. You will be asked to specify center point of circle.
- Click to specify the center point for the circle; refer to Figure-14. You will be asked to specify circumferential point of circle to define diameter.

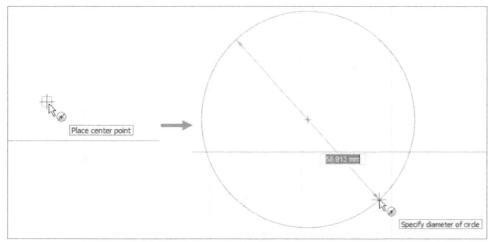

Figure-14. Creation of center diameter circle

- Click to specify the circumferential point or enter desired value of diameter in the dynamic input box.

2-Point Circle

The **2-Point Circle** tool is used to create circle by specifying two circumferential points. The procedure to use this tool is discussed next.

- Click on the **2-Point Circle** tool of **Circle** cascading menu from **CREATE** drop-down and specify the first point for circle; refer to Figure-15.

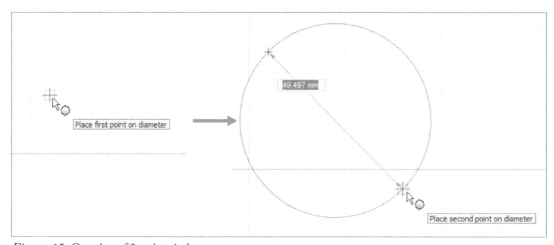

Figure-15. Creation of 2-point circle

- Specify the second point on the canvas screen or enter the diameter dimension in the dynamic input box and press **ENTER** key.

3-Point Circle

The **3-Point Circle** tool is used to create circles using 3 circumferential points as references. The procedure to use this tool is discussed next.

- Click on **3-Point Circle** tool from **Circle** cascading menu of **CREATE** drop-down.
- Click on the screen to specify the first point, second point and third point of circle; refer to Figure-16. Note that you can also select on other entities to define circumferential points for circle.

Figure-16. Creation of 3-point circle

- After specifying points, right-click on the screen and click **OK** button from **Marking menu** to complete the process. You can also press **ESC** key to exit the circle tool.
- If you want to add dimensions then right-click on the selected circle and click on the **Sketch Dimension** tool from **Marking menu**. You can also select **Sketch Dimension** tool from **SKETCH** drop-down.

2-Tangent Circle

The **2-Tangent Circle** tool is used to create a circle which is tangent to two selected lines. The procedure to use this tool is discussed next.

- Select **2-Tangent Circle** tool of **Circle** cascading menu from **CREATE** drop-down.
- Click at desired locations on lines that should be tangent to the circle; refer to Figure-17. Preview of circle will be displayed.

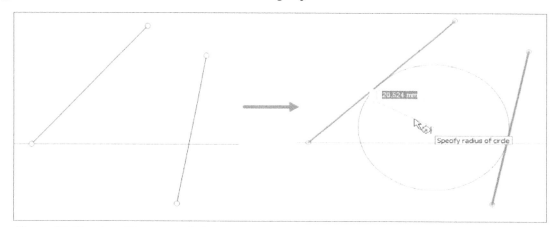

Figure-17. Creation of 2-tangent circle

- Enter the desired radius value of the circle in the dynamic input box and press **ENTER** to create a circle or click at the desired location to define diameter of the circle.
- Press **ESC** to exit the tool.

3-Tangent Circle

The **3-Tangent Circle** tool is used to create a circle using three tangent lines. The procedure to use this tool is discussed next.

- Click on **3-Tangent Circle** tool of **Circle** cascading menu from **CREATE** drop-down.
- Select three lines to be tangent to the circle. You can also use window selection to select the lines; refer to Figure-18. The preview of circle will be displayed.
- Right-click on the screen and click **OK** button from **Marking menu** to create the circle. You can also press **ESC** key to exit the tool.

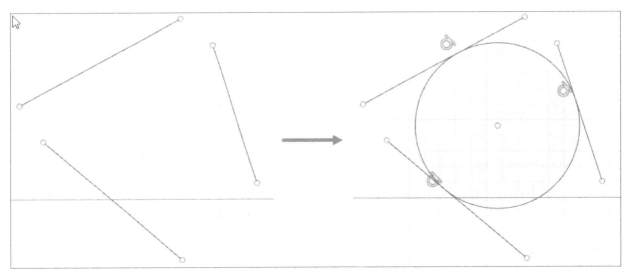

Figure-18. Creation of 3-tangent circle

Arc

The **Arc** tool is used to create arcs. There are three tools in the **Arc** cascading menu; **3-Point Arc**, **Center Point Arc**, and **Tangent Arc**; refer to Figure-19.

Figure-19. Arc cascading menu

The tools of **Arc** cascading menu are discussed next.

3-Point Arc

The **3-Point Arc** tool is used to create an arc using three points (start point, end point, and circumferential point). To use this tool, you need to specify two end points and one circumferential point of the arc. The procedure to use this tool is discussed next.

- Click on **3-Point Arc** tool of **Arc** cascading menu from **CREATE** drop-down. You will be asked to specify points for arc.
- Click on the desired location to specify the start point of the arc; refer to Figure-20.

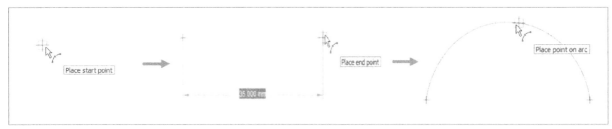

Figure-20. Creation of 3-point arc

- Click on the screen to specify the end point of the arc.
- Click at desired location to define the radius of arc. The arc will be created.
- Press **ESC** to exit the tool.

Center Point Arc

The **Center Point Arc** tool is used to create arc by defining center point, start point, and end point of the arc. The procedure is given next.

- Click **Center Point Arc** tool of **Arc** cascading menu from **CREATE** drop-down. You will be asked to specify center point of the arc.
- Click on the screen canvas to specify the center point of arc.
- Click to specify the start point of the arc or enter desired value of radius in dynamic input box.
- Enter the desired angle value in dynamic input box to define length of arc or click on the screen to specify the end point of the arc; refer to Figure-21.

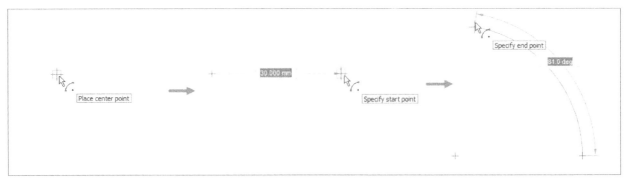

Figure-21. Creation of center point arc

- The arc will be displayed. Right-click on the screen and click **OK** button from **Marking menu** to exit the tool. You can also press **ESC** key to exit the tool.

Tangent Arc

The **Tangent Arc** tool is used to create arc tangent to selected entity.

- Click on the **Tangent Arc** tool from **Arc** cascading menu in **CREATE** drop-down.
- Click near the end point of an entity (line, arc or curve) from screen to specify the start point of the arc; refer to Figure-22. A rubber-band arc will be attached to cursor starting from selected point.
- Click at the desired location to specify the end point of the arc.

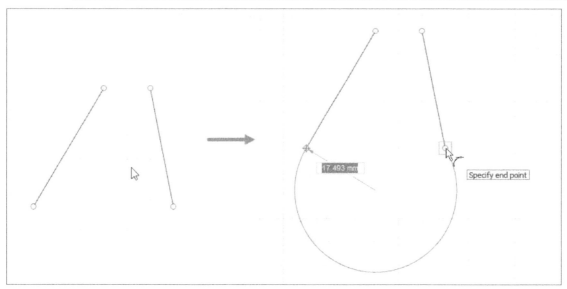

Figure-22. Creation of tangent arc

- Right-click on the screen and click **OK** button from **Marking menu** to complete the process. You can also press **ESC** key to exit the arc tool.

What happens when you try to create an arc at corner location where two entities meet and selected point is common to both the entities; refer to Figure-23. Will the arc be created tangent to line 1 or line 2? What if the arc is being created tangent to line 1 but we want to create it tangent to line 2. In such conditions, after selecting end point, move the cursor in line with entity to be tangent for few millimeters and then specify the end point at desired location; refer to Figure-24.

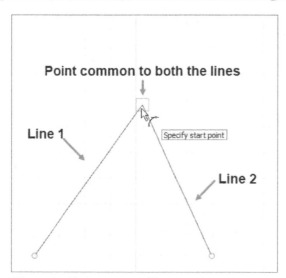

Figure-23. Tangent arc problem at corner point

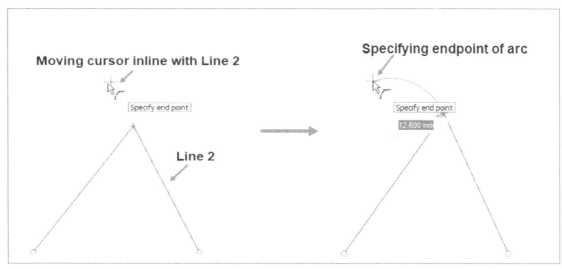

Figure-24. Creating arc tangent to line2

Polygon

The **Polygon** tool is used to create polygon of desired number of sides. There are three tools to create polygon in **Polygon** cascading menu; **Circumscribed Polygon**, **Inscribed Polygon**, and **Edge Polygon**; refer to Figure-25. The tools to create the polygons are discussed next.

Figure-25. Polygon cascading menu

Circumscribed Polygon

Use the **Circumscribed Polygon** tool to create a polygon formed outside the reference circle. Note that midpoints of polygon lines will lie on the reference circle. The procedure to use this tool is discussed next.

- Click on the **Circumscribed Polygon** tool from **Polygon** cascading menu in **CREATE** drop-down; refer to Figure-25. You will be asked to specify center point of the reference circle.

- Click on the screen to specify the center point of the polygon; refer to Figure-26. You will be asked to specify radius of reference circle.

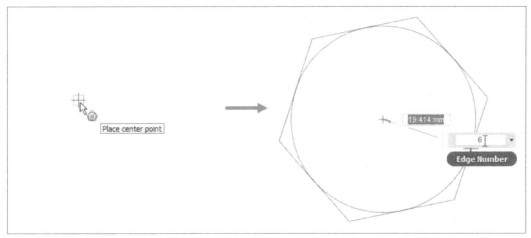

Figure-26. Creation of circumscribed polygon

- Enter the value of radius in the edit box and press **TAB** to activate **Edge Number** edit box.
- Specify desired number of edges of the polygon in **Edge Number** edit box.
- After specifying the parameters, press **ENTER** to create polygon.

Inscribed Polygon

The **Inscribed Polygon** tool is used to create a polygon formed inside the reference circle. The procedure to use this tool is discussed next.

- Click on **Inscribed Polygon** of the **Polygon** cascading menu from **CREATE** drop-down. You will be asked to specify center point of reference circle.
- Click on the screen to specify the center point of the circle; refer to Figure-27.
- Enter the distance between center point of polygon and vertex of polygon edge in dynamic input box.
- Press **TAB** and specify the value of number of edges in **Edge Number** dynamic input box.
- Press **ENTER** to create polygon.

Figure-27. Creation of inscribed polygon

Edge Polygon

The **Edge Polygon** tool is used to create a polygon by defining single edge and number of edges of the polygon. The procedure to use this tool is discussed next.

- Click the **Edge Polygon** tool of the **Polygon** cascading menu from **CREATE** drop-down. You will be asked to specify start and end points of the edge line.
- Click on the screen to select the start point and end point of edge. You can also enter the value of angle and length of the edge in dynamic input boxes; refer to Figure-28. After entering the value in dynamic input boxes, move the cursor to desired side of edge where you want to create the polygon.
- Specify the value of number of edges of polygon in **Edge Number** input box.

Figure-28. Creation of edge polygon

- Press **ENTER** or click in the desired side to create the polygon.

Ellipse

The **Ellipse** tool is used to create ellipses in the sketch. The procedure to create an ellipse is discussed next.

- Click on **Ellipse** tool of **CREATE** drop-down from **Toolbar**; refer to Figure-29. You will be asked to specify center point for ellipse.

Figure-29. Ellipse tool

- Click on the screen to specify the center point for ellipse.
- Move the cursor in desired direction and specify the value of major diameter in dynamic input box. You can also specify the value of angle in **Angle** dynamic input box if you want major axis to be inclined.

- Click on the screen and move the cursor upward/downward. You will be asked to specify length of minor axis. Enter the desired value of minor diameter in the input box; refer to Figure-30. The ellipse will be created.

Figure-30. Creation of ellipse

- Right-click on the screen and click **OK** button to exit this tool.

Slot

The **Slot** tool is used to create slots. There are five tools in **Slot** cascading menu; **Center to Center Slot, Overall Slot, Center Point Slot, Three Point Arc Slot**, and **Center Point Arc Slot**; refer to Figure-31.

Figure-31. Slot cascading menu

The tools of **Slot** cascading menu are discussed next.

Creating Center To Center Slot

The **Center To Center Slot** tool is used to create the linear slot defined by the distance of slot arc centers and width of slot. The procedure to use this tool is discussed next.

- Click on **Center To Center Slot** tool of **Slot** cascading menu from **CREATE** drop-down.
- Click on the screen to specify the center point of first arc of slot. You will be asked to specify center point of other arc of slot.
- Click to specify the point or enter desired parameters in the input boxes.
- Move the cursor upward/downward. You will be asked to specify width of slot/ diameter of slot arc.
- Enter the value in dynamic input box or click on the screen; refer to Figure-32. The slot will be created.

Figure-32. Creation of center to center slot

Creating Overall Slot

The **Overall Slot** tool creates a linear slot defined by total length and total width. The procedure to use this tool is discussed next.

- Click on **Overall Slot** tool of **Slot** cascading menu from **CREATE** drop-down.
- Click on the screen to specify the start point of the slot; refer to Figure-33. You will be asked to specify end point of slot.

Figure-33. Creation of overall slot

- Click on the screen to specify the end point of the slot or enter the distance between start point and end point in the dynamic input box.
- Move the cursor upward/download and enter the width of slot in dynamic input box or click at desired location.
- Press **ENTER** to create the slot and exit the tool.

Creating Center Point Slot

The **Center Point Slot** tool is used to create a linear slot which is defined by center point of slot, location of arc center, and width of slot. The procedure to use this tool is discussed next.

- Click on **Center Point Slot** tool of **Slot** cascading menu from **CREATE** drop-down.
- Click on the screen to specify the center of slot; refer to Figure-34.

Figure-34. Creation of center point slot

- Click to specify the half length of the center to center distance of the slot.

- Specify the value of width for slot in the dynamic input box and press **ENTER** key. The slot will be created.

Creating Three Point Arc Slot

The **Three Point Arc Slot** tool is used to create a slot along specified arc with defined width. The procedure to use this tool is given next.

- Click on the **Three Point Arc Slot** tool from **Slot** cascading menu of **CREATE** drop-down. You will be asked to specify the start point of center arc.
- Click at the desired location. You will be asked to specify end point of center arc.
- Click to specify the end point of arc. You will be asked to specify a circumferential point of the arc.
- Click at the desired location and move the cursor upward/downward. Preview of arc will be displayed with dynamic width value.
- Enter the desired value of slot width in dynamic input box and the press **ENTER** to create the slot; refer to Figure-35.

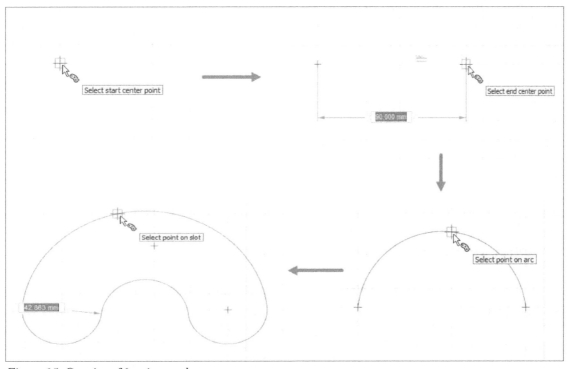

Figure-35. Creation of 3-point arc slot

Creating Center Point Arc Slot

The **Center Point Arc Slot** tool is used to create an arc slot by specifying center point of arc, start & end point of arc, and width of slot. The procedure to use this tool is given next.

- Click on the **Center Point Arc Slot** tool from the **Slot** cascading menu of **CREATE** drop-down in the **Toolbar**. You will be asked to specify the center of arc.
- Click at the desired location. You will be asked to specify the start point of the arc.
- Click at the desired location or enter desired value of arc radius in the dynamic input box. You will be asked to specify the end point of arc.
- Click at the desired location to specify end point or enter the desired value of angular span of arc in the dynamic input box. You will be asked to specify the width of slot.

- Click to specify the slot width or enter the desired value in dynamic input box to create the slot; refer to Figure-36.

Figure-36. Creation of center point arc slot

Spline

The **Spline** tools are used to create spline curves. There are two tools in **Spline** cascading Menu; **Fit Point Spline** and **Control Point Spline**; refer to Figure-37.

Figure-37. Spline cascading menu

The tools of **Spline** cascading menu are discussed next.

Fit Point Spline

The **Fit Point Spline** tool is used to create spline curve through the selected points. It is a freeform curve creation tool. The procedure to use this tool is discussed next.

- Click **Fit Point Spline** tool from **Spline** cascading menu of **CREATE** drop-down from **Toolbar**; refer to Figure-37.
- Click on the screen to specify the start point for the spline. You will be asked to specify next point of spline.
- Specify the other points at desired locations to form spline of desired shape; refer to Figure-38.

- After specifying desired number of points, click on the **Tick** (**Create and Continue**) button to end the spline path.
- Press **ENTER** or **ESC** to exit the tool.

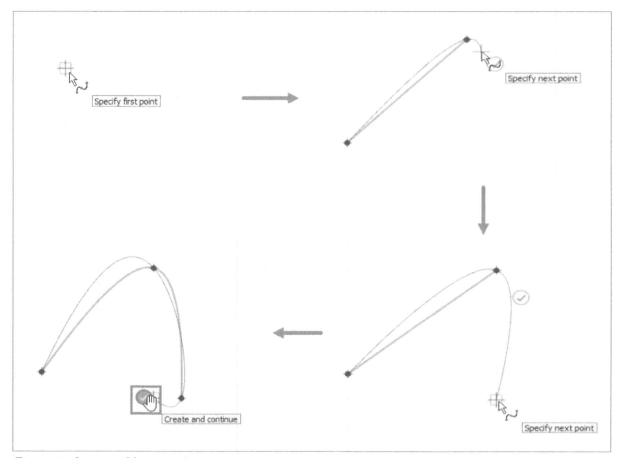

Figure-38. Creation of fit point spline

Control Point Spline

The **Control Point Spline** tool is used to create the spline curve driven by the selected control points. The procedure to use this tool is discussed next.

- Click **Control Point Spline** tool from **Spline** cascading menu of **CREATE** drop-down from **Toolbar**; refer to Figure-37.
- Click on the screen to specify the start point for the spline. You will be asked to specify next point of spline.
- Specify the other points at desired locations to form spline of desired shape; refer to Figure-39.
- After specifying desired number of points, click on the **Tick** (**Create and Continue**) button to end the spline path.
- Press **ENTER** or **ESC** to exit the tool.

Figure-39. Creation of control point spline

Conic Curve

The **Conic Curve** tool creates a curve driven by points and rho value. The shape of the curve can be elliptical, parabolic, or hyperbolic depending on the value of Rho. The procedure to use this tool is discussed next.

- Click on **Conic Curve** tool from the **CREATE** drop-down; refer to Figure-40.

Figure-40. Conic Curve tool

- Click on the screen to specify the start point of the conic curve.
- Click on the screen to specify the end point of the conic curve.
- Click on the screen to specify control point.
- Enter the **Rho** value in **Rho** dynamic input box for the conic curve; refer to Figure-41. The curve will be created. The value of rho lies between **0** to **0.99**.

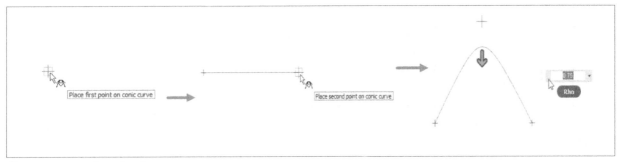

Figure-41. Creation of conic curve

Point

The **Point** tool is used to create sketch points. Sketch points find their major usage when creating surfaces. The point give the flexibility to parametrically change the surface design.

- Click on **Point** tool of the **CREATE** drop-down from **Toolbar**; refer to Figure-42.

Figure-42. Point tool

- Click at desired locations in the sketch canvas to create points; refer to Figure-43.

Figure-43. Creation of point

- Press **ESC** key to exit this tool or click **OK** button from **Marking menu**.

Text

The **Text** tool is used to create text which can be used for embossing/engraving on a solid model. The **Text** tool is also used to create notes and other information for the model.

- Click on **Text** tool of the **CREATE** drop-down from **Toolbar**; refer to Figure-44. You will be asked to specify location of the text.

Figure-44. Text tool

- Click at the desired location to place text. The **TEXT** dialog box will be displayed; refer to Figure-45.

Figure-45. TEXT dialog box

- Click in the **Text** edit box and enter the desired text. Preview of text will be displayed in real-time.
- Click in **Height** edit box and enter the desired value of height for text.
- Click in **Angle** edit box and enter the desired value of angle for rotating text from current base line; refer to Figure-46.

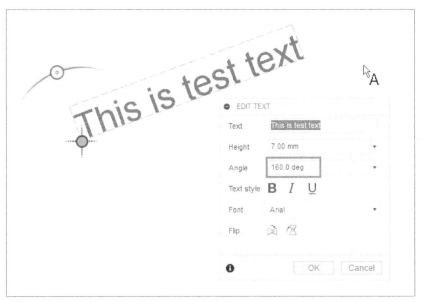

Figure-46. Angle specified for text

- Select the desired style for text in **Text Style** section. You can set the text as bold, italic, and underline by selecting respective buttons.

- Click on the **Font** drop-down and select the desired font for text. There are various single line text fonts available in this drop-down which are used for CAM to name or mark the part. These fonts are of **.shx** format like **cdm.shx**.
- If you want to flip the text then select the desired button from the **Flip** section.
- Click **OK** button of the **TEXT** dialog box to complete the process.

After creating the text, you can edit it anytime by double-clicking on it in sketch mode.

Mirror

The **Mirror** tool is used to create mirror copy of the selected entities with respect to a reference called mirror line. The procedure to create the mirror entities is given next.

- Click on **Mirror** tool of **CREATE** drop-down from **Toolbar**; refer to Figure-47. The **MIRROR** dialog box will be displayed; refer to Figure-48.

Figure-47. Mirror tool

Figure-48. MIRROR dialog box

- The **Objects** selection button is active by default and you are asked to select the objects. Select the entities or sketch whose mirror copy is to be created.

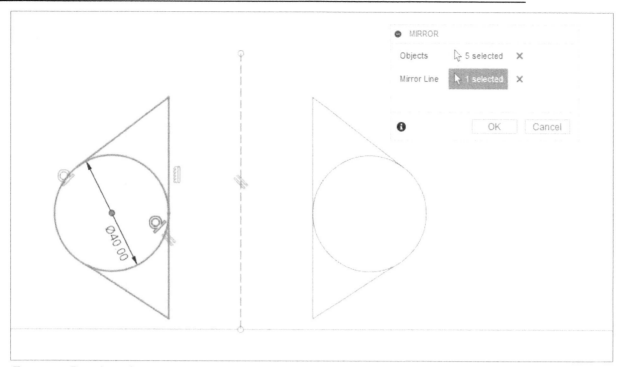

Figure-49. Procedure of mirror

- Click on **Select** button of **Mirror Line** section and select the reference line for creating mirror copy. The preview of mirror will be displayed; refer to Figure-49.
- If preview of mirror is as per your requirement then click on **OK** button from **MIRROR** dialog box to complete the process.

Sometimes, we need to create multiple copies of the sketch entities like in sketch of keyboard or piano. For such cases, Autodesk Fusion 360 provides two tools, **Circular Pattern** and **Rectangular Pattern**. These tools are discussed next.

Circular Pattern

The **Circular pattern** tool is used to create multiple copies of an entity in circular fashion. The procedure to use this tool is discussed next.

- Click on **Circular Pattern** tool of **CREATE** drop-down from **Toolbar**; refer to Figure-50. The **CIRCULAR PATTERN** dialog box will be displayed; refer to Figure-51.

Figure-50. Circular Pattern tool

Figure-51. CIRCULAR PATTERN dialog box

- The **Objects** selection button is active by default and you are asked to select the objects. Select the entities or sketch to apply the circular pattern.
- Click on **Select** button for **Center Point** section and select the reference point to be used as center point for circular pattern. The preview of circular pattern will be displayed; refer to Figure-52.

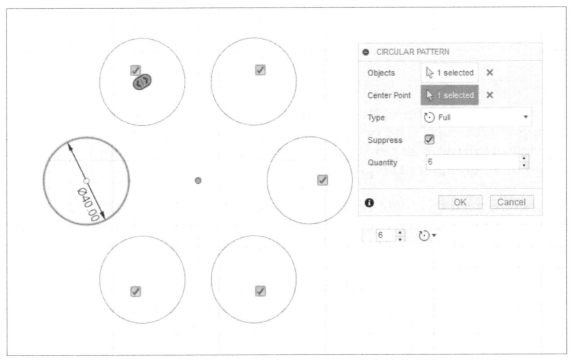

Figure-52. Creation Of circular pattern

- Select **Full** option from **Type** drop-down if you want to create a pattern over full 360 round. Select the **Angle** option from **Type** drop-down if you want to define the span of pattern in angle value. Select the **Symmetric** option from **Type** drop-down if you want to create a circular pattern symmetric to the center line; refer to Figure-53.

Figure-53. Tools of type drop down

- Select the **Suppress** check box if you want to suppress any copy in pattern and then clear the check box for that entity in the preview to be suppressed. Clear the **Suppress** check box from the dialog box to generate all instances of pattern.
- Click in the **Quantity** edit box and enter the desired value for number of copies of object to be created in the circular pattern. You can also set the quantity by moving drag handle.
- After specifying the parameters, click on **OK** button from **CIRCULAR PATTERN** dialog box to complete the process.

Rectangular Pattern

The **Rectangular Pattern** tool is used to create multiple copies of an entity in horizontal and vertical direction. You can create pattern in two linear directions at the same time. The procedure to create rectangular pattern is given next.

- Click on the **Rectangular Pattern** tool of **CREATE** drop-down from **Toolbar**; refer to Figure-54. A **RECTANGULAR PATTERN** dialog box will be displayed; refer to Figure-55.

Figure-54. Rectangular Pattern tool

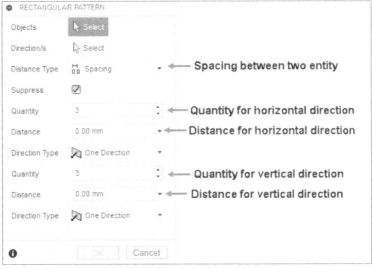

Figure-55. RECTANGULAR PATTERN dialog box

- The **Objects** section button is active by default and you are asked to select the objects. Select the sketch or entities for rectangular pattern.
- Click on **Select** button of **Direction/s** section and select the reference lines for directions of rectangular pattern. If you do not select reference lines then patterns are automatically create along horizontal and vertical axes; refer to Figure-56.

Figure-56. Rectangular pattern direction

- Select **Extent** option from **Distance Type** drop-down if you want to specify the total span in which object copies will be created. Select **Spacing** from **Distance Type** drop-down to set distance between two consecutive copies of object. In our case, we are selecting **Extent** option.
- Select the **Suppress** check box if you want to suppress any entity in the pattern.
- Click in the **Quantity** edit box and enter the desired value for number of copies.
- Click in the **Distance** edit box and enter the desired distance within which copies will be created; refer to Figure-57.

Figure-57. Creation of rectangular pattern

- Select **One Direction** option from **Direction Type** drop-down if you want to create copies in only one direction. Select **Symmetric** option from **Direction Type** drop-down if you want to create copies in both sides of selected direction.
- Similarly, specify the parameters for other direction.
- After specifying the parameters, click **OK** button from **RECTANGULAR PATTERN** dialog box to complete the process.

Project/Include

The tools in this cascading menu are used to project edges/curves of selected solids or surfaces on the sketch. These tools will be discussed later in this book while working with 3D models. Hover on the **Project/Include** option of **CREATE** drop-down from **Toolbar** to display **Project/Include** cascading menu; refer to Figure-58.

Figure-58. Project or Include cascading menu

Sketch Dimension

The **Sketch Dimension** tool is used to dimension the entities automatically based on selections. This tool can create different type of dimension like horizontal, vertical, diameter, radius, or inclined dimensions. The procedure to use this tool is discussed next.

- Click on the **Sketch Dimension** tool of **CREATE** drop-down from **Toolbar**; refer to Figure-59.

Figure-59. Sketch dimension tool

- Select the entity you want to dimension and then click at the desired distance to place dimension; refer to Figure-60. Based on how you move the cursor, the dimension will be horizontal, vertical or inclined. So, after selecting an inclined line, you need to move the cursor in different ways starting from the object to get different type of dimensions. If you want to create inclined dimension for a line then move the cursor perpendicular to the line after selecting it. If you want to create horizontal dimension of an inclined line then move the cursor straight along horizontal axis. In the same way, move the cursor straight vertically to create vertical dimension of an inclined line. This technique can also be applied while dimensioning two points.

Figure-60. Applying the dimension

SKETCH EDITING TOOL

The standard tools to edit sketch entities are categorized in this section. The tools in this section are discussed next.

Fillet

The **Fillet** tool is used to create fillet at the corners created by intersection of two entities. Fillet is sometimes also referred to as round. The procedure to use this tool is discussed next.

*   Click on **Fillet** tool of **MODIFY** drop-down from **Toolbar**; refer to Figure-61. You will be asked to select the entities.

Figure-61. Fillet tool

*   Select the first entity and then second entity.
*   Enter the value of radius in floating window; refer to Figure-62. The fillet will be created.

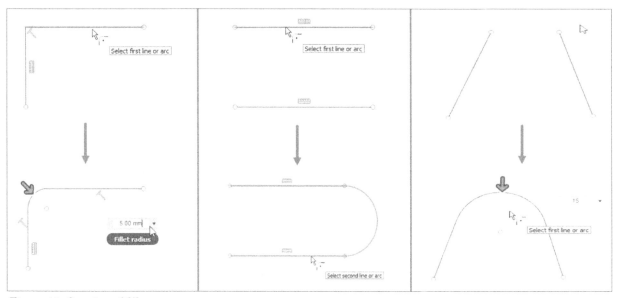

Figure-62. Creation of fillet

Trim

The **Trim** tool is used to remove unwanted portion of a sketch entity. While removing the segments, the tool considers intersection point as the reference for trimming. The procedure to use this tool is discussed next.

- Click on **Trim** tool of **MODIFY** drop-down from **Toolbar**; refer to Figure-63.

Figure-63. Trim tool

- Click on the entity to trim. You can also trim multiple entities by clicking on them.
- The entity will be trimmed. Figure-64 shows the procedure of trimming.

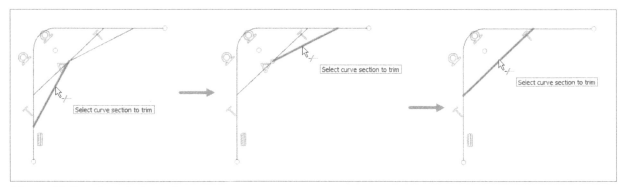

Figure-64. Procedure of trim tool

- Press **ESC** key to exit this tool.

Extend

The **Extend** tool does the reverse of **Trim** tool. This tool is available below the **Trim** tool. The **Extend** tool extends the sketch entities up to the nearest intersecting entities. The procedure to use this tool is discussed next.

*   Click on the **Extend** tool of **MODIFY** drop-down from **Toolbar**; refer to Figure-65.

Figure-65. Extend tool

*   Hover the cursor on the entity that you want to extend. Preview of the extension will display.
*   Click on the entity if the preview is as per your requirement. Figure-66 shows the process of extending entities.

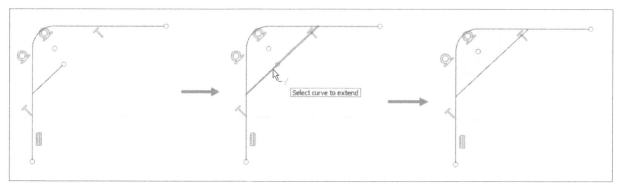

Figure-66. Procedure of extend tool

*   Press **ESC** key to exit this tool.

Break

The **Break** tool is used to break the entity at selected reference points. The procedure to use this tool is discussed next.

*   Click on **Break** tool of **MODIFY** drop-down from **Toolbar**; refer to Figure-67.

Figure-67. Break tool

- Hover the cursor on the entity. The preview will be displayed of break. Note that there must be any intersecting curve on selected entity to apply break.
- If preview is as per your requirement then click on the entity to break; refer to Figure-68.

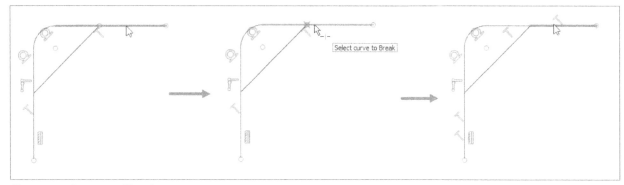

Figure-68. Creation of break

- Press **ESC** key to exit this tool.

Sketch Scale

The **Sketch Scale** tool is used to enlarge or reduce the size of selected entities with respect to the selected point based on specified scale factor. The procedure to use this tool is discussed next.

- Click on the **Sketch Scale** tool of **MODIFY** drop-down from **Toolbar**; refer to Figure-69. The **SKETCH SCALE** dialog box will be displayed; refer to Figure-70.

Figure-69. Sketch Scale tool

Figure-70. SKETCH SCALE dialog box

- The **Entities** selection box is active by default. Click on the entities to be scaled.
- Click on **Select** button of **Point** section and select the reference point about which selected entities will be scaled up/down. The updated **SKETCH SCALE** dialog box will be displayed; refer to Figure-71. Make sure the point to be selected as reference has not been selected during entities selection.

- Click in the **Scale Factor** edit box or dynamic input box and enter the desired value for scale. The preview will be displayed. You can also set the scaling value by moving the drag handle from screen. A value between **0** to **1** will reduce the size and value higher than **1** will increase the size of selected entities.
- If preview is as per your requirement then click on the **OK** button of **SKETCH SCALE** dialog box to complete the process.

Figure-71. Procedure of sketch scale

Offset

The **Offset** tool is used to create copies of the selected entities at a specified distance. If you are the user of **AutoCAD** then this is the most common tool used for creating layouts. The procedure to use this tool is discussed next.

- Click on **Offset** tool of **MODIFY** drop-down from **Toolbar**; refer to Figure-72. The **OFFSET** dialog box will be displayed; refer to Figure-73.

Figure-72. Offset tool

Figure-73. OFFSET dialog box

- The **Sketch Curves** selection is active by default. Select the entities for offset. The updated **OFFSET** dialog box will be displayed.

- Select the **Chain Selection** check box if you want to select all the entities in current chain. Otherwise, clear the check box if you want to select only segments of chain for offset.
- Click in the **Offset Position** edit box and enter the desired distance for offset; refer to Figure-74. You can also set the offset distance by moving the drag-handle from screen.

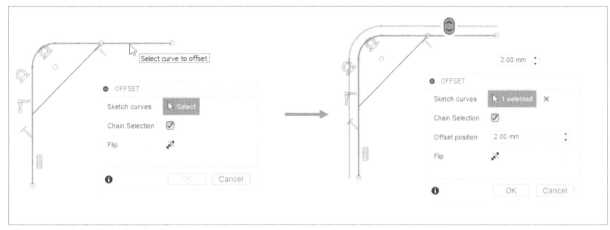

Figure-74. Procedure of offset

- Click **OK** button of **OFFSET** dialog box to finish the process.

SKETCH PALETTE

When sketch mode is active, the **SKETCH PALETTE** dialog box is displayed at bottom right corner of Fusion 360 screen. This dialog box contain commonly used sketch options and sketch constraints; refer to Figure-75.

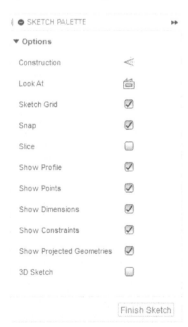

Figure-75. SKETCH PALETTE dialog box

The various tools of sketch Palette are discussed next.

Options

In **Options** section of **SKETCH PALETTE** dialog box, there are various options to activate or deactivate sketch functions. These options are discussed next.

- **Construction-** Select this option while create any sketch object like line, circle, rectangle etc. The object will be created as construction geometry; refer to Figure-76. Click again on this option to return to normal sketching mode.

Figure-76. Creating construction geometry

- **Look At-** If due to any reason, you have rotated the model while sketching and want to make the sketching plane parallel to screen again then click on the **Look At** button once.

- **Sketch Grid-** This option controls the display of sketch grid. To view grid, select the **Grid** check box otherwise clear the check box to hide.

- **Snap-** This option controls the grid Snap. To activate grid snapping, select **Snap** check box and clear the **Snap** check box to disable. Note that the snapping of key points like end point, intersection point, mid point etc. will still be active even if you clear the **Snap** check box.

- **Slice-** This option cuts the solid/surface part using **Sketch Plane** if it is coming before sketching plane while creating sketch. This tool does not change the geometry because it is only a display option. To enable, select the **Slice** check box and clear the **Slice** check box to disable.

- **Show Profile-** This option is used to display closed profiles in the sketch. This tool is useful to check geometry when you are going to apply protrusion tools like **Extrude** or **Revolve** later on the sketch. If your sketch is not a closed profile then you cannot create solid protrusions using that sketch. To enable this tool, select the **Show Profile** check box and to disable it clear the check box.

- **Show Points-** The **Show Points** option is used to display points at the end of different open sketch entities. Select the check box to enable this option.

- **Show Dimensions-** This option is used to display the dimensions of entities. Select the check box to enable this option.

- **Show Constraints**- This option is used to display or hide the constraints in the sketch. Constrains are used to restrict the movement of objected in defined fashion. To display constraints in the sketch, select the **Constraints** check box and clear the check box to hide constraints.

- **Show Projected Geometries**- This tool is used to display the projected geometries on the sketch. Select the check box to enable and clear the check box to disable this option. Note that projected geometries are generally displayed in dark pink color.

- **3D Sketch**- This option enables to pull sketch objects out of the sketch plane and create a 3D sketch. To enable this tool, select the **3D Sketch** check box and to disable it clear the check box.

Feature Options

The **Feature Options** section of **SKETCH PALETTE** is displayed when sketch creation tools like rectangle, circle, slot, polygon, and so on are active which have variation in defining their parameters; refer to Figure-77. Select the desired option from the **Feature Options** section to switch to different input style for same tool.

Figure-77. SKETCH PALETTE when Circle tool is active

CONSTRAINTS

The tools in **CONSTRAINTS** panel of **SKETCH** contextual tab are used to apply constraints to the sketch; refer to Figure-78. Constraints are used to restrict the shapes/position of sketch entities with respect to other entities.

Figure-78. CONSTRAINTS panel

- Make sure the **Show Constraints** check box is selected from **SKETCH PALETTE** dialog box before working with constraints; refer to Figure-79.

Figure-79. Show Constraints check box

Various constraints available in Autodesk Fusion are discussed next.

The **Horizontal/Vertical Constraint** makes one or more selected lines to become horizontal/Vertical. To apply this constraint, click on the **Horizontal/Vertical** button and select the entities. Press **ESC** to exit the tool. You can also make two points horizontally or vertically in-line by using this constraint.

What if you were trying to make a line vertical constrained but it is becoming horizontal constrained. In such cases, you should drag the end point of line towards vertical reference and then apply the Horizontal/Vertical constraint.

The **Coincident Constraint** makes selected point to be coincident with a line, arc, circle, or ellipse. To apply this constraint, select the **Coincident** button from **CONSTRAINTS** panel in **SKETCH** contextual tab and select the entities for coincident. Press **ESC** to exit the tool.

The **Tangent Constraint** makes selected arc, circle, spline, or ellipse to become tangent to other arc, circle, spline, ellipse, line, or edge. To apply this constraint, click on the **Tangent** button and select the required entity. Press **ESC** to exit the tool; refer to Figure-80.

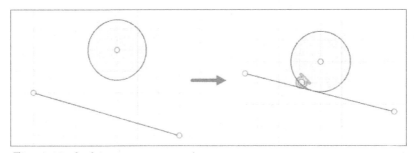

Figure-80. Applying tangent constraint

The **Equal Constraint** makes the selected lines to have equal length and the selected arcs, or circles to have equal radii/diameter. To apply this constraint, click on the **Equal** button and select required entity to apply the equal constraint; refer to Figure-81. Press **ESC** to exit the tool.

Figure-81. Applying equal constraint

The **Parallel Constraint** makes the selected lines parallel to each other. To apply this constraint, click on the **Parallel** button and then select the desired entities; refer to Figure-82. Press **ESC** to exit the tool.

Figure-82. Applying parallel constraint

The **Perpendicular Constraint** makes the selected lines perpendicular to each other. To apply this constraint, click on the **Perpendicular** button and select the entities; refer to Figure-83. Press **ESC** to exit the tool.

Figure-83. Applying perpendicular constraint

The **Fix/Unfix Constraint** makes the selected entity to be fixed at current position. If you apply this constraint to a line or an arc, its location will be fixed but you can change its size by dragging the endpoints or specifying value. To apply this constraint, click on the **Fix/Unfix** button and select the entities. Press **ESC** to exit the tool.

Fix option is useful when you want to restrict the movement of an entity while applying other constraints. Like in Figure-84, if you want the arc to move in place of line then you can fix the line by applying **Fix** constraint before applying **Midpoint** constraint.

The **Midpoint Constraint** makes selected point of an entity to be placed on the midpoint of another sketch entity. To apply this constraint, click on the **Midpoint** button. Select the point and then select the entity whose midpoint is to be used for constraining; refer to Figure-84. Press **ESC** to exit the tool.

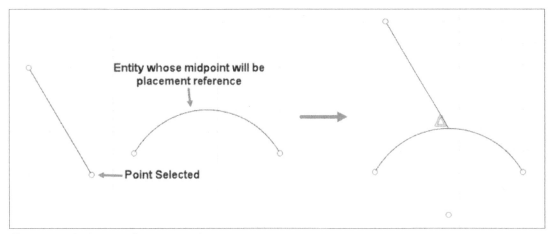

Figure-84. Applying midpoint constraint

The **Concentric Constraint** makes selected arc or circle to share the same center point with other arc, circle, point, vertex or circular edge. To apply this constraint, click the **Concentric** button and then select the two entities to apply the concentric constraint; refer to Figure-85. Press **ESC** to exit the tool.

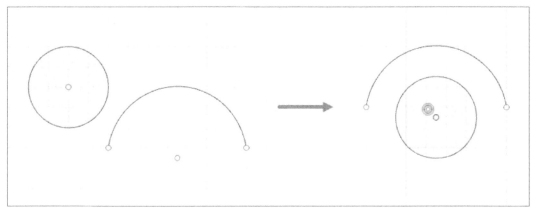

Figure-85. Applying concentric constraint

The **Collinear Constraint** makes the selected lines to lie on the same infinite line; refer to Figure-86. To use this constraint, select the **Collinear constraint** button and select the entities. Press **ESC** to exit the tool.

Figure-86. Applying collinear constraint

⊏⌐⊐ The **Symmetry Constraint** makes two selected lines, arcs, points, and ellipses to remain symmetric about a reference line. To apply this constraint, click on the **Symmetric** button and select the two objects to be symmetric about the reference line. You will be asked to select reference object. Select the line to be used as symmetry reference. The constraint will be applied; refer to Figure-87. Press **ESC** to exit the tool.

Figure-87. Applying symmetry constraint

The **Curvature Constraint** is used to creates a curvature continuous (G2) condition between selected sketch entities which meet at sharp vertex. To use this tool, click on **Smooth** button and select the desired entities near sharp vertex; refer to Figure-88. Press **ESC** to exit the tool.

While applying curvature constraint to splines, make sure you select the splines not the control handles.

Figure-88. Applying curvature constraint

Except for Horizontal/Vertical and Fix constraint, you can also select an external entity such as an edge, plane, axis, or sketch curve of an external sketch as reference to apply the constraint.

PRACTICAL 1

Create the sketch as shown in Figure-89. Also, dimension the sketch as per the figure.

Figure-89. Practical 1

Steps to be Performed:

Below is the step by step procedure of creating the sketch shown in the Figure-89.

Starting Sketching Environment

- Start **Autodesk Fusion 360** if not started already.
- Select the **New Design** tool from **File** menu to start a new design; refer to Figure-90.
- Select the **Create Sketch** tool from **CREATE** drop-down; refer to Figure-91. You will be asked to select a sketching plane; refer to Figure-92.

Figure-90. New Design tool

Figure-91. Create Sketch tool

Figure-92. Select plane for sketch

- Select the "**Top**"(XY) plane for sketching.

Creating Lines

- Click on the **Line** button from **CREATE** drop-down or press **L** key from keyboard to select line. The **Line** tool will become active and you will be asked to select the start point.
- Click on the origin and move the cursor towards right; refer to Figure-93.

Figure-93. Starting creation of line

- Type **30** in the dimension box displayed near line and press **TAB** key to lock the dimension. Click on the screen to create a line.
- Move the cursor vertically upwards and type the value **40** in the dimension box and press **TAB** key to lock the dimension and then click on the screen to complete the line.
- Move the cursor towards right and type **20** in the dimension box. Lock the dimension as discussed earlier and click on screen; refer to Figure-94.

Figure-94. Sketch after specifying 20 value

- Move the cursor upward and specify the value as **55** in the dimension box. Press **TAB** key to lock the dimension and then click on the screen to complete the line.
- Move the cursor left and specify the value as **20** in the dimension box. Press **TAB** key to lock the dimension and then click on the screen to complete the line.
- Move the cursor upwards and specify the value as **40** in the dimension box. Press **TAB** key to lock the dimension and then click on the screen to complete the line.
- Move the cursor towards left and specify **30** in the dimension box press **TAB** key to lock the dimension and then click on the screen to complete the line.
- Move the cursor downward and click on the origin to close the sketch. Press **ESC** to exit the line tool.

The sketch after performing the above steps is displayed as shown in Figure-95.

Figure-95. Final practical 1

PRACTICAL 2

In this practical, we will create the sketch as shown in Figure-96.

Figure-96. Practical 2

Steps to be performed:

Below is the step by step procedure of creating the sketch shown in the Figure-96.

Starting Sketching Environment

*   Start **Autodesk Fusion 360** if not started already.
*   Select the **New Design** tool from **File** menu to start a new design.
*   Select the **Create Sketch** tool from **CREATE** drop-down.
*   After selecting this tool, you need to select the **plane** for creating sketch.
*   Select the **Top Plane** to create the sketch.

Creating Lines

*   Click on the **Line** button from **CREATE** drop-down or press **L** key. You are asked to specify the start point of the line.
*   Click on the origin and move the cursor towards right. Specify **25** in the dimension box and press **TAB** key to lock the dimension. Click on the screen to complete the line.
*   Move the cursor downward and specify **6** in the dimension box. Lock the dimension as discussed earlier and click on screen.
*   Move the cursor to the left and specify **12** in the dimension box. Lock the dimension as discussed earlier and click on screen
*   Move the cursor downwards and enter **50** in the dimension box. Till this point, our sketch should display like Figure-97.

Figure-97. Sketch after creating lines

Creating Arcs

- Select the **Tangent Arc** tool from **Arc** cascading menu in **CREATE** drop-down.
- Click on the end point of the vertical line recently created and move the cursor downwards in such a way that the end point of arc is in-line with the origin.
- Specify the dimension value **13** in the dimension box and press **ENTER** to complete the arc; refer to Figure-98.

Figure-98. Arc creation

Note that you can also create tangent arc by dragging the cursor while creating line using **Line** tool. To specify dimension of tangent arc, you need to drag the cursor while creating line, hold the left click, specify the radius value for tangent arc, and then release the left click.

Creating Fillet

- Click on the **Fillet** tool from **MODIFY** drop-down/panel in the **SKETCH** contextual tab in the **Toolbar**.
- Select the lines as shown in Figure-99.
- Enter the value as **3** in the radius box.

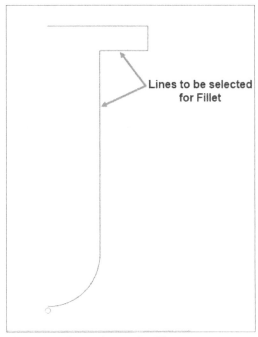

Figure-99. Line selection for fillet

Creating Mirror Copy

- Press **L** key and create a line from origin to end point of the Arc.
- Press **ESC** key from keyboard to exit the tool.
- Now, select the newly created line, right-click on it and select **Normal Construction** from **Marking menu** or select the newly created line and press x from keyboard to convert line into construction geometry. Press **ESC** to exit selection.
- Select the **Mirror** tool from **CREATE** drop-down and select all the entities we have sketched except construction line; refer to Figure-100.

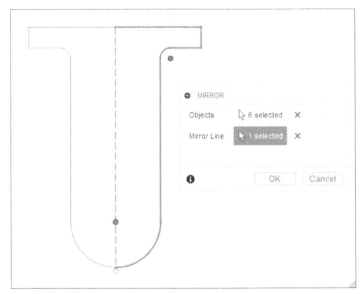

Figure-100. Entities selected for creating mirror

- Click on the **Mirror Line** selection button in the dialog box and select the construction line from sketch. Preview of mirror feature will be displayed.
- Click **OK** button from the **MIRROR** dialog box.

Creating Circle and Lines to complete.

- Click on the **Center Diameter Circle** tool from **Circle** cascading menu.
- Click at the center point of the bottom arc and move the cursor; refer to Figure-101.

Figure-101. Circle creation

- Enter the dimension as **13** in the input box.
- Click on the **Line** tool from **CREATE** drop-down and click anywhere on the center line (except mid point and end points) to specify the start point of the line; refer to Figure-102.

Figure-102. Point selected on centerline

- Move the cursor horizontally towards right and specify the value as **9**. Press **TAB** and click on the screen.

- Move the cursor vertically downwards and click when line passes the arc; refer to Figure-103.

Figure-103. Vertical line created

- Press **ESC** to exit the tool. Click on the **Trim** tool from **MODIFY** drop-down and remove the extra portion outside the arc. Press **ESC** to exit the **Trim** tool.
- Mirror both the lines as we did earlier. The sketch should display as shown in Figure-104.

Figure-104. Sketch after all sketching operation

Dimensioning Sketch

Some of the dimensions are applied automatically while creating sketch. To create rest of the dimensions, click on the **Sketch Dimension** tool from **CREATE** panel/drop-down. Dimension symbol will get attached to cursor.

• Click on the arc and place the dimension at proper spacing if not created already. Enter the radius in dynamic input box as 13 and press **ENTER.**
• Click on the two lines as shown in Figure-105.

Figure-105. Lines to be selected for dimensioning

• Click to place the dimension at its proper place. In the dynamic input box, enter the value as 40.

Similarly, dimension all the entity in the sketch until the sketch is fully defined. The final sketch after dimensioning will be displayed as shown in Figure-106. You can delete the extra dimensions before applying real dimensions.

Figure-106. Final sketch

FULLY DEFINED, UNDER-DEFINED, AND OVER-DEFINED SKETCHES

Till this point, you have worked on various sketching tools and you have created sketch for two practical sessions. You might have noticed that some entities are displayed in blue color while some are displayed in bold black color. Also, there are dimensions which are enclosed in bracket. Here, we will discuss why these colors and different dimensions appear.

Fully Defined Sketches

A fully defined sketch is the one whose specifications can not be changed unintentionally. In some complex sketches, when you change dimension of one entity, the dimension of other entity gets changed automatically. If you have the sketch fully defined then the dimension of the entities will not change unintentionally. In technical terms, a fully defined sketch is the one in which entities have zero degree of freedom. In Autodesk Fusion, the sketch that is fully defined will be displayed in bold black color; refer to Figure-107. In a fully defined sketch, if you try to drag any entity of the sketch then it will not move because its degree of freedom is zero. A fully defined sketch is always recommended for creating features in CAD.

Figure-107. Fully defined sketch

Under Defined Sketches

An under-defined sketch is the one in which all the required dimensions are not applied. An under-defined sketch is displayed in blue color in Autodesk Fusion 360. When you change value of a dimension or drag an entity in the under-defined sketch then other entities may change shape/size accordingly. An under-defined sketch is not recommended for CAD modeling.

Over Defined Sketches

An over defined sketch is the one where more dimensions are applied than those required to fully define the sketch. In over-defined sketches, extra dimensions are bound by parenthesis like the **50** dimension in Figure-106.

PRACTICAL 3

Create the sketch as shown in Figure-108. Also, dimension the sketch as per the figure.

Figure-108. Practical 3

Steps to be performed:

Below is the step by step procedure of creating the sketch shown in Figure-108.

Starting Sketching Environment

- Start **Autodesk Fusion 360** if not started already.
- Select the **New Design** tool from **File** menu to start a new design.
- Select the **Create Sketch** tool from **CREATE** drop-down.
- On selecting this tool, you will be asked to select a plane for creating sketch.
- Select the **Top Plane** to create the sketch.

Creating Lines

- Select **Line** tool from **CREATE** drop-down and create a vertical line starting from origin and moving upward. (No need of dimensions, just make it a long one as it is going to be centerline.)
- Select the line and right-click on this line. Marking menu will be displayed. Select **Normal/Construction** tool to make this line as a center line; refer to Figure-109. Press ESC to exit eh

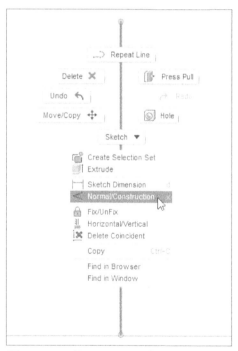

Figure-109. Creating centerline

- Press **L** key to start **Line** tool again and click at the end point of center line to create a line.
- Move the cursor towards right and specify the value as **15** in the dimension box. Press **TAB** key to lock the dimension and click on the screen.
- Move the cursor upward with some outward angle. Specify length as **35** in dimension box. Press **TAB** key to lock the dimension and switch to angle dimension. Specify the angle value as **93** degree and click on the screen.
- Move the cursor to the left, specify the value as **7** in the length input box and **140** degree in angle input box; refer to Figure-110.

Figure-110. Creating lines with dimensions

Creating Mirror copy

- Select the **Mirror** tool from **CREATE** drop-down and select the entities we have sketched except center line for mirror.
- Click on the **Mirror Line** selection button and select the center line of sketch as mirror line. Preview of mirror will be displayed; Figure-111.

Figure-111. Preview of mirror

- Click **OK** button from **MIRROR** dialog box to complete the mirror copy.
- Now, select **Line** tool and create a line joining the open ends of sketch; refer to Figure-112.

Figure-112. Joining the open ends of sketch

- Create a vertical line from one end of the sketch of length **25** mm as shown in Figure-113.

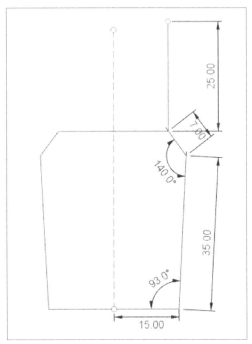

Figure-113. Creating line from right side of sketch

Creating Arcs

- Click **Tangent Arc** tool from **Arc** cascading menu in **CREATE** drop-down.
- Click on the end point of vertical line recently created and move the cursor upwards. Create three consecutive arc joining each other; as shown in Figure-114. Press **ESC** to exit the tool.
- Select **Sketch Dimension** tool from **CREATE** drop-down or press **D** key to select this tool.

- Apply radius dimensions to three arc as **10, 22,** and **7** respectively; refer to Figure-115. Make sure horizontal and vertical constraints are applied to the straight lines in the sketch.

Figure-114. Creating three consecutive arcs

Figure-115. After sketch dimension on arc

- Select the **Line** tool and create a line joining end of recently created arc to horizontal line in the sketch; refer to Figure-116. Press **ESC** tool to exit the command.

Figure-116. Line to be created

You may find that there is not a smooth transition between newly created line and arc as in our case. In such cases, apply the tangent constraint between line and arc; refer to Figure-117.

Figure-117. Applying tangent constraint for smooth transition

Dimensioning Sketch

- Select the unwanted dimensions and delete them by pressing **DELETE** key.
- Click on the **Sketch Dimension** tool or press **D** key to select the tool.
- Select the entity and apply the dimension; refer to Figure-118.

Figure-118. Select entities for dimension

- Drag the dimension to proper place.

Similarly, dimension all the other entities in the sketch until it is fully defined. The final sketch after dimensioning will be displayed; as shown in Figure-119.

Figure-119. Final sketch of practical 3

Following are some sketches for practice.

PRACTICE 1
Create the sketch as shown in Figure-120.

Figure-120. Practice 1

PRACTICE 2
Create the sketch as shown in Figure-121.

Figure-121. Practice 2

PRACTICE 3

Create the sketch as shown in Figure-122.

Figure-122. Practice 3

PRACTICE 4

Create the sketch as shown in Figure-123.

Figure-123. Practice 4

To get more exercise, mail us at cadcamcaeworks@gmail.com

SELF ASSESSMENT

Q1. In Autodesk Fusion 360, which of the following workspace has tool to start a new sketch?

a. RENDER
b. DESIGN
c. DRAWING
d. SIMULATION

Q2. Which of the following shortcut key can be used to convert selected line into a construction line?

a. L
b. c
c. y
d. x

Q3. While the Line tool is active in sketch, if you drag the cursor then a tangent arc is created. (T/F)

Q4. Which of the following tool is not available in Autodesk Fusion Sketch mode to create circle?

a. Center Radius Circle
b. 3-Point Circle
c. 3-Tangent Circle
d. 2-Point Circle

Q5. Which of the following Polygon tool should be used to create polygon if distance between two parallel edges of polygon and number of edges are given?

a. Circumscribed Polygon
b. Inscribed Polygon
c. Edge Polygon
d. All of the above.

FOR STUDENT NOTES

Chapter 3

3D Sketch and SolidModeling

Topics Covered

The major topics covered in this chapter are:

- *Solid Modeling*
- *Operation drop-down*
- *Loft Tool*
- *Rib Tool*
- *Multiple Holes*
- *Torus Tool*
- *Circular Pattern*
- *Project/Include Tools*

3D SKETCHES

3D Sketches are those sketches which are not confined to single plane. Assume a line connecting end points of two lines in YZ and ZX planes; refer to Figure-1. Such a sketch can be called 3D Sketch; refer to Figure-2.

Figure-1. 3D line

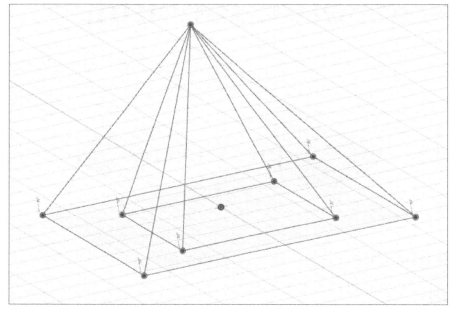

Figure-2. Example of 3D sketch

In Autodesk Fusion 360, there are no specific tools for creating 3D sketches except a check box to enable or disable 3D sketching in **SKETCH PALETTE**. So, we are back to basics of plane orientations for creating 3D sketches. The process of creating a 3D sketch is explained next with the help of an example.

Creating 3D Sketch

Create the sketch of frame as shown in Figure-3.

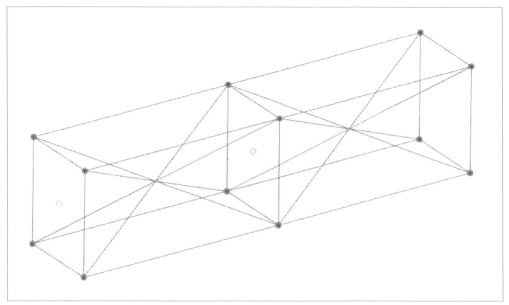

Figure-3. Load bearing frame sketch

Creating Base Sketches and Planes

- After starting a new design file in Autodesk Fusion, click on the **Create Sketch** button from the **CREATE** drop-down. You will be asked to select a sketching plane.
- Select the XY plane as sketching plane and create a center point rectangle as shown in Figure-4.

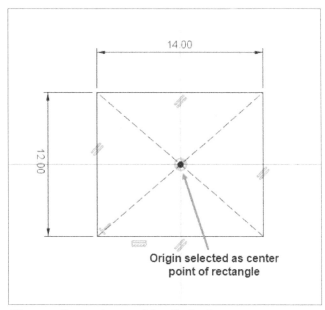

Figure-4. Rectangle created for 3D sketch

- Nope! Don't exit the sketching environment yet!! Select the whole sketch by window selection; refer to Figure-5 and press **CTRL+C** from keyboard. This will keep a copy of current sketch in clipboard memory of software.
- Click on the **Finish Sketch** button from **FINISH SKETCH** panel of the **Toolbar** to exit sketching environment.

Figure-5. Window selection

- Click on the **Offset Plane** tool from the **CONSTRUCT** drop-down of the **SOLID** tab in the **Toolbar** and select **XY Plane** from **Origin** node of **BROWSER**; refer to Figure-6. (You will learn more about the plane and construction geometries later in this chapter.)

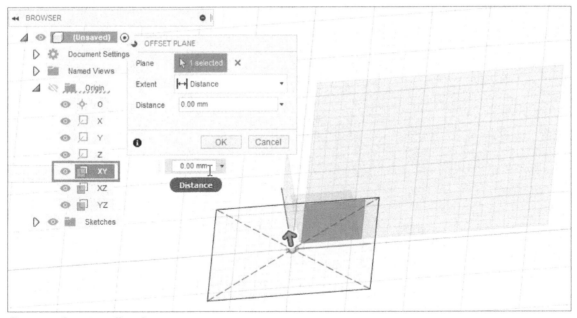

Figure-6. Creating offset plane

- Specify the distance value as **300** in **OFFSET PLANE** dialog box and click on the **OK** button. A new plane will be create at a distance of **300** from XY plane.
- Click again on the **Offset Plane** tool from the **CONSTRUCT** drop-down in the **Toolbar** and create another plane at an offset distance of **300** from earlier created plane; refer to Figure-7.

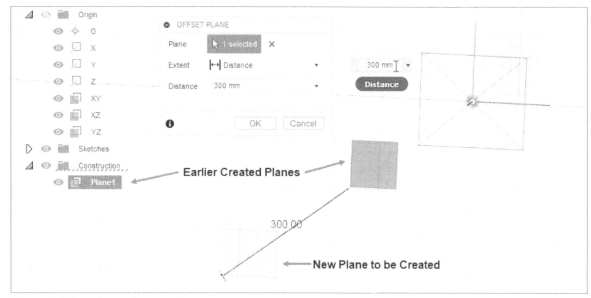

Figure-7. New plane to be created

- Select **Plane1** from the **Construction** node in **BROWSER** and click on the **Create Sketch** button from **CREATE** drop-down in the **Toolbar**. The sketching environment will be activated.
- Press **CTRL+V** from keyboard to paste earlier copied sketch. The **MOVE/COPY** dialog box will be displayed with sketch pasted; refer to Figure-8.

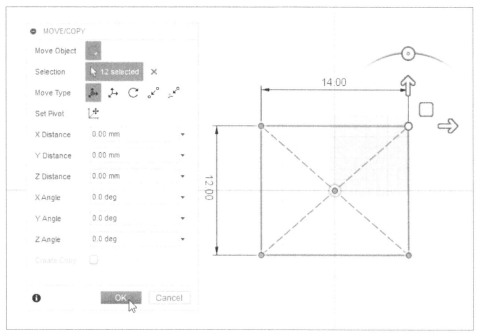

Figure-8. Sketch pasted with MOVE COPY dialog box

- There is no need to change any parameter because our sketch is well constrained and same as we wanted. Click on the **OK** button from the dialog box and exit the sketch environment.
- Create the same sketch on other offset plane. The sketches will be displayed as shown in Figure-9.

Figure-9. Sketches after copy paste

Creating 3D Lines

(Till the time, this book is authored, we are able to use only lines and splines for creating 3D sketches.)

- Click on the **Preferences** option from the **User Account** drop-down at the top-right corner of the application window. The **Preferences** dialog box will be displayed. (This dialog box has been discussed earlier in Chapter 1.)
- Select the **Design** option from **General** node at the left in the dialog box. The options will be displayed as shown in Figure-10.

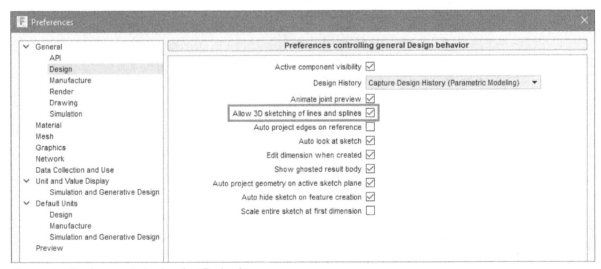

Figure-10. Preferences dialog box for 3D sketching

- Select the **Allow 3D sketching of lines and splines** check box as highlighted in above figure and click on the **OK** button from the dialog box.

Now, we are ready to create 3-dimensional lines.

- Click on the **Create Sketch** tool from the **CREATE** drop-down in the **Toolbar** and select any of the sketching plane. The sketching plane will become parallel to screen.
- Rotate the model by using **SHIFT+Middle Mouse Button (MMB)**.
- Click on the **Line** tool from **CREATE** drop-down and hover the cursor on earlier created sketches. You will find that the snap points of all the sketches get highlighted when you hover the cursor over them.
- Now what left is just clicks and clicks. Join various points of sketches to form frame sketch as shown in Figure-11.

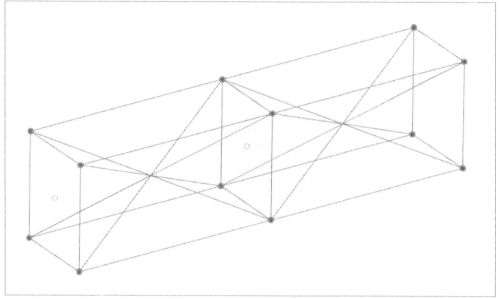

Figure-11. Sketch created for frame

- Click on the **Finish Sketch** tool from the **FINISH SKETCH** panel of the **Toolbar** to exit the sketching environment. So, it is the property of snap points for various elements that allow creating 3D sketch entities.

SELECTION TOOLS

You have earlier selected the objects by clicking on them or by making a window to select them. In Autodesk Fusion, sometimes you will reach in situations where only features are to be selected or only faces are to be selected. In such cases, we apply selection filters. You can also define the pattern by which we will be selecting objects using the options in **SELECT** drop-down of the **Toolbar**; refer to Figure-12. These tools are discussed next.

Figure-12. Select drop down

Select Tool

This tool is always active while working in Autodesk Fusion. Because of this tool, you are able to select any tool from toolbar or object from canvas.

Window Selection

This tool is active by default when you start working on Autodesk Fusion. This tool is used to activate window selection mode. You can activate this tool by selecting it from **SELECT** drop-down or by pressing **1** key from keyboard (Note that 1 is not to be pressed from **NUMPAD** on your keyboard). After activating window selection mode, there are two ways in which you can create window to select objects; Window selection and Cross Window selection (sometimes called Cross selection). Click in the canvas and drag the cursor towards right to perform window selection. Release the button when you have formed window of desired size. Click in the canvas and drag the cursor towards left to perform cross window selection. Both the selection methods and their uses are given in Figure-13 and Figure-14.

Figure-13. Window selection mode

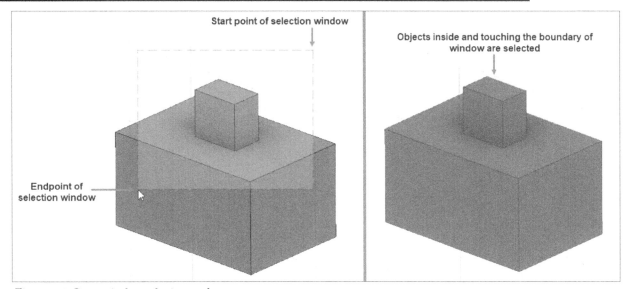

Figure-14. Cross window selection mode

Freeform Selection

Click on the **Freeform Selection** tool from **SELECT** drop-down or press **2** from keyboard to activate this selection mode. Click and drag the cursor to create a freeform boundary for selection. Dragging cursor towards right will make objects completely inside the boundaries selected and dragging cursor towards left will make objects inside or touching the boundaries selected.

Paint Selection

Click on the **Paint Selection** tool from **SELECT** drop-down or press **3** from keyboard to activate this selection mode. In this selection mode, all the objects over which cursor passes while dragging will be selected.

Selection Tools

The selection tools discussed earlier are conventional selection tools. You can also select the objects by theirs names, types, and sizes. These tools are available in the **Selection Tools** cascading menu of **SELECT** drop-down; refer to Figure-15.

Figure-15. Selection Tools cascading menu

Select By Name Method

- Click on the **Select By Name** tool from the **Selection Tools** cascading menu of **SELECT** drop-down in the **Toolbar**. The **SELECT BY NAME** dialog box will be displayed; refer to Figure-16.

Figure-16. SELECT BY NAME dialog Box

- Type the name of object to be selected in the **Name** edit box of the dialog box.
- Select the **Bodies** check box to allow selection of bodies and select the **Components** check box to allow selection of components.
- Click on the **Find** button in the dialog box. All the components and bodies matching the specified name will be selected; refer to Figure-17.

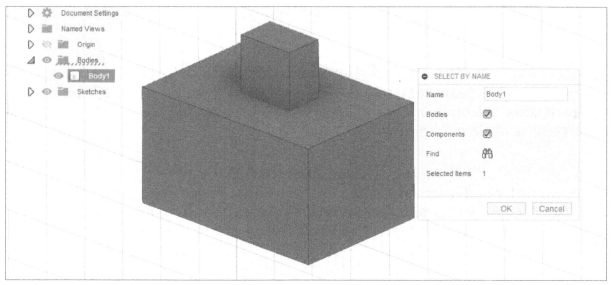

Figure-17. Bodies selected by name

- Click on the **OK** button from the dialog box to complete the process.

Select By Boundary Method

The **Select By Boundary** method is used to select objects which fall under define shape of cylinder, box, or sphere. The procedure to use this method is given next.

- Click on the **Select By Boundary** tool from the **Selection Tools** cascading menu of **SELECT** drop-down. The **SELECT BY BOUNDARY** dialog box will be displayed; refer to Figure-18.

Figure-18. SELECT BY
BOUNDARY dialog box

- Select the desired option from the **Boundary Shape** drop-down to define the shape of selection boundary.
- Click on the desired point in the model to place centroid of boundary shape. Preview of boundary will be displayed; refer to Figure-19.

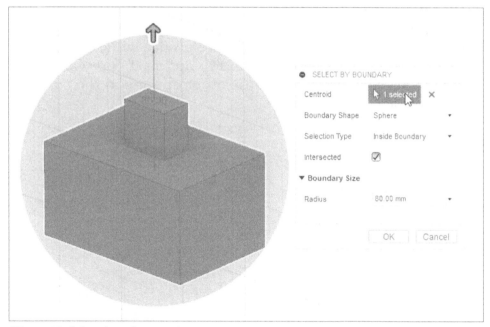

Figure-19. Sphere boundary preview

- Specify desired parameters in the **Boundary Size** section to define size of boundary shape.
- Select the **Inside Boundary** option from the **Selection Type** drop-down if you want to select the objects inside the boundary. Select the **Outside Boundary** option from the **Selection Type** drop-down if you want to select the objects outside the boundary shape.
- Select the **Intersected** check box if you want to select all the objects that are intersecting with created boundary shape.
- Click on the **OK** button from the dialog box to make selection.

Select By Size Method

The select by size method is used when you want to select the entities based on their sizes. The procedure for using this method is given next.

- Click on the **Select By Size** tool from the **Selection Tools** cascading menu of the **SELECT** drop-down in **Toolbar**. The **SELECT BY SIZE** dialog box will be displayed; refer to Figure-20.

Figure-20. SELECT BY SIZE dialog box

- Specify the range of size within which entities will be select and then click on the **OK** button.

Selection Priority

The options in **Selection Priority** cascading menu of **SELECT** drop-down in **Toolbar** are used to define which entities will be given preference while selecting objects; refer to Figure-21. Select the **Select Body Priority** option if you want to select bodies in place of faces/edges. Similarly, select the other options in the cascading menu to select respective entities.

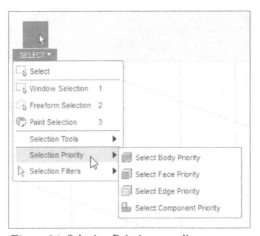

Figure-21. Selection Priority cascading menu

Selection Filters

The check boxes in **Selection Filters** cascading menu are used to define which objects can be selected and which objects cannot be selected; refer to Figure-22. Select the desired check boxes to activate selections of respective objects. In default condition, the **Select All** check box is selected.

Figure-22. Selection Filters cascading menu

SOLID MODELING

Till this point, we have worked on 2D sketches and have created on Top or Front plane. We have also created 3D sketches. Now, we will learn the tools for solid modeling.

Solid modeling is the most advanced method of geometric modeling in three dimensions. Solid modeling is the representation of the solid objects in your computer in digital form. Various tools to perform solid modeling are available in the **SOLID** tab of **Toolbar**. We will learn about various tools and commands used to create solid models in next topic.

CREATE DROP-DOWN

In **Create** drop-down, there are various 3D modeling tools used to create and manage solid objects; refer to Figure-23. These tools are discussed next.

Figure-23. CREATE drop down

New Component

Click on **New Component** tool from **Create** drop-down; refer to Figure-24. A new component will start. You will find use of this tool later in Assembly chapter of the book. (No! we are not skipping this tool, we have discussed it later :-)

Figure-24. New Component

Extrude

The **Extrude** tool is used to create a solid volume by adding height to the selected sketch. In other words, this tool adds material in the direction perpendicular to the plane of sketch by using the boundaries of sketch. The procedure to use this tool is discussed next.

• Create a closed profile sketch as discussed in previous chapter.

- After creating sketch, exit the sketch environment by selecting the **Finish Sketch** tool from **Toolbar** or **Right-click** outside the sketch and select **Finish Sketch** from the **Sketch** drop-down in **Marking menu**; refer to Figure-25.

Figure-25. Sketch for extrusion

- Click on **Extrude** tool of **Create** drop-down from **Toolbar**; refer to Figure-26. The **EXTRUDE** dialog box will be displayed; refer to Figure-27.

Figure-26. Extrude tool

Figure-27. EXTRUDE dialog box

- Profile selection is active by default. Select the sketch to be extruded by clicking on the shaded area in the sketch. If your sketch has multiple closed profiles then make sure to select correct shaded area. For example, in Figure-25 we can select inside the circle, outside the circle, or both to create extrusion. The extruded body will be of the shape selected here.

Start drop-down

- There are three tools in **Start** drop-down; refer to Figure-28.

Figure-28. Start drop down

- Select **Profile Plane** tool, if you want to extrude the sketch starting from current sketching plane; refer to Figure-29.

Figure-29. Extrude starting from profile plane

- Click on **Offset Plane** tool if you want to extrude the sketch starting from some offset distance. The updated **EXTRUDE** dialog box will be displayed; refer to Figure-30.

Figure-30. Offset plane in EX-
TRUDE dialog box

- Click in **Offset** edit box and enter desired value of distance between starting of extrusion and sketch plane; refer to Figure-31.

Figure-31. Extruding with offset

- Select the **From Object** option from **Start** section, if you want to extrude the profile starting from selected surface/face (or at a distance from selected face) of another body.
- After selecting **From Object** option, click on **Select** button of **Object** section and select the object from where you are going to start the extrude; refer to Figure-32.

Figure-32. From object tool

- Click in **Distance** edit box and specify the height of extrusion. You can also drag the Arrow handle displayed on the sketch upward to define extrude height.
- If you want to create tapered walls of extrude feature then specify desired angle value in the **Taper Angle** edit box. You can specify both positive and negative values in this edit box. You can also use the rotation handle displayed in the preview to specify taper value. Applying taper angle is also called draft in some software.

Direction drop-down

- There are three tools in **Direction** drop-down of **EXTRUDE** dialog box; refer to Figure-33.

Figure-33. Direction drop down

- Click on **One Side** option from **Direction** drop-down if you want to specify the height of extrusion in one direction.
- Click on **Two Sides** option from **Direction** drop-down if you want to specify the height of extrusion in both upward and downward directions of sketching plane; refer to Figure-34. The options to specify parameters for side 1 and side 2 will be displayed in the dialog box.

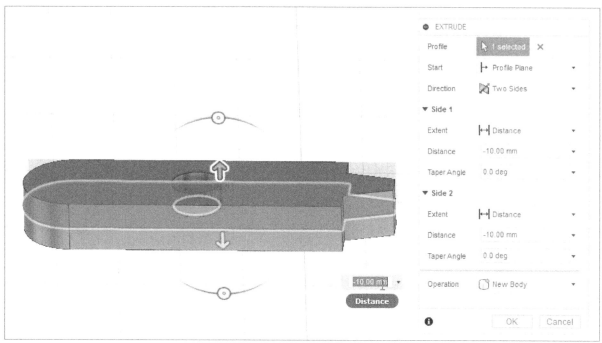

Figure-34. Extrude with two sides

- Click on **Symmetric** option from **Direction** drop-down if you want to specify the height of extrusion symmetric in both upward and downward directions of sketching plane. You will be asked to specify height of extrusion for one side and the profile will be extruded symmetrically on the other side with same value. Select the **Half length** or **Whole length** button from **Measurement** section as required; refer to Figure-35.

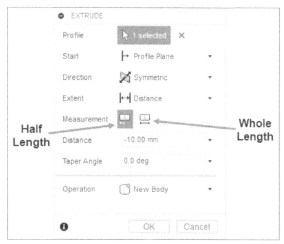

Figure-35. Extrude with symmetric direction

Extent drop-down

- Select **Distance** in **Extent** drop-down from **EXTRUDE** dialog box if you want to set the height of extrusion manually. Click in the **Height** edit box and specify the desired height.
- Select **To Object** option from **Distance** drop-down if you want to define a surface/face at which extrusion will end; refer to Figure-36. After selecting this option, click on the face or surface up to which extrusion is to be created.

Figure-36. To object extrude

- Click on **All** tool, if you want to cut through the model or part from extrusion. The extrusion will goes through from the body of model; refer to Figure-37. If you want to add material in place of removing then select the **Join** option from the **Operation** drop-down in the dialog box.

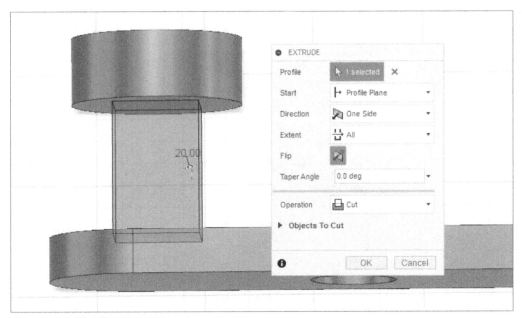

Figure-37. All tool in Extent drop down

- Click on the **Flip** button to reverse direction of extrusion.

Operation drop-down

- There are five options in **Operation** drop-down of **EXTRUDE** dialog box; refer to Figure-38. These options are discussed next.

Figure-38. Operation drop down

- Select **Join** option of **Operation** drop-down if you want to combine the extrude feature with intersecting bodies; refer to Figure-39.

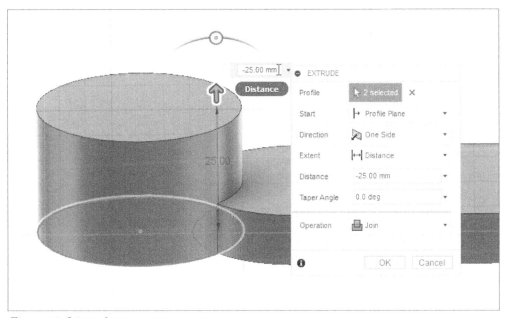

Figure-39. Join tool

- Select **Cut** option if you want to remove material from base body by using current extrude feature; refer to Figure-40.

Figure-40. Cut tool

- Select **Intersect** option from **Operation** drop-down if you want to create the region commonly bounded by extrude feature and intersecting solid bodies; refer to Figure-41.

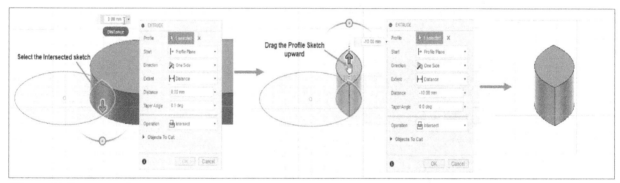

Figure-41. Intersect tool

- Select **New Body** option from **Operation** drop-down if you want to create a new body. A new body creation becomes important when you are creating molds and want all the tool bodies to be individual objects.
- Select the **New Component** option from **Operation** drop-down if you want to create a new component of the current extrude feature. New components are created for assembly. You will learn more about this option later in the book.

Revolve

Revolve tool is used to create a solid volume by revolving a sketch about selected axis. In other words, if you revolve a sketch about an axis then the volume covered by revolving sketch boundary is called revolve feature. The procedure to use this tool is discussed next.

- Create a closed profile sketch with a center line as discussed in previous chapter.
- Click on **Revolve** tool from **CREATE** drop-down of **Toolbar**; refer to Figure-42. The **REVOLVE** dialog box will be displayed; refer to Figure-43.

Figure-42. Revolve tool

Figure-43. REVOLVE dialog box

- Click on **Select** button for **Profile** selection from **REVOLVE** dialog box and then select the sketch for profile from the screen canvas.
- Click on **Select** button for **Axis** selection from **REVOLVE** dialog box and then select the sketch edge, line or center line from the screen canvas; refer to Figure-44.

Figure-44. Region selected for revolve

- After selecting the entities, the preview of revolve feature will be displayed; refer to Figure-45.

Figure-45. Preview of revolve feature

- Specify the desired value of revolve angle in the **Angle** dynamic input box. You can also set the value of angle by moving the drag handle; refer to Figure-46.

Figure-46. Moving the drag handle

Direction drop-down

The options in **Direction** drop-down are used to define in which direction profile will be revolved.

- Select **One Side** option to revolve the profile in one direction.
- Select **Two Side** option from **Direction** drop-down if you want to revolve the profile in both sides with different revolution angles; refer to Figure-47.

Figure-47. Two side tool

- Select the **Symmetric** option from **Direction** drop-down if you want to revolve the model in both direction with same angle i.e. symmetrically.

Type

- Select the **Angle** option from **Type** drop-down if you want to revolve the profile by specified angle.
- Select the **To** option from **Type** drop-down if you want to revolve the model up to a plane, face, surface, or vertex; refer to Figure-48.

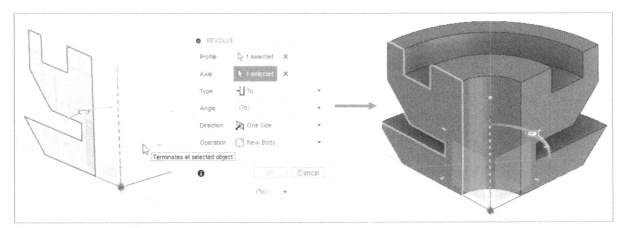

Figure-48. Preview of To option

- Select the **Full** option from **Type** drop-down if you want to revolve the profile to 360 degree angle.
- Set the other options as discussed earlier.
- Click **OK** button from **REVOLVE** dialog box to create the feature.

Sweep

The **Sweep** tool is used to create a solid volume by moving a sketch along the selected path. In other words, if you move a sketch along a path then the volume that is covered by moving sketch boundary is called sweep feature. Note that to create a solid sweep feature, you will need two sketches, one for the profile and another for the path already created in the canvas. The steps to use this tool are discussed next.

*   Click on **Sweep** tool from **CREATE** drop-down; refer to Figure-49. The **SWEEP** dialog box will be displayed; refer to Figure-50.

Figure-49. Sweep tool

Figure-50. SWEEP dialog box

In this dialog box, there are three options in **Type** drop-down to create sweep feature; **Single Path**, **Path + Guide Rail**, and **Path + Guide Surface**. The procedures to create sweep feature by using these options are discussed next.

Single Path

The **Single Path** tool sweeps the selected profile along a single path.

*   Click on the **Select** button of **Profile** section from the **SWEEP** dialog box and select the sketch for profile from the canvas screen.
*   Click on the **Select** button of **Path** section from **SWEEP** dialog box and select the path from the canvas screen; refer to Figure-51. Note that few more options are now available in the dialog box.

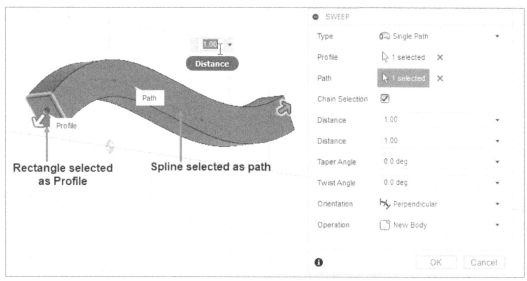

Figure-51. Selection of sketch and path

- Select the **Chain Selection** check box if you want select chain of entities connected with path curve being selected; refer to Figure-52.

Figure-52. Selecting path with and without chain selection

- The distance in the **Distance** edit boxes are not the actual distance value rather it is the percentage of total distance along the path. **1** is the maximum value which is the total path distance of sweep. Enter **0.5** value in the edit box to create the sweep along only half length of the path. You can also adjust the length of the sweep by entering value in dynamic input box or by moving the drag arrow handles displayed on the model.
- Click in the **Taper Angle** edit box and specify the desired angle value to apply draft to the faces of feature.
- Click in the **Twist Angle** edit box and specify the angle value by which you want to twist the profile along path while creating sweep feature; refer to Figure-53.

Figure-53. Preview of twisted sweep feature

- The options in the **Orientation** drop-down of **SWEEP** dialog box are used to define how the profile is pulled along the sweep path.
- **Perpendicular** option is the default selection of **Orientation** drop-down. This option creates the sweep feature in such that profile section is always perpendicular to the path. This allow more curvature on the path; refer to Figure-54.

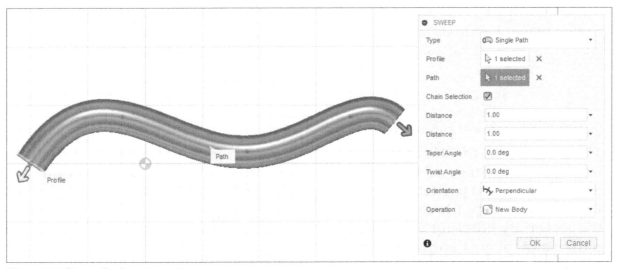

Figure-54. Perpendicular orientation

- **Parallel** option of **Orientation** drop-down creates sweep feature in such a way that the profile section is always parallel to its original orientation; refer to Figure-55.

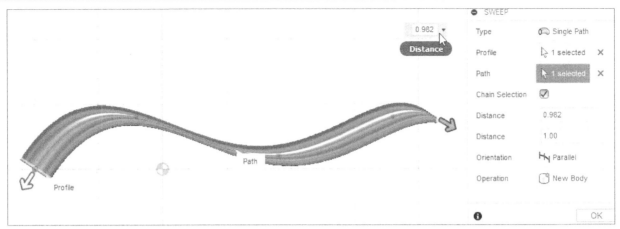

Figure-55. Parallel orientation

- After specifying the parameters, click on **OK** button to create the sweep feature.

Path + Guide Rail

Selecting this option sweeps the selected sketch along the path and uses the guide rail to control the shape. The procedure to use this tool is discussed next.

- Select the **Path + Guide Rail** option of **Type** drop-down from **SWEEP** dialog box. The options in the dialog box will be displayed as shown in Figure-56.

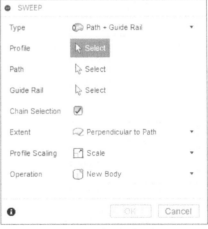

Figure-56. Path + Guide Rail option

- Click on the **Select** button for **Profile** from the **SWEEP** dialog box and then select the sketch created for profile from the canvas screen.
- Click on the **Select** button for **Path** from **SWEEP** dialog box and then select the sketch/edge for path from the canvas screen.

Note that you can also select edges of solids/surfaces as path or guide rails and faces of solids as profile section.

- Click on the **Select** button for **Guide Rail** from the **SWEEP** dialog box and then select the sketch for guide from the canvas screen; refer to Figure-57. Preview of sweep feature will be displayed and additional options will be available in the **SWEEP** dialog box.

Figure-57. Selection of entities for path + guide rail

- Click in the **Extent** drop-down and select the **Perpendicular to Path** option if you want to create the sweep feature till the profile is perpendicular to path. Select the **Full Extents** option from the drop-down if you want to create sweep till the end point of path.

- Specify the desired values for distance in **Path Distance** and **Guide Rail Distance** edit boxes as discussed earlier. Note that the **Guide Rail Distance** edit box will be available only when **Full Extents** option is selected in the **Extents** drop-down.

- Select the **Scale** option from **Profile Scaling** drop-down in **SWEEP** dialog box, if you want to equally scale the profile in both X and Y direction; refer to Figure-58. **The profile will be scaled up depending on the distance between path and guide rail.**

- Select the **Stretch** option from **Profile Scaling** drop-down if you want to scale the profile in X direction only. In this way, profile will keep following guide rail while moving along the path; refer to Figure-58.

- Click on **None** option from **Profile Scaling** drop-down, if you don't want to scale the profile along sweep. On selecting this option, guide rail is used as an orientation guide only; refer to Figure-58.

Figure-58. Preview of profile orientation

Note that the profile, path and guide rail are same in all three cases.

- The tools of **Operation** drop-down are same as discussed earlier in this book. Click on the **OK** button from the dialog box to create the features.

Path + Guide Surface

This option sweeps the selected sketch along the path and uses the guide surface to control the shape. The procedure to use this tool is discussed next.

- Select the **Path + Guide Surface** option of **Type** drop-down from **SWEEP** dialog box. The options in the dialog box will be displayed as shown in Figure-59.

Figure-59. Path + Guide Surface option

- Select the profile for sweep and click on the **Select** button for Path.
- Select the curve/edge for path and click on the **Select** button for Guide Surface.
- Select the surface by which you want to control the shape of sweep feature; refer to Figure-59. Preview of feature will be displayed.

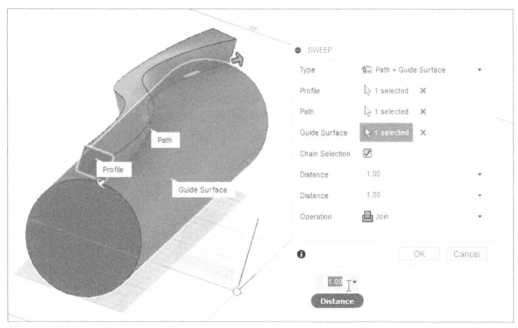

Figure-60. Sweep feature created using guide surface

- Set the parameters as discussed earlier and click on the **OK** button to create the feature.

Part file of this example is available in resources folder of this book. you can try different combinations of sweep for this example.

CONSTRUCTION GEOMETRY

Till now, we have created all the features on default planes but sometimes, we need to create features that cannot be created on default planes. In such cases, we create some construction geometries. Construction geometries are used as references for other features. Some of the well known entities that come under construction geometries are:

- Planes
- Axes
- Points
- Coordinate Systems
- Curves
- Sketches

You have learned about sketches earlier in the book. Now, we will work on other features. All the tools for construction geometry features are available in the **Construct** drop-down; refer to Figure-61. These tools are discussed next.

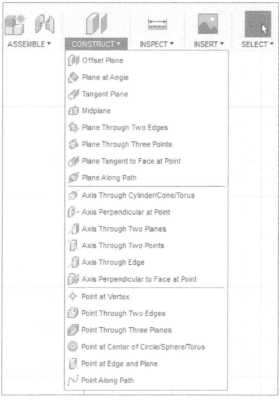

Figure-61. CONSTRUCT panel drop down

Offset Plane

The **Offset Plane** tool is used to create a plane at specified distance from a face/plane reference. The procedure to use this tool is discussed next.

- Click on the **Offset Plane** tool of **Construct** drop-down from **Toolbar**; refer to Figure-62. The **OFFSET PLANE** dialog box will be displayed; refer to Figure-63.

Figure-62. Offset Plane tool

Figure-63. OFFSET PLANE
dialog box

- Plane selection is active by default. Click on the plane/face of model to be used as reference for offset plane; refer to Figure-64. The preview for offset plane will be displayed.

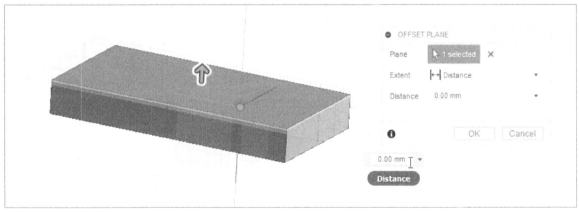

Figure-64. Selection of plane for creating offset plane

- Click in the **Distance** edit box of **OFFSET PLANE** dialog box and enter the distance at which you want to create the plane. You can also set the distance by moving the drag handle.
- After specifying the distance for offset plane, click on the **OK** button from **OFFSET PLANE** dialog box. The plane will be created; refer to Figure-65.

Figure-65. Preview of offset plane

Plane at Angle

The **Plane at Angle** tool is used to create a plane at specified angle. The procedure to use this tool is discussed next.

- Click on the **Plane at Angle** tool of **Construct** drop-down from **Toolbar**; refer to Figure-66. The **PLANE AT ANGLE** dialog box will be displayed; refer to Figure-67.

Figure-66. Plane at Angle tool

Figure-67. PLANE AT ANGLE dialog box

- **Line** selection of **PLANE AT ANGLE** dialog box is active by default. Click on the line/ edge/axis from the model as reference for creating a plane. The updated **PLANE AT ANGLE** dialog box will be displayed; refer to Figure-68.

Figure-68. Updated PLANE AT ANGLE dialog box

- Specify the desired angle value in **Angle** edit box or drag the handle.
- After specifying the angle for plane, click on the **OK** button from **PLANE AT ANGLE** dialog box. The plane will be created; refer to Figure-69.

Figure-69. Preview of plane at angle

Tangent Plane

The **Tangent Plane** tool is used to create a plane tangent to the selected face/surface. The procedure to use this tool is discussed next.

- Click on the **Tangent Plane** tool of **Construct** drop-down from **Toolbar**; refer to Figure-70. The **TANGENT PLANE** dialog box will be displayed; refer to Figure-71.

Figure-70. Tangent Plane tool

Figure-71. TANGENT PLANE dialog box

- The **Face** selection of **TANGENT PLANE** dialog box is active by default. Click on the round face of model to which plane should be tangent. The updated dialog box will be displayed; refer to Figure-72.

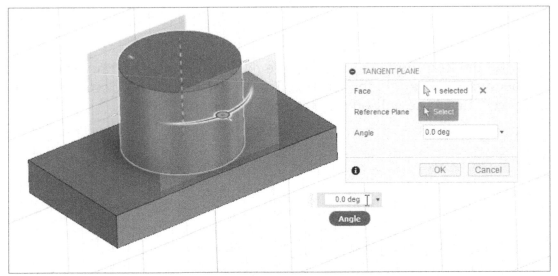

Figure-72. Updated TANGENT PLANE dialog box

- Selection of **Reference Plane** is optional. If you want to select the reference plane to define orientation of the tangent plane then click on the **Select** button of **Reference Plane** section and click on plane/face. The plane will orient accordingly to selected plane.
- Click in the **Angle** edit box and specify the angle of plane with respect to the reference plane. If you have not specified reference plane then angle will be calculated from original position. You can also set the angle by moving the drag handle.
- After specifying the parameters, click on the **OK** button from **TANGENT PLANE** dialog box to create a tangent plane; refer to Figure-73.

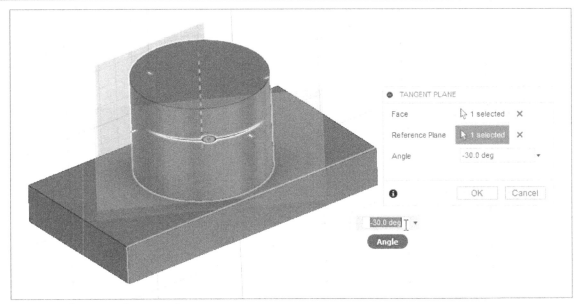

Figure-73. Preview of tangent plane

Midplane

The **Midplane** tool is used to create a plane at the midpoint of two faces/planes. The procedure to use this tool is discussed next.

*   Click on the **Midplane** tool of **Construct** drop-down from **Toolbar**; refer to Figure-74. The **MIDPLANE** dialog box will be displayed; refer to Figure-75.

Figure-74. Midplane tool

Figure-75. MIDPLANE dialog box

*   Now, you need to select two plane or faces to create a mid plane; refer to Figure-76.

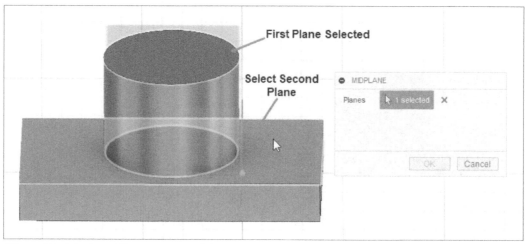

Figure-76. Selection of face to create midplane

• After selecting the second plane or face, preview of plane will be displayed; refer to Figure-77.

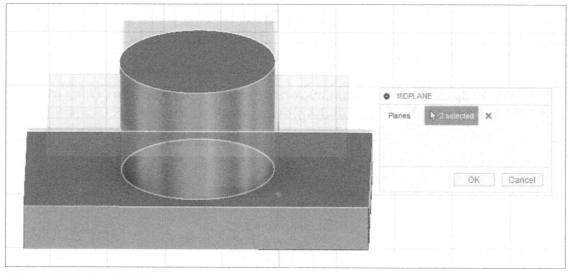

Figure-77. Preview of midplane

• Click on the **OK** button from the dialog box. The plane will be created.

Plane Through Two Edges

The **Plane Through Two Edges** tool is used to create a plane with the reference as two linear edges. The procedure to use this tool is discussed next.

• Click on the **Plane Through Two Edges** tool of **Construct** drop-down from **Toolbar**; refer to Figure-78. The tool will be activated and the **PLANE THROUGH TWO EDGES** dialog box will be displayed; refer to Figure-79.

Figure-78. Plane Through Two Edges tool

Figure-79. PLANE THROUGH
TWO EDGES dialog box

- Click on two straight edges of model to create plane; refer to Figure-80.

Figure-80. Selection of edges

- On selecting the second edge, the preview of plane will be displayed; refer to Figure-81.

Figure-81. Preview of plane through two edges

- Click on the **OK** button from the dialog box to create the plane.

Plane Through Three Points

The **Plane Through Three Points** tool is used to create a plane with the help of three points as reference. The procedure to use this tool is discussed next.

- Click on the **Plane Through Three Points** tool of **CONSTRUCT** drop-down from Toolbar; refer to Figure-82. The **PLANE THROUGH THREE POINTS** dialog box will be displayed; refer to Figure-83.

Figure-82. Plane Through Three Points tool

Figure-83. PLANE THROUGH THREE POINTS dialog box

- Select three points from model as reference to create a plane; refer to Figure-84.

Figure-84. Selection of points for creating plane

- After selecting the third point, the preview of plane will be displayed along with model; refer to Figure-85. Click on the **OK** button from the dialog box.

Figure-85. Preview of plane through three points

Plane Tangent to Face at Point

The **Plane Tangent to Face at Point** tool is used to create a plane which is tangent to selected face and aligned to selected point. The procedure to use this tool is discussed next.

- Click on the **Plane Tangent to Face at Point** tool of **CONSTRUCT** drop-down from **Toolbar**; refer to Figure-86. The **PLANE TANGENT TO FACE AT POINT** dialog box will be displayed; refer to Figure-87.

Figure-86. Plane Tangent to Face at Point tool

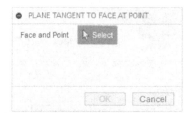

*Figure-87. PLANE TANGENT TO
FACE AT POINT dialog box*

- Click on the model to select a point and face; refer to Figure-88. You can select round as well as flat faces in this case.

Figure-88. Selection of point and face

- On selecting the second face or point, preview of plane will be displayed; refer to Figure-89. Click on the **OK** button from the dialog box to create the plane.

Figure-89. Preview of plane tangent to face at point

Plane Along Path

The **Plane Along Path** tool is used to create a plane along selected path. The plane will be perpendicular to the path at selected point. The procedure to use this tool is discussed next.

- Click on the **Plane Along Path** tool of **CONSTRUCT** drop-down from **Toolbar**; refer to Figure-90. The **PLANE ALONG PATH** dialog box will be displayed; refer to Figure-91.

Figure-90. Plane Along Path tool

Figure-91. PLANE ALONG PATH dialog box

- **Path** selection of **PLANE ALONG PATH** dialog box is active by default. Click on the edge/curve from model as reference for plane; refer to Figure-92.

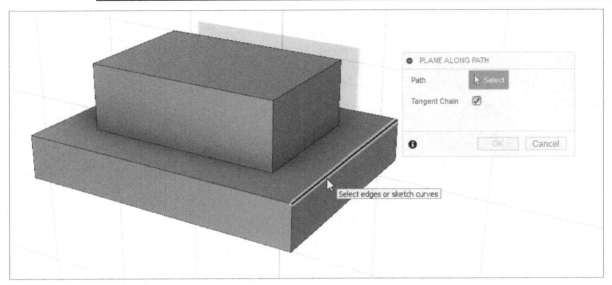

Figure-92. Selection of path

- On selecting the path, the updated **PLANE ALONG PATH** dialog box will be displayed along with the preview of plane; refer to Figure-93.

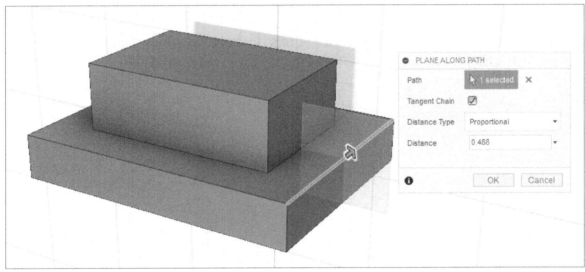

Figure-93. Preview of plane along path

- Click in the **Distance** edit box and specify the distance of plane in percentage between 0 to 1. You can also adjust the distance by moving the drag handle.
- After specifying the parameters, click on the **OK** button from **PLANE ALONG PATH** dialog box. The plane will be created.

Till now we have created plane through different references. In next section, we will create axis through different references.

Axis Through Cylinder/Cone/Torus

The **Axis Through Cylinder/Cone/Torus** tool is used to create axis through center of Cylinder, Cone, or Torus body. The procedure to use this tool is discussed next.

- Click on the **Axis Through Cylinder/Cone/Torus** tool of **CONSTRUCT** drop-down from **Toolbar**; refer to Figure-94. The **AXIS THROUGH CYLINDER/CONE/TORUS** dialog box will be displayed; refer to Figure-95.

Figure-94. Axis Through Cylinder Cone Torus tool

*Figure-95. AXIS THROUGH CYLIN-
DER CONE TORUS dialog box*

- Click on the round face of Cylinder, Cone, or Torus from model, preview of the axis will be displayed; refer to Figure-96. Click on the **OK** button from the dialog box to create the axis.

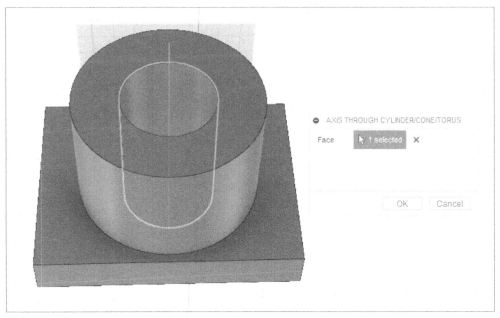

Figure-96. Preview of axis of cylinder

Axis Perpendicular at Point

The **Axis Perpendicular at Point** tool is used to create an axis perpendicular to the selected face at selected point. The procedure to use this tool is discussed next.

- Click on the **Axis Perpendicular at Point** tool of **Construct** drop-down from **Toolbar**; refer to Figure-97. The tool will be activated and **AXIS PERPENDICULAR AT POINT** dialog box will be displayed; refer to Figure-98.

Figure-97. Axis Perpendicular at Point tool

*Figure-98. AXIS PERPENDICULAR
AT POINT dialog box*

- Click at desired location on the face of model; refer to Figure-99.

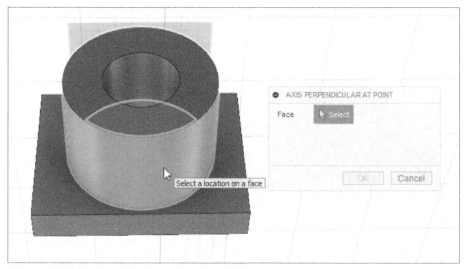

Figure-99. Selection of face for axis

- After selecting the point on any face, preview of axis will be displayed; refer to Figure-100. Click on the **OK** button from the dialog box to create axis.

Figure-100. Preview of axis perpendicular at point

Axis Through Two Planes

The **Axis Through Two Planes** tool is used to create an axis at the intersection of two planes or planer faces. The procedure to use this tool is discussed next.

- Click on the **Axis Through Two Planes** tool of **CONSTRUCT** drop-down from **Toolbar**; refer to Figure-101. The **AXIS THROUGH TWO PLANES** dialog box will be displayed; refer to Figure-102.

Figure-101. Axis Through Two Planes tool

Figure-102. AXIS THROUGH TWO PLANES dialog box

- Planes selection of **AXIS THROUGH TWO PLANES** dialog box is active by default. You need to select two planes to create an axis; refer to Figure-103.

Figure-103. Selection of planes for creating axis

- On selecting the second plane, preview of axis will be displayed; refer to Figure-104.

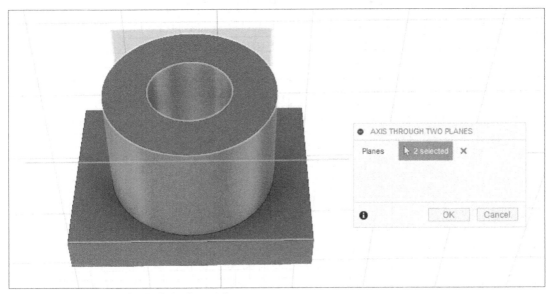

Figure-104. Preview of axis through two planes

- Click on the **OK** button from the dialog box to create the axis.

Axis Through Two Points

The **Axis Through Two Points** tool is used to create an axis passing through two reference points. The procedure to use this tool is discussed next.

- Click on the **Axis Through Two Points** tool of **CONSTRUCT** drop-down from **Toolbar**; refer to Figure-105. The tool will be activated and **AXIS THROUGH TWO POINTS** dialog box will be displayed; refer to Figure-106.

Figure-105. Axis Through Two Points tool

Figure-106. AXIS THROUGH TWO POINTS dialog box

- Select the two points from model; refer to Figure-107. Preview of axis will be displayed. Click on the **OK** button from the dialog box to create the axis.

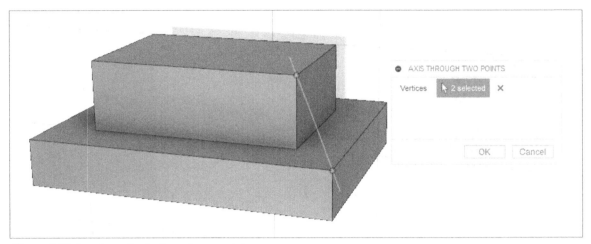

Figure-107. Preview of axis through two points

Axis Through Edge

The **Axis Through Edge** tool is used to create an axis on the selected edge/axis. The procedure to use this tool is discussed next.

- Click on the **Axis Through Edge** tool of **Construct** drop-down from **Toolbar**; refer to Figure-108. The tool will be activated and **AXIS THROUGH EDGE** dialog box will be displayed; refer to Figure-109.

Figure-108. Axis Through Edge tool

Figure-109. AXIS THROUGH EDGE dialog box

- Click on desired edge of model to create the axis; refer to Figure-110. Preview of axis will be displayed.

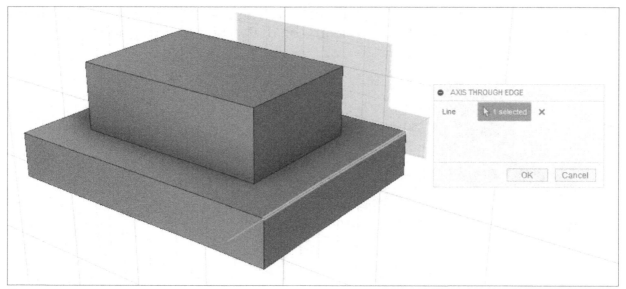

Figure-110. Preview of axis through edge

- Click on the **OK** button from the dialog box to create the axis.

Axis Perpendicular to Face at Point

The **Axis Perpendicular to Face at Point** tool is used to create an axis by using a face and a point as reference. The procedure to use this point is discussed next.

- Click on the **Axis Perpendicular to Face at Point** tool of **CONSTRUCT** drop-down from **Toolbar**; refer to Figure-111. The tool will be activated and **AXIS PERPENDICULAR TO FACE AT POINT** dialog box will be displayed; refer to Figure-112.

Figure-111. Axis Perpendicular to Face at Point tool

Figure-112. AXIS PERPENDICULAR TO FACE AT POINT dialog box

- Click on the model to select the point and face as a reference for creating plane; refer to Figure-113.

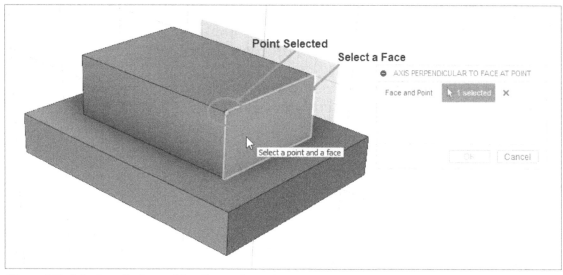

Figure-113. Selection of point and face for creating axis

- On selecting the face, preview of axis will be displayed; refer to Figure-114.

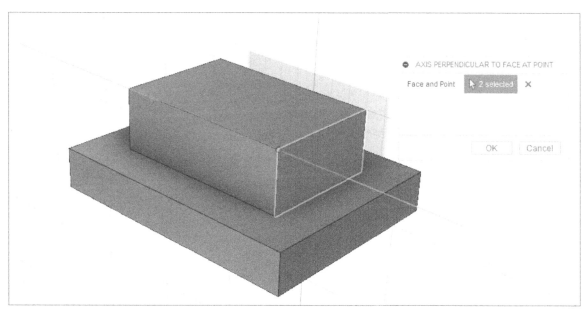

Figure-114. Preview of axis perpendicular to face at point

Note that axis will always be created passing through the point.

Till now, we have learned to created plane and axis. In next topics, we will learn the procedure to create points. Points can be used as origin, coordinate system location, or reference for other features. The tools to create points are discussed next.

Point at Vertex

The **Point at Vertex** tool is used to create a point by selecting any vertex of the model. The procedure to use this tool is discussed next.

- Click on the **Point at Vertex** tool of **CONSTRUCT** drop-down from **Toolbar**; refer to Figure-115. The tool will be activated and **POINT AT VERTEX** dialog box will be displayed; refer to Figure-116.

Figure-115. Point at Vertex tool

Figure-116. POINT AT VERTEX dialog box

- Click on the vertex of model to create a constructional point; refer to Figure-117.

Figure-117. Preview of point at vertex

Note that you can create only one point at a time using this tool.

- Click on the **OK** button from the dialog box to create point.

Point Through Two Edges

The **Point Through Two Edges** tool is used to create a point at intersection of two edges/axes intersecting each other. The procedure to use this tool is discussed next.

- Click on the **Point Through Two Edges** tool of **Construct** drop-down from **Toolbar**; refer to Figure-118. The tool is activated and **POINT THROUGH TWO EDGES** dialog box will be displayed; refer to Figure-119.

Figure-118. Point Through Two Edges tool

*Figure-119. POINT THROUGH
TWO EDGES dialog box*

- Select the two intersecting lines on the model to create point; refer to Figure-120.

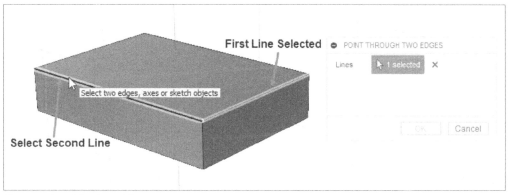

Figure-120. Selection of lines to create point

- On selecting the second line, preview of point will be displayed. Click on the **OK** button from the dialog box to create the point; refer to Figure-121.

Figure-121. Point created through two edges

Point Through Three Planes

The **Point Through Three Planes** tool is used to create a point at the intersection of three planes/faces. The procedure to use this tool is discussed next.

*   Click on the **Point Through Three Planes** tool of **CONSTRUCT** drop-down from **Toolbar**; refer to Figure-122. The tool will be activated and **POINT THROUGH THREE PLANES** dialog box will be displayed; refer to Figure-123.

Figure-122. Point Through Three Planes tool

Figure-123. POINT THROUGH
THREE PLANES dialog box

*   Select the three intersecting planes/faces from the model; refer to Figure-124.

Figure-124. Selection of three planes to create point

*   On selecting the third plane, preview of the constructional point will be displayed; refer to Figure-125.

Figure-125. Preview of point through three planes

• Click on the **OK** button from the dialog box to create the point.

Point at Center of Circle/Sphere/Torus

The **Point at Center of Circle/Sphere/Torus** tool is used to create a point at the center of selected circle/sphere/torus. The procedure to use this tool is discussed next.

• Click on the **Point at Center of Circle/Sphere/Torus** tool of **Construct** drop-down from **Toolbar**; refer to Figure-126. The tool will be activated and respective dialog box will be displayed; refer to Figure-127.

Figure-126. Point at Center of Circle Sphere Torus tool

Figure-127. POINT AT CENTER OF CIRCLE SPHERE TORUS dialog box

• Select the circle, or round face of sphere/torus to create the center point. Preview of point will be displayed; refer to Figure-128.

Figure-128. Preview of point at center

• Click on the **OK** button from the dialog box to create the point.

Point at Edge and Plane

The **Point at Edge and Plane** tool is used to create a point with the help of edge and plane as references. The procedure to use this tool is discussed next.

• Click on the **Point at Edge and Plane** tool of **CONSTRUCT** drop-down from **Toolbar**; refer to Figure-129. The tool will be activated and respective dialog box will be displayed; refer to Figure-130.

Figure-129. Point at Edge and Plane tool

Figure-130. POINT AT EDGE AND PLANE dialog box

• Select the edge and plane/face to create a point at the intersection; refer to Figure-131.

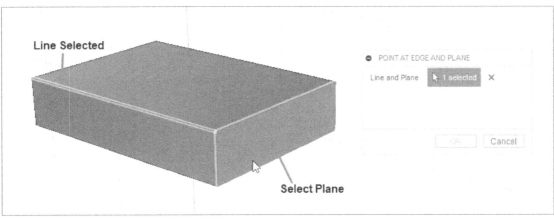

Figure-131. Selection of edge and plane

- On selecting the plane, preview of point will be displayed. Click on the **OK** button from the dialog box to create the point; refer to Figure-132.

Figure-132. Point at edge and plane created

Point Along Path

The **Point Along Path** tool is used to create a point along selected path. The procedure to use this tool is discussed next.

- Click on the **Point Along Path** tool of **CONSTRUCT** drop-down from **Toolbar**; refer to Figure-133. The **POINT ALONG PATH** dialog box will be displayed; refer to Figure-134.

Figure-133. Point Along Path tool

Figure-134. POINT ALONG PATH dialog box

- **Path** selection of **POINT ALONG PATH** dialog box is active by default. Click on the edge/curve from model as reference for point. On selecting the path, the updated **POINT ALONG PATH** dialog box will be displayed; refer to Figure-135.

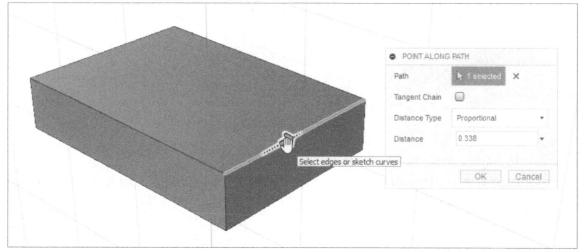

Figure-135. Selection of path to create point

- Click in the **Distance** edit box and specify the distance of point in percentage between 0 to 1. You can also adjust the distance by moving the drag handle.
- After specifying the parameters, click on the **OK** button from **POINT ALONG PATH** dialog box. The point will be created; refer to Figure-136.

Figure-136. Point along path created

PROJECT/INCLUDE TOOLS

There are various tools in **Project/Include** cascading menu of **CREATE** drop-down in **Toolbar** of **Sketch** mode, which are used to generated sketch entities on current sketching plane or surfaces by using edges, faces, and other geometries of selected objects; refer to Figure-137. You can also generate intersection curves using 3D objects. The tools in this cascading menu are given next.

Figure-137. Project Include cascading menu

Project Tool

The **Project** tool is used to project selected surface/face/edge/point/sketch of other features on selected sketching plane. Like, you can project the boundaries of selected face on the sketching plane. The procedure to use this tool is given next.

• Click on the **Project** tool from **Project/Include** cascading menu of **SKETCH** drop-down in the **Toolbar** after activating sketch on desired sketching plane. The **PROJECT** dialog box will be displayed; refer to Figure-138.

Figure-138. PROJECT dialog box

• Hover the cursor at desired geometry. Preview of project feature will be displayed; refer to Figure-139.

Figure-139. Preview of projected geometry

- Click at the desired face/edge/point/curve to project it on sketching plane. You can select multiple objects to project them on sketching plane.
- Click on the **OK** button from the dialog box to apply projection.

Intersect Tool

The **Intersect** tool is used when you want to create sketch geometries at the intersection of selected object and intersecting active sketching plane. The procedure to use this tool is given next.

- Start a sketch on desired plane.
- Click on the **Intersect** tool from **Project/Include** cascading menu of the **CREATE** drop-down in the **Toolbar**. The **INTERSECT** dialog box will be displayed; refer to Figure-140 and you will be asked to select the objects that are intersecting with current sketching plane.

Figure-140. INTERSECT dialog box

- Select the objects that are intersecting with current sketching plane and their intersection curves are to be generated; refer to Figure-141.

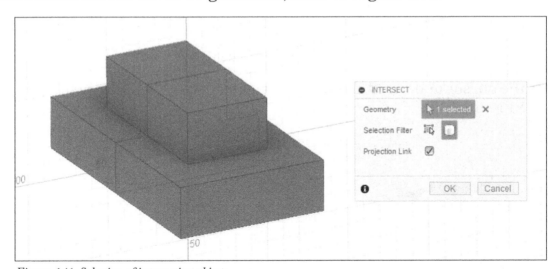

Figure-141. Selection of intersecting objects

- On selecting the objects that are intersecting with current sketching plane, a preview of the intersection curve will be displayed. Click on the **OK** button to create the generated curves; refer to Figure-142.

Figure-142. Intersection curves generated

Include 3D Geometry Tool

The **Include 3D Geometry** tool is used to include the boundaries of selected objects in current sketch. Note that this tool will not project the curves on selected sketching plane but you can use the curves for other purposes like as a reference. The procedure to use this tool is given next.

- Start a sketch on desired plane.
- Click on the **Include 3D Geometry** tool from the **Project/Include** cascading menu of the **CREATE** drop-down in **Toolbar**. You will be asked to select the 3D geometry to be included in current sketch.
- Select the desired object. Boundary curves of selected object will be created on itself; refer to Figure-143.

Figure-143. Boundary curves generated

- Press **ESC** to exit the tool.

Project to Surface Tool

The **Project to Surface** tool is used to project selected curves on the selected faces/ surfaces. The procedure to use this tool is given next.

- Click on the **Project to Surface** tool from the **Project/Include** cascading menu of the **CREATE** drop-down in the **Toolbar**. The **PROJECT TO SURFACE** dialog box will be displayed; refer to Figure-144. You will be asked to select a sketching plane.

Figure-144. PROJECT TO
SURFACE dialog box

- Select the plane which is parallel to face/surface on which sketch is to be projected. The sketching environment will become active. Click on the **Project to Surface** tool, the **PROJECT TO SURFACE** dialog box will be displayed; refer to Figure-145.

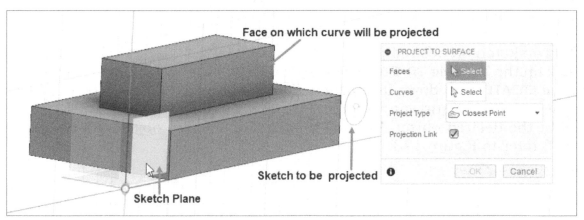

Figure-145. Selection for project to surface tool

- Select the face(s) on which you want to project selected curves.
- Click on the **Select** button for Curves from the dialog box and select the curves to be projected. Preview of projection will be displayed; refer to Figure-146.

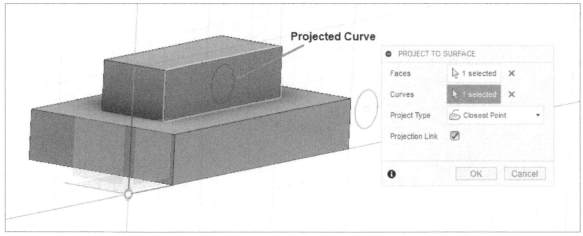

Figure-146. Preview of projected curve

- Select the **Closest Point** option from the **Project Type** drop-down if your object is well within the boundaries of selected face or you want to projects along the surface vector to the closest point on the faces; refer to Figure-146. If some of the part of curve is outside the nearest surface then rest of the curve will not be projected; refer to Figure-147. Select the **Along Vector** option from the **Project Type** drop-down if you want to define the direction along which the curve will be projected and select a direction references like, edge, axis, face, or plane. Preview of the projection will be displayed; refer to Figure-148.

Figure-147. Closest point projection

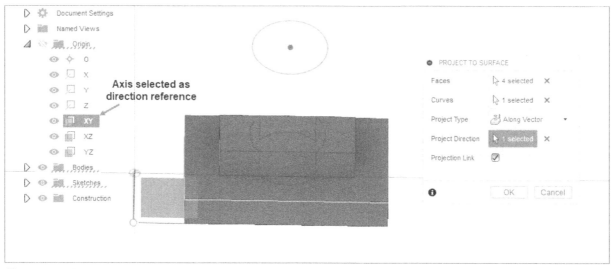

Figure-148. Projection along selected axis

- Click on the **OK** button from the dialog box to create projection.

Intersection Curve Tool

The **Intersection Curve** tool is used to create projection curves generated by selected curve and selected surfaces/faces. The procedure to use this tool is given next.

- Start a new sketch on the plane perpendicular to projection direction.
- Click on the **Intersection Curve** tool from the **Project/Include** cascading menu of the **CREATE** drop-down in **Toolbar**. The **INTERSECTION CURVE** dialog box will be displayed; refer to Figure-149.

Figure-149. INTERSECTION CURVE dialog box

- Select the curve that you want to projected and then select the faces/surfaces on which curve is to be projected. Preview of intersection curve will be displayed; refer to Figure-150.

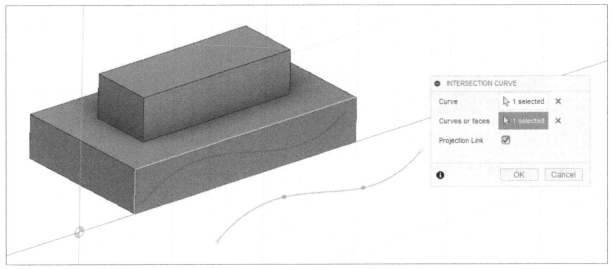

Figure-150. Preview of intersection curve

- Click on the **OK** button from the dialog box to create curves.

SELF ASSESSMENT

Q1. Discuss the procedure of cutting material from a body.

Q2. Which tool is used to combine two bodies?

Q3. Discuss the use of Sweep tool with example?

Q4. Discuss the procedure of creating plane using Offset Plane tool with example.

Q5. Create a plane tangent to the face of model.

Q6. Create a plane using three points as reference.

Q7. Create a plane using edge of a model as reference.

Q8. Create a point at the center of cylinder.

Chapter 4

Advanced 3D Modeling

Topics Covered

The major topics covered in this chapter are:

- *Loft Tool*
- *Web Tool*
- *Multiple Holes Tool*
- *Torus Tool*
- *Rectangular Pattern*
- *Thicken Tool*
- *Create Mesh Tool*

INTRODUCTION

In the last chapter, we have learned the procedure to use some 3D modeling tools and creating the constructional geometry. In this chapter, we will use the constructional geometry tools with some advanced 3D modeling tools. The tools are available in panel of MODEL workspace.

LOFT

The **Loft** tool is used to create a solid volume by joining two or more sketches created on different planes; refer to Figure-1. The procedure to use this tool is given next.

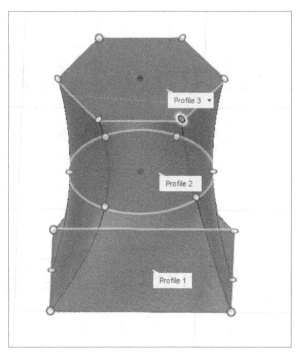

Figure-1. Lofted feature

- Click on the **Loft** tool from **CREATE** drop-down in the **Toolbar**; refer to Figure-2. The **LOFT** dialog box will be displayed as shown in Figure-3.

Figure-2. Loft tool

Figure-3. LOFT dialog box

- By default, **Profiles** selection box is active and you are asked to select sketches for loft feature. You can also select faces/surfaces as profile for loft.
- Click one by one on the sketches created at different planes. Note that you need to select the sketches in order by which they can be joined to each other successively. The preview of loft will be displayed; refer to Figure-4.

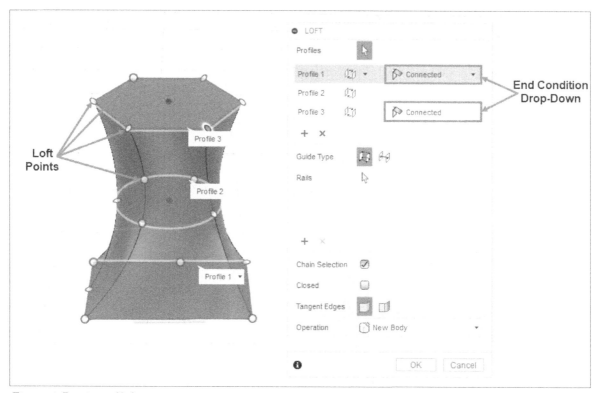

Figure-4. Preview of loft

- To make adjustments to the loft, you can move the loft points along the profile edge.

- Click the **End condition** drop-down of **Profile 1** from **Profiles** selection box. The options will be displayed as per the geometry selected.

If you have selected sketches only as profiles then **Connected** and **Direction** options are available in the drop-down; refer to Figure-5. If you have selected sketches and faces of model or only faces of the model as profiles then **Connected (G0)**, **Tangent(G1)**, and **Curvature(G2)** options are available in the **End condition** drop-down; refer to Figure-6. If you have selected a point as profile at the end then **Sharp** and **Point Tangent** options will be available in the **End condition** drop-down; refer to Figure-7.

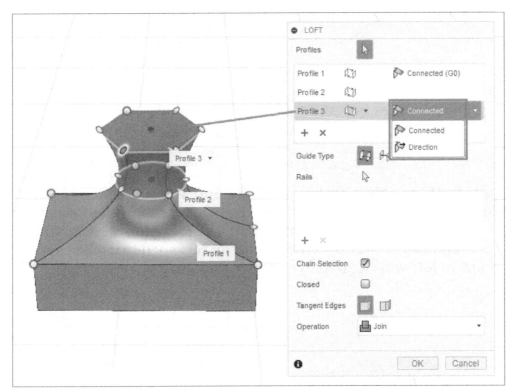

Figure-5. End condition options for sketch profile in loft

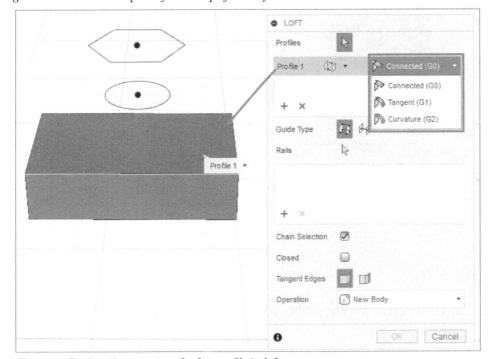

Figure-6. End condition options for face profile in loft

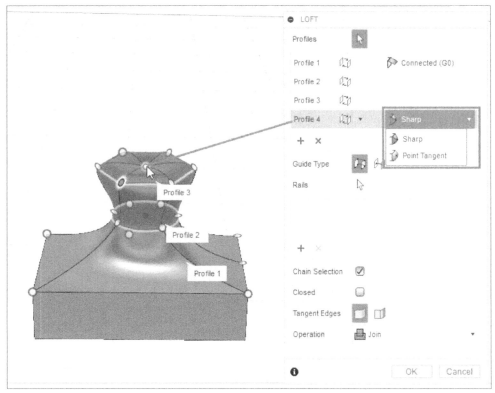

Figure-7. End condition options for point profile in loft

- Select the desired end condition option from the **End condition** drop-down. One line explanation of each end condition option is given in Figure-8.

Figure-8. End condition

- Select the **Direction** option from the **End Condition** drop-down. The updated **LOFT** dialog box will be displayed with options to specify **Takeoff Weight** and **Takeoff Angle**; refer to Figure-9. As the name suggests, these options are used to specify scale and angle at which loft will start or end at selected profile.

Figure-9. Updated LOFT dialog box

- If you have selected **Tangent**, **Curvature**, or **Point Tangent** option from the **End Condition** drop-down then **Tangency Weight** edit box is displayed in the dialog box to specify scale factor of tangency.
- Enter the value as **4** in **Takeoff Weight** edit box and specify the outward angle in **Takeoff Angle** edit box by **20** degree. You will find a bulge in the loft feature; refer to Figure-10.

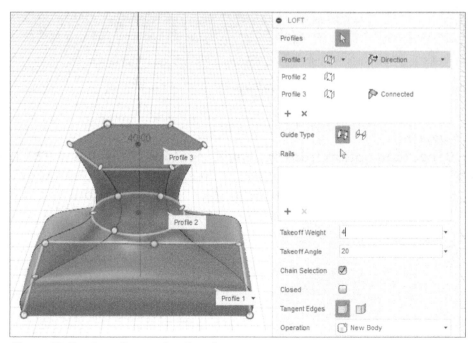

Figure-10. Preview after entering the value

- Select the **Chain Selection** check box if you also want to select the adjacent edges and included as one profile. Clear the check box if you want to select the each edge of profile individually. This check box hardly has any effect in **Model** workspace but you will find its uses in **Patch** and **Sculpt** workspaces while create loft feature.

- After setting desired parameters, click **OK** button of **LOFT** dialog box to create the loft feature.

Loft feature can be very useful in joining two faces or surfaces to create solid volume; refer to Figure-11. You can adjust the shape of loft by using the drag points on the edges.

Figure-11. Creating loft using surface and face

Guide Type

There are two ways to control transition between profiles of loft; using **Rails** and using **Centerline**. **Rails** are 2D or 3D curves that affect the loft shape between sections at boundaries. To refine the shape of loft, you need to add number of rails. These rails must intersect each section and terminate on or beyond the first and last sections. **Rails** must be tangentially continuous. A **Centerline** tool is a type of rail to which the loft sections are held normal. It behaves like a sweep path. Centerline lofts maintain a more consistent transition between the cross-sectional areas of selected loft sections. Center lines follow the same criteria as rails, except they need not intersect the sections and only one centerline can be selected. We have discussed two examples next for tent and ring which use rails and centerline respectively.

Using Rails

- To select rails for the loft, click the **Rails** button in **Guide Type** section; refer to Figure-12.

Figure-12. Rails and Centerline tool

- In this case, we have created a sketch of tent like structure using a rectangle and four arcs (to be used as rail) on different planes; refer to Figure-13.

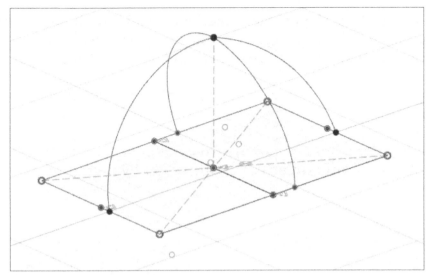

Figure-13. Sketch for using Rails tool

- Select the **Loft** tool from **CREATE** drop-down. The **LOFT** dialog box will be displayed.
- Select the rectangle and point of the sketch in **Profiles** section of **LOFT** dialog box. The preview of model will be shown.
- Click on the **Arrow** selection button of **Rails** from **Guide Type** section box, to select the rails for the loft.
- Select the four arcs of the model; refer to Figure-14.

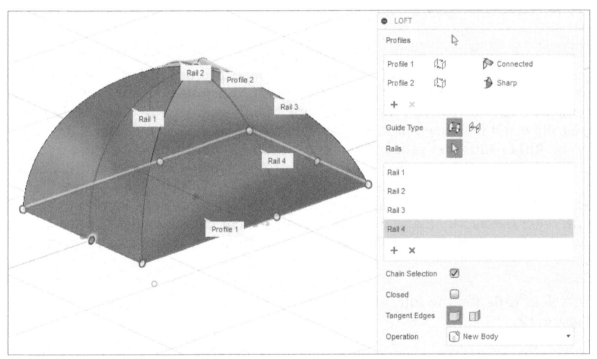

Figure-14. Preview of loft on selecting Rails

- Click **OK** of **LOFT** dialog box to complete the process of making loft. The shape of loft will be modified according to rails selected.

Using Centerline

- To use the **Centerline** guide type, we have created a sketch of ring like structure with the help of circle and rectangle on different planes; refer to Figure-15.

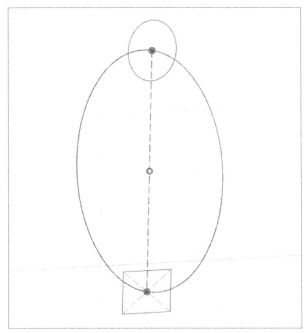

Figure-15. Sketch of ring

- Select the **Loft** tool from **CREATE** drop-down. The **LOFT** dialog box will be displayed.
- Select the circle and rectangle as profile in **Profiles** section of **LOFT** dialog box.
- Since these two profiles are coplanar, you may not get any preview and an error might welcome you.
- Click on **Centerline** button from **Guide Type** section and select the circle to be used as center line. The preview will be displayed; refer to Figure-16.

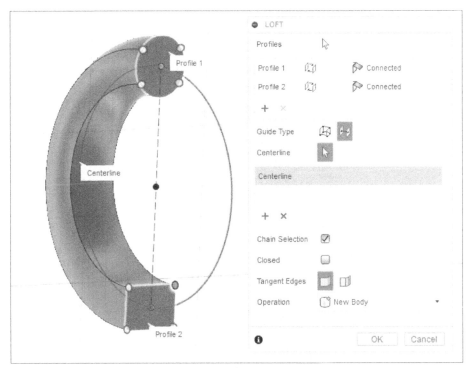

Figure-16. Preview of loft on selecting centerline

- By default, **Closed** check box is clear so you will be getting half of the ring. Select the **Closed** check box to complete the loft. Preview of the loft feature will be modified; refer to Figure-17.

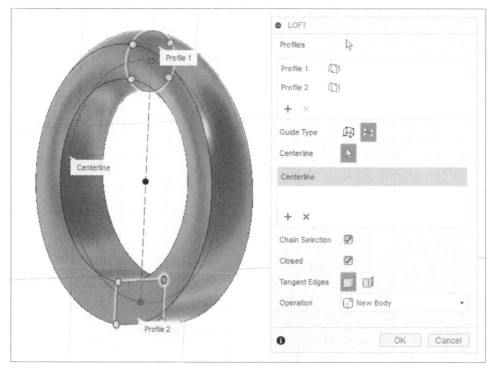

Figure-17. Preview of loft on selecting closed centerline

- Click **OK** button of **LOFT** dialog box to complete the process.
- The tools of **Operation** drop-down are same as discussed earlier.

RIB

The **Rib** tool is used to create supporting features in the model by using curve(s). The procedure to use this tool is discussed next.

- Click on **Rib** tool from **CREATE** drop-down; refer to Figure-18 or right-click on the screen canvas and select **Rib** from **Create** cascading menu in **Marking menu**. The **RIB** dialog box will be displayed; refer to Figure-19. Note that the curve for rib should be created in such a way that its projection is within solid faces of the model; refer to Figure-20.

Figure-18. Rib tool

Figure-19. RIB dialog box

Figure-20. Sketch for rib

- The **Curve** section of **RIB** dialog box is active by default. Select the sketch curve joining edges of solid model to create rib. The updated **RIB** dialog box will be displayed; refer to Figure-21.

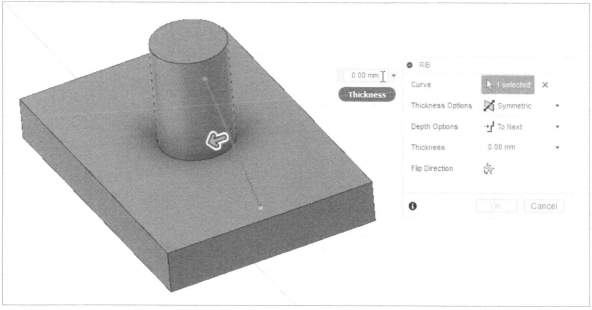

Figure-21. Updated RIB dialog box

- Select the **Symmetric** option from **Thickness Options** drop-down to set the thickness of rib on both side of curve. Select **One Direction** option from **Thickness Options** drop-down to apply the thickness of rib in one direction or one side.
- Enter the desired value of thickness in **Thickness** edit box or floating window.
- Select the **To Next** option in **Depth Options** drop-down from **RIB** dialog box to create the rib up to next surface or model; refer to Figure-22.

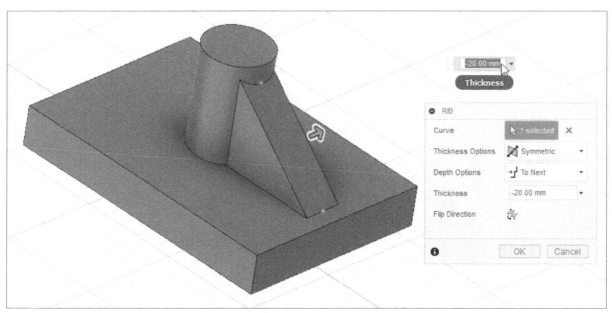

Figure-22. To Next tool in Rib

- Select the **Depth** option from **Depth Options** drop-down to specify the depth of rib. Type the numerical value of depth in **Depth** edit box or adjust the depth by moving the **Drag arrow**.
- You can also enter the value of depth in minus(-) to reverse the direction of depth in **Depth** edit box; refer to Figure-23.

Figure-23. Depth tool in Rib

- Click on the **Flip Direction** button to flip the direction of rib.
- After specifying the parameters, click **OK** button of **RIB** dialog box complete the process.

WEB

The **Web** tool works like **Rib** tool which is used to create geometry from sketch curves that intersect with pre-existing bodies. The **Web** tool uses multiple curves to create several merged ribs at once. The procedure to use this tool is discussed next.

- Click on **Web** tool from **CREATE** drop-down of **SOLID** tab in the **Toolbar**; refer to **Figure-24**. The **WEB** dialog box will be displayed; refer to Figure-25.

Figure-24. Web tool

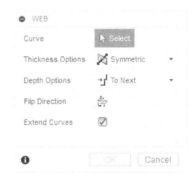

Figure-25. WEB dialog box

- The **Curve** selection is active by default. Select the sketch to create web; refer to Figure-26.

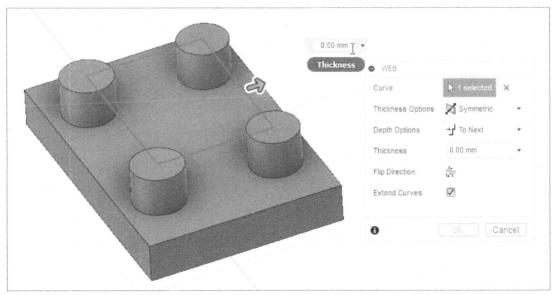

Figure-26. Selecting the sketch

- Enter the desired value of thickness in the **Thickness** edit box or floating window. You can also set the thickness by moving the drag handle.

- The options for **Thickness options** and **Depth Options** drop-downs are same discussed earlier.
- Preview of rib will be displayed according to parameters specified; refer to Figure-27.
- Click **OK** button from **WEB** dialog box to complete the process.

Figure-27. Preview of web

HOLE

The **Hole** tool is used to create holes that comply with the real machining tools. With the help of **Hole** tool, three types of holes are created. The procedure to use this tool is discussed next.

- Click on **Hole** tool from **CREATE** drop-down or right-click on the screen canvas and select **Hole** of **Create** cascading menu from **Marking** menu; refer to Figure-28. The **HOLE** dialog box will be displayed; refer to Figure-29.

Figure-28. Hole tool

Figure-29. HOLE dialog box

- There are two types of tools in **Placement** section which are discussed next.

Single Hole

- Click on **Single Hole** button from **Placement** section to create one hole. The **Select** button for **Face** section will be activated.
- Select the face/plane on which you want to create hole. The updated **HOLE** dialog box will be displayed with preview of hole; refer to Figure-30.

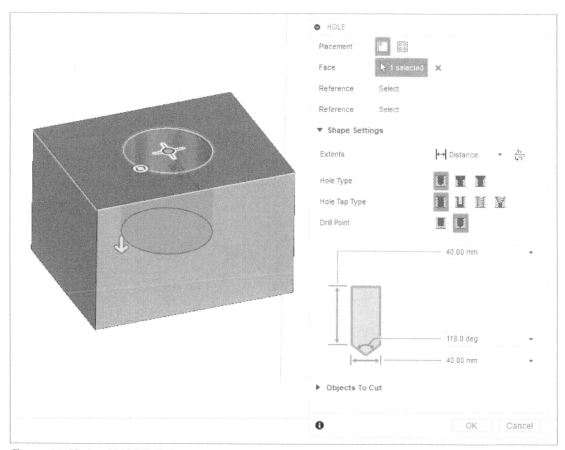

Figure-30. Updated HOLE dialog box

- Click on **Select** button of first **Reference** section from **HOLE** dialog box, click at the center of hole and then click at the edge from where you want to specify the distance of hole; refer to Figure-31.

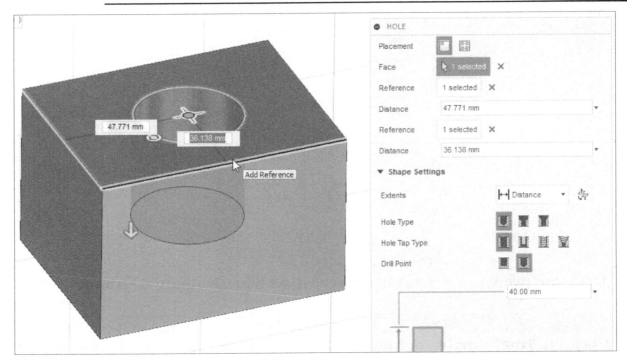

Figure-31. Add reference

- Enter the desired value of distance in the dynamic input box or **Distance** edit box in dialog box. Click on another edge to define other reference and set the desired distance value.
- Click on **Simple** button in **Hole Type** section to create simple hole of specified dimensions.
- Click on **Counterbore** button in **Hole Type** section to create a counterbore hole and specify the dimension in their respective edit box at the bottom in the dialog box; refer to Figure-32.

Figure-32. Counterbore hole

- Click on **Countersink** button in **Hole Type** drop-down to create a countersink hole and specify the dimension in their respective edit box at the bottom in the dialog box; refer to Figure-33.

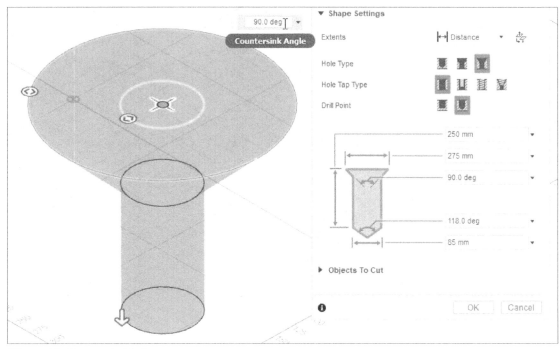

Figure-33. Countersink hole

- Click on the desired button in the **Hole Tap Type** section to define the tapping inside the hole. Select the **Simple** button to create straight holes without tapping.
- Select the **Clearance** button to create standard holes with defined fit. The options will be displayed accordingly; refer to Figure-34. Select the desired options to define size of hole.
- Select the **Tapped** button to create holes as per their class and designation in standard hole profile database; refer to Figure-35. Select the desired options to define shape and size of hole. If you want to model threads created by tapping in the hole then select the **Modeled** check box. Preview of hole will be displayed with selected thread type; refer to Figure-36.

Figure-34. Options for clearance hole tap type

Figure-35. Options for tapped hole tap type

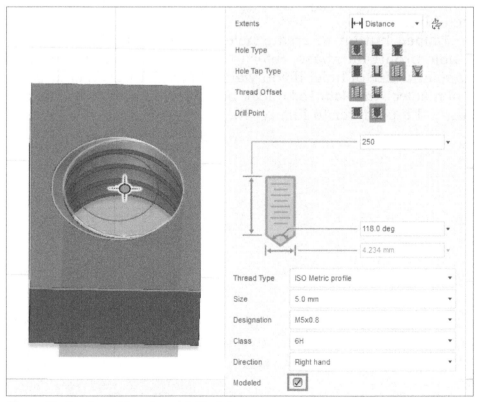

Figure-36. Preview of threads modeled in hole

- Select the **Distance** option from **Extent** drop-down to specify the distance of hole in the model. Select the **To** option from **Extent** drop-down to set the length of hole up to next model or face. Select the **All** option from **Extent** drop-down to create a hole passing through all the features in its path.
- Click on **Flip Direction** option to reverse the direction of hole.
- Expand the **Objects To Cut** node and select check boxes for bodies that you want to be cut by the hole.
- After specifying the parameters, click **OK** button of **HOLE** dialog box to complete the process; refer to Figure-37.

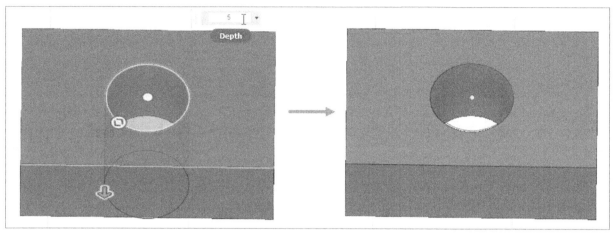

Figure-37. Preview of hole

Multiple Holes

The **Multiple Holes** button in **HOLE** dialog box is used to multiple similar hole at a time. To use this tool, you must have sketch points already created on the model where you want to cut holes. The procedure to use this tool is discussed next.

- Click on the **Multiple Holes** button in **Placement** section from **HOLE** dialog box. The **Sketch Point** selection tool will be activated. Select the sketch points for defining positions of holes; refer to Figure-38.

Figure-38. Sketch for multiple holes

- Set the other options as discussed earlier.
- After specifying the parameters, click **OK** button from **HOLE** dialog box to finish the process. The preview will be displayed; refer to Figure-39.

Figure-39. Preview of multiple holes

THREAD

The **Thread** tool is used to cut helical thread on cylindrical faces. Using this tool, you can save the custom threads in library. The Procedure to use this tool is discussed next.

- Click on the **Thread** tool from the **CREATE** drop-down in the **Toolbar**; refer to Figure-40. The **THREAD** dialog box will be displayed; refer to Figure-41.

Figure-40. Thread tool

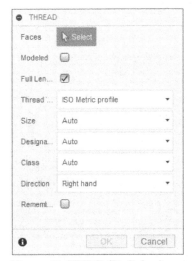

Figure-41. THREAD dialog box

- The **Faces** selection of **THREAD** dialog box is active by default. Select the round faces to which threads are to be applied.

- Select the **Modeled** check box to create the model feature of thread otherwise it will be created as cosmetic feature.
- On selecting **Modeled** check box, preview of thread will be displayed; refer to Figure-42.

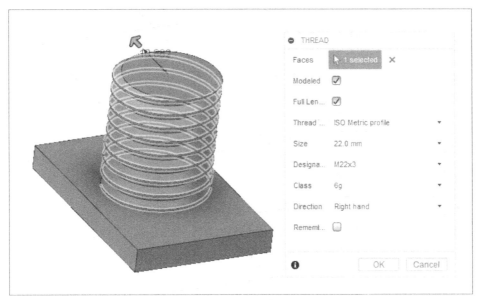

Figure-42. Preview of thread on selecting Modeled check box

- Clear the **Full Length** check box to specify the length of thread on the selected face. Otherwise, thread will be created up to the entire length of selected face.
- Click on the **Thread Type** drop-down to select the type of thread profile; refer to Figure-43. Most of the engineering thread profiles are available in this drop-down.

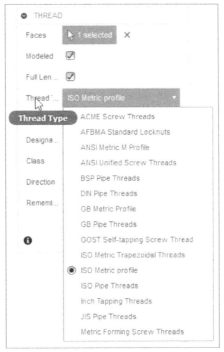

Figure-43. Thread Type drop down

- Click on the **Size** drop-down and select the desired size of thread. You can also adjust the size by using the **Drag Handle**.
- Click on the **Designation** drop-down and select the designation of thread; refer to Figure-44.

Figure-44. Thread Designation drop down

- Click on the **Class** drop-down and select the class of thread.
- Click on **Direction** drop-down and select the direction for thread; refer to Figure-45.

Figure-45. Thread Direction drop down

- Select the **Remember Size** check box to remember these thread setting for the next time, when the **Thread** tool will be invoked.
- Click **OK** button from **THREAD** dialog box to create the thread; refer to Figure-46.

Figure-46. Thread created in solid

BOX

The **Box** tool is used to create a rectangular box on selected work plane. The procedure to use this tool is discussed next.

*   Click on **Box** tool in **CREATE** drop-down from **Toolbar**; refer to Figure-47. You will be asked to select the plane for creating the sketch for box.

Figure-47. Box tool

*   Select **Top** plane or any other desired plane/face.
*   Click on the screen to specify the first point of sketch.
*   Move the cursor to display preview of rectangle and click at desired location to specify other corner of rectangle. You can also enter the numerical value of **Length** and **Width** in their specific edit box; refer to Figure-48.

Figure-48. Entering dimension for rectangle

- You can toggle between these two edit box by pressing **TAB** key. The **Box** dialog box will be displayed along with the preview of box; refer to Figure-49.

Figure-49. Preview of box with BOX dialog box

- Specify the desired value of height in the **Height** edit box of the **BOX** dialog box.
- The options of **Operation** section were discussed earlier.
- Click **OK** button from the **BOX** dialog box to create the box; refer to Figure-50.

Figure-50. Box created

CYLINDER

This tool is used to create a cylindrical body by adding depth to a circular region. The procedure to use this tool is discussed next.

- Click on **Cylinder** tool in **CREATE** drop-down from **Toolbar**; refer to Figure-51. You are asked to select plane for creating base sketch. Select the desired plane/face.

Figure-51. Cylinder tool

- Click on the screen to specify the center point of base circle.
- Enter the desired value of diameter in the floating window and press **ENTER** to create a sketch of circle; refer to Figure-52.

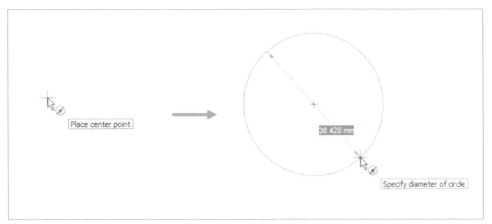

Figure-52. Specifying diameter of circle to create cylinder

- The **CYLINDER** dialog box will be displayed along with preview of cylinder; refer to Figure-53.

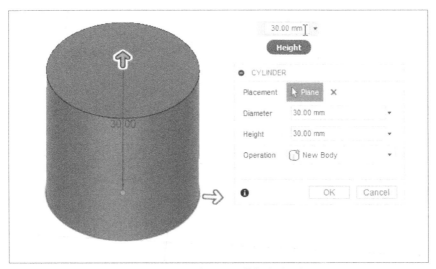

Figure-53. Preview of cylinder with CYLINDER dialog box

- If you want to edit the diameter of cylinder then click in the **Diameter** edit box of **CYLINDER** dialog box and specify the desired value.
- Click in the **Height** edit box and specify the height of cylinder.
- Click **OK** button from the **CYLINDER** dialog box to create the cylinder; refer to Figure-54.

Figure-54. Cylinder created

SPHERE

The **Sphere** tool is used to create a T-spline, solid, or surface sphere on a work plane or face. The procedure to use this tool is discussed next.

- Click on the **Sphere** tool in **CREATE** drop-down from **Toolbar**; refer to Figure-55.

Figure-55. Sphere tool

- You are asked to select the plane for creating the sketch for circle. Select the desired plane/face.
- Click on the screen at desired location to specify the center point of sphere. The **SPHERE** dialog box will be displayed along with the preview of sphere; refer to Figure-56.

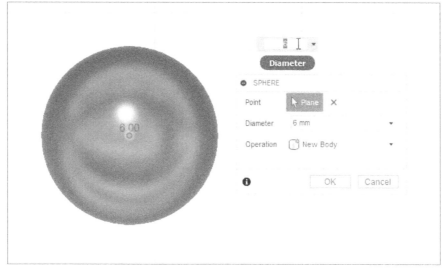

Figure-56. Preview of sphere with SPHERE dialog box

- Click in the **Diameter** edit box and specify the desired value of diameter for sphere.
- The options of **Operation** drop-down are same as discussed earlier.
- Click **OK** button of **SPHERE** dialog box to finish the process; refer to Figure-57.

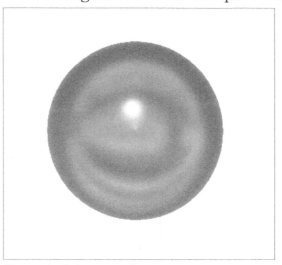

Figure-57. Sphere created

TORUS

The **Torus** tool is used to create T-spline, solid, or surface torus on a work plane or face. The procedure to use this tool is discussed next.

- Click on **Torus** tool in **CREATE** drop-down from **Toolbar**; refer to Figure-58. You are asked to select the plane/face for creating the center circle of torus. Select the desired face/plane.

Figure-58. Torus tool

- Click on the screen to specify the center point of sketch. Specify the diameter of torus in dynamic input box and press **ENTER**; refer to Figure-59. The **TORUS** dialog box will be displayed along with the preview of Torus; refer to Figure-60.

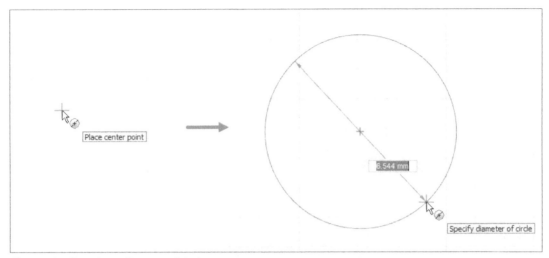

Figure-59. Specifying diameter of circle to create torus

Figure-60. Preview of torus with TORUS dialog box

- If you want to edit the diameter of circle earlier created then click in the **Inner Diameter** edit box and specify the desired value.
- Click in the **Torus Diameter** edit box and enter the diameter of torus. You can also adjust the diameter of torus by moving the drag handle.
- Select the **On Center** option of **Position** drop-down from **TORUS** dialog box, if you want to use inner circle as center of the torus. Select the **Inside** option of **Position** drop-down if you want to position the torus inside of the inner circle. Select the **Outside** option of **Position** drop-down if you want to position the torus section outside of the inner circle.

- The options of **Operation** drop-down are same as discussed earlier.
- Click **OK** button of **TORUS** dialog box to finish the process; refer to Figure-61.

Figure-61. Torus created

COIL

The **Coil** tool is used for creating helix-based features like springs. The procedure to use this tool is discussed next.

- Click on the **Coil** tool of **CREATE** drop-down from **Toolbar**; refer to Figure-62. You will be asked to select a face/plane to create base sketch.

Figure-62. Coil tool

- Click on the desired face/plane. You will be asked to specify center of the base circle.
- Click on the screen to specify the center point of sketch. Type the desired value of diameter of coil in dynamic input box and press **ENTER**; refer to Figure-63.

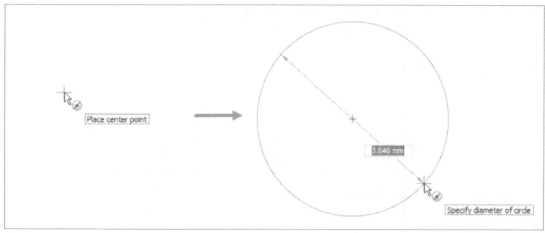

Figure-63. Specifying diameter of circle to create coil

- The **COIL** dialog box will be displayed along with the preview of coil; refer to Figure-64.

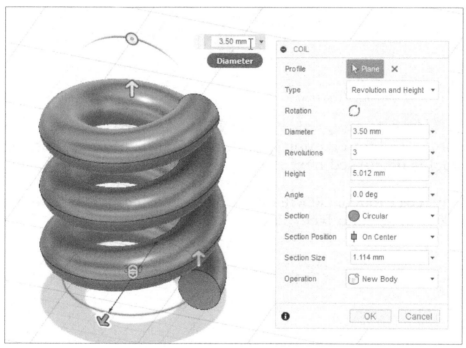

Figure-64. Preview of coil with COIL dialog box

- Select the **Revolution and Height** option from **Type** drop-down if you want to create the coil by specifying number of revolutions in the coil and height of coil. Select the **Revolution and Pitch** option from **Type** drop-down if you want to create the coil by specifying number of revolutions in the coil and distance between two successive turns of the coil. Select the **Height and Pitch** option from **Type** drop-down to specify total height of the coil and distance between two successive turns of the coil. Select the **Spiral** option from **Type** drop-down to create a spiral coil. Note that the options in the dialog box will be modified based on your selection in **Type** drop-down. In our case, we are selecting the **Revolution and Height** option; refer to Figure-65.

Figure-65. Coil Type drop down

- Click on the **Rotation** button to flip the rotation side of coil to clockwise or counterclockwise direction; refer to Figure-66.

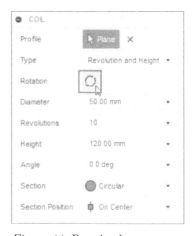

Figure-66. Rotation button

- Click in the **Diameter** edit box and enter the desired value to change the diameter of coil.
- Click in the **Revolutions** edit box and enter the desired value for number of revolutions of coil.
- Click in the **Height** edit box and specify the total height of coil. You can also set the height of coil by moving the drag handle.
- Click in the **Angle** edit box and specify the desired angle value to create taper coil.
- Select **Circular** option of **Section** drop-down from **COIL** dialog box to set the circular profile of coil. Select the **Square** option from **Section** drop-down to set square profile of coil. Select **Triangular(External)** option of **Section** drop-down to set the external triangular profile of coil. Select **Triangular(Internal)** option of **Section** drop-down to set internal triangular profile of coil; refer to Figure-67.

Figure-67. Coil Section drop down

- Select **On Center** option of **Section Position** drop-down from **COIL** dialog box to position the coil in such a way that the base circle is at center of the coil. Click on the **Inside** button of **Section Position** drop-down if you want to position the coil inside the base circle. Click on the **Outside** section of **Section Position** drop-down if you want to position the coil outside the base circle.
- Click in the **Section Size** edit box and specify the size of coil section. If section is circle then this will be diameter and if section is triangle or square then it will be length of one edge of section.
- The options of **Operations** drop-down were discussed earlier.
- Click **OK** button of **COIL** dialog box to finish the process of creating a coil; refer to Figure-68.

Figure-68. Coil created

PIPE

The **Pipe** tool is used to create pipes of different sections that follow a selected path. The procedure to use this tool is discussed next.

- Click on **Pipe** tool of **CREATE** drop-down from **Toolbar**; refer to Figure-69. The **PIPE** dialog box will be displayed and you will be asked to select a path for pipe; refer to Figure-70.

Figure-69. Pipe tool

Figure-70. PIPE dialog box

- Select the sketch or edge of a model for path of the pipe; refer to Figure-71.

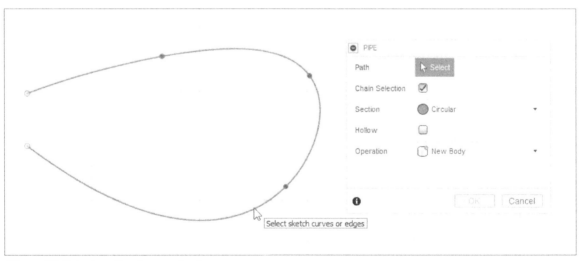

Figure-71. Selection of path to create pipe

- On selecting the path, the updated **PIPE** dialog box will be displayed. Click in the **Distance** edit box and enter the desired value. The value of distance lies between 0 to 1. You can also set the distance (length) of pipe on the selected path by moving the drag handle.
- The options of **Section** drop-down were discussed earlier in **Coil** tool.
- Click in the **Section Size** edit box and specify the diameter of pipe.
- Select the **Hollow** check box to create a hollow pipe. The updated **PIPE** dialog box will be displayed along with the preview of pipe; refer to Figure-72.

Figure-72. Preview of pipe with PIPE dialog box

- Click in the **Section Thickness** edit box and specify thickness of pipe.
- The options of **Operation** drop-down were discussed earlier in this book.
- Click **OK** button of **PIPE** dialog box to complete the process of creating the pipe; refer to Figure-73.

Figure-73. Pipe created

PATTERN

The **Pattern** tool is used to create copies of features or bodies at regular intervals. There are three tools in **Pattern** cascading menu; refer to Figure-74. These tools are discussed next.

Figure-74. Pattern cascading menu

Rectangular Pattern

The **Rectangular Pattern** tool is used to create copies of objects in one or two directions. The procedure to use this tool are discussed next.

- Click on **Rectangular Pattern** tool of **Pattern** cascading menu from **CREATE** drop-down; refer to Figure-75. The **RECTANGULAR PATTERN** dialog box will be displayed; refer to Figure-76.

Figure-75. Rectangular Pattern tool in solid

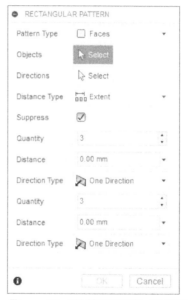

Figure-76. RECTANGULAR PAT-TERN dialog box in solid

- Select **Faces** option from **Pattern Type** drop-down if you want to select faces for pattern. Select **Bodies** from **Pattern Type** drop-down if you want to select bodies for creating copies. Select **Features** from **Pattern Type** drop-down if you want to select features for creating copies. Select **Components** from **Pattern Type** drop-down if you want to select component for creating copies; refer to Figure-77.

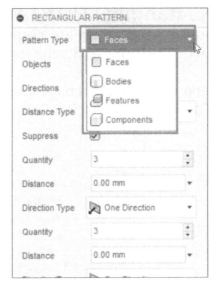

Figure-77. Pattern Type drop down

- We are using **Bodies** option from **Pattern Type** drop-down. Select the body for creating its copies; refer to Figure-78.

Figure-78. Selection of body for rectangular pattern

- Click on **Select** button of **Directions** option and select the default axes or edges of the model to define direction in which copies will be created; refer to Figure-79.

Figure-79. Selection of direction

- Select the **Extent** option from **Distance Type** drop-down if you want to specify total length within which copies will be created. Select the **Spacing** option from **Distance Type** drop-down to set the distance between two consecutive instances of object. In our case, we have selected **Extent** option.
- Select the **Suppress** check box if you want to suppress any instance of pattern.
- Click in the **Quantity** edit box and specify the number of instances to be created in the pattern along selected direction.
- Click in **Distance** edit box and specify the distance value within which pattern instances will be created. You can also set the distance by moving the drag handle.
- Select the **One Direction** option from **Direction Type** drop-down if you want to create the copies in one side of selected direction. Click on **Symmetric** option from **Direction Type** drop-down to create the copies in both sides of selected direction.
- Similarly, specify the quantity, distance, and direction type for other direction.
- After specifying the parameter, click **OK** button from **RECTANGULAR PATTERN** dialog box to finish the process; refer to Figure-80.

Figure-80. Solid model after applying rectangular pattern tool

Circular Pattern

The **Circular Pattern** tool is used to create copies of selected objects around selected axis/edge. The procedure to use this tool is discussed next.

• Click on **Circular Pattern** tool from **Pattern** cascading menu; refer to Figure-81. The **CIRCULAR PATTERN** dialog box will be displayed; refer to Figure-82.

Figure-81. Circular Pattern tool in solid

Figure-82. CIRCULAR PATTERN dialog box in solid

• Select the desired option from **Pattern Type** drop-down. The options of **Pattern Type** drop-down are same as discussed in **Rectangular Pattern** tool.
• **Objects** selection is active by default. Select the component to be patterned; refer to Figure-83.

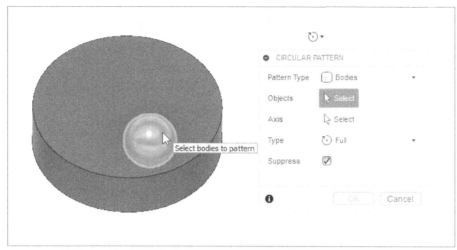

Figure-83. Selection of body for circular pattern

- Click on **Select** button of **Axis** section and select the edge/axis about which the circular pattern will be created.
- Select the **Full** option from **Type** drop-down if you want to create the copies of object around 360 degree path. Select **Angle** option from **Type** drop-down if you want to create the copies within specified angle range. Click on **Symmetric** option from **Type** drop-down if you want to create copies symmetrically in specified angle range.
- Select the **Suppress** check box if you want to suppress the any instance of pattern.
- Click in the **Quantity** edit box and enter the number of copies to be created in pattern.
- After specifying the parameters, click on the **OK** button from **CIRCULAR PATTERN** dialog box to finish the process; refer to Figure-84.

Figure-84. Solid model after applying circular pattern tool

Pattern on Path

The **Pattern on Path** tool is used to create copies of the selected object along selected path. The procedure to use this tool is discussed next.

- Click on the **Pattern on Path** tool of **Pattern** cascading menu from **CREATE** drop-down; refer to Figure-85. The **PATTERN ON PATH** dialog box will be displayed; refer to Figure-86.

Figure-85. Pattern on Path tool

Figure-86. PATTERN ON PATH dialog box

- Click on **Faces** from **Pattern Type** drop-down. Other options of **Pattern Type** drop-down are same as discussed earlier.
- **Objects** selection is selected by default. Select the faces for creating the copies; refer to Figure-87.

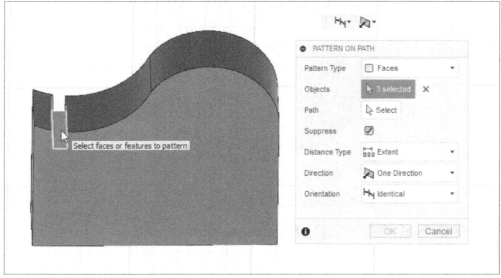

Figure-87. Selection of faces

- Click on **Select** button for **Path** option and select the path for creating copies.

- On selecting path, the updated **PATTERN ON PATH** dialog box will be displayed; refer to Figure-88.

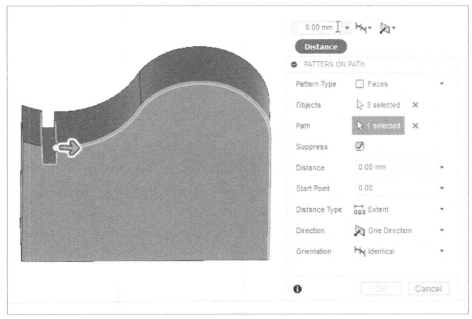

Figure-88. Updated PATTERN ON PATH dialog box on selection of path

- Select the **Suppress** check box if you want to suppress the any instance of pattern.
- Click in the **Distance** edit box and specify the distance value along the path.
- Click in the **Quantity** edit box and specify the number of copies to be created.
- The **Start Point** option is used specify the distance from the start point to place where the first pattern instance will be created. It is shown in the screen canvas as a **white point** and determines the starting point of the selected path. It can be set to any value between zero and one using the **Start Point** edit box, but it is easier to adjust it manually by dragging the start point; refer to Figure-89.

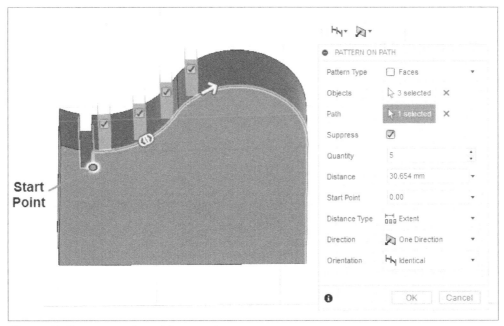

Figure-89. Pattern creation with start point

- The options of **Distance Type** and **Direction** drop-down were discussed earlier in this chapter.
- Select **Path Direction** option of **Orientation** drop-down if you want to rotate each instance according to the pattern path. Select the **Identical** option of **Orientation** drop-down to keep the instances in the same orientation as the original object.
- Click **OK** button from **PATTERN ON PATH** dialog box to complete the process of creating the copies; refer to Figure-90.

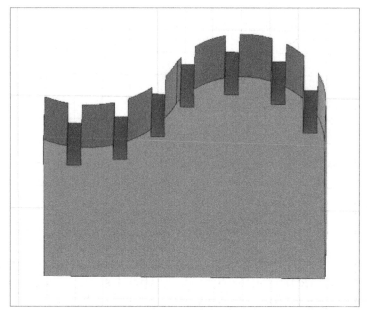

Figure-90. Solid model after applying pattern on path tool

MIRROR

The **Mirror** tool is used to create mirror copy of selected objects to the opposite side of a selected face or plane. The procedure to use this tool is discussed next.

- Click on **Mirror** tool of **CREATE** drop-down from **Toolbar**; refer to Figure-91. The **MIRROR** dialog box will be displayed; refer to Figure-92.

Figure-91. Mirror tool in solid

Figure-92. MIRROR dialog box in solid

- Select the desired option from **Pattern Type** drop-down to select respective objects for mirroring. The other options of **Pattern Type** section have already been discussed earlier.
- Select the bodies to be mirrored.

- Click on **Select** button of **Mirror Plane** section and select the plane/face to be used as mirror plane. Preview of mirror copy will be displayed; refer to Figure-93.

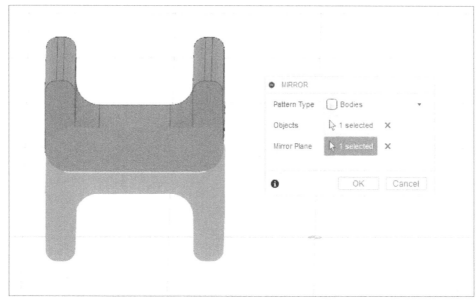

Figure-93. Preview of mirror on selection of plane

- If you have selected **Features** in **Pattern Type** drop-down then **Compute Option** drop-down will also be displayed in the dialog box; refer to Figure-94. Select the Optimized option if you want to copy of feature with minimum processing time and less flexibility to individually change features later. Select Identical option if you want to create copy of feature using same background programming which was used while creating the base feature. Select the adjust option if you want to recompute each instance of the feature as a separate feature.

Figure-94. Compute Option in MIRROR dialog box

- Click **OK** button of **MIRROR** dialog box to finish the process of creating mirror copy; refer to Figure-95.

Figure-95. Solid model after applying mirror tool

THICKEN

The **Thicken** tool is used to add thickness to surfaces to make them solid. (You will learn about surfaces in Chapter 9 Surface Modeling of this book.) The procedure to use this tool is discussed next.

- Open any file that has surfaces or create a surface by following basic tools of Chapter 9 of this book.
- Click on **Thicken** tool of **CREATE** drop-down from **Toolbar**; refer to Figure-96. A **THICKEN** dialog box will be displayed; refer to Figure-97.

Figure-96. Thicken tool

Figure-97. THICKEN dialog box

- **Faces** selection is active by default. Select the surface to add thickness; refer to Figure-98.

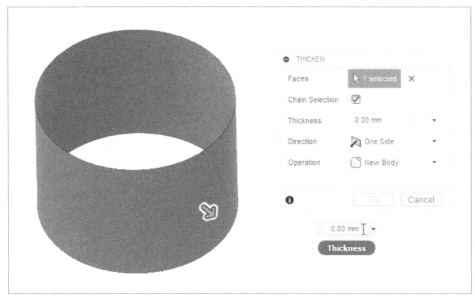

Figure-98. Selection of faces to add thickness

- Click in the **Thickness** edit box of dialog box and specify desired value of thickness.
- Click on **One Side** option from **Direction** drop-down to apply the thickness to one side of surface. Click on **Symmetric** option from **Direction** drop-down to apply the thickness to both sides of surface equally. In our case, we have selected **Symmetric** option.
- The options of **Operation** drop-down were discussed earlier in this chapter.
- Click **OK** button of **THICKEN** dialog box to finish the process; refer to Figure-99.

Figure-99. Solid model after applying thicken tool

BOUNDARY FILL

The **Boundary Fill** tool is used to create a volume from bounded by selected planes, bodies, and surfaces. This volume is called cell and can be used to cut, add, or create new body in the model. The procedure to use this tool are discussed next.

- Click on **Boundary Fill** tool of **CREATE** drop-down from **Toolbar**; refer to Figure-100. The **BOUNDARY FILL** dialog box will be displayed; refer to Figure-101.

Figure-100. Boundary Fill tool

Figure-101. BOUNDARY FILL dialog box

- **Select Tools** selection is active by default. Select the bodies/planes/surfaces for boundary fill; refer to Figure-102.

Figure-102. Selection for boundary fill

- Click on **Select** button of **Select Cells** section and select the check boxes for cells to be created.
- The tools of **Operation** section were discussed earlier in this chapter.
- Click **OK** button of **BOUNDARY FILL** dialog box to finish the process; refer to Figure-103. If the parent body is overlapping with new boundary fill bodies then hide the parent body using eye icon in **BROWSER** to check the result.

Figure-103. Result of boundary fill after hiding parent body

CREATE FORM

The **Create Form** tool is used to create or modify the form of model using freestyle editing tools. Clicking this tool takes you to **Form** mode. You will learn more about **Form** mode later in Chapter 12 and 13 of this book. The procedure to use this tool is discussed next.

- Click on **Create Form** tool of **CREATE** drop-down from **Toolbar**; refer to Figure-104. The **Form mode** will be activated and related toolbar will be displayed; refer to Figure-105.

Figure-104. Create Form tool

Figure-105. Form mode

- Now, create or modify the model as desired.
- Click **Finish Form** button from **Toolbar** to exit the **Form mode** and return to **Model Workspace**; refer to Figure-106.

Figure-106. Finish Form button

CREATE BASE FEATURE

The **Create Base Feature** tool inserts a base feature operation in the **Timeline**. Any operations performed on the design while in a base feature are not recorded in the **Timeline**. This tool is used when you want to safeguard some of the operations while sharing the file.

- Click on **Create Base Feature** tool of **CREATE** drop-down from **Toolbar**; refer to Figure-107. The tools in the **Toolbar** will be same as for **Model** workspace.

Figure-107. Create Base Feature tool

- Do the desired operation that you do not want to record in **Timeline** and then click on **FINISH BASE FEATURE** button from **Toolbar** to exit the mode; refer to Figure-108.

Figure-108. Finish Base Feature button

CREATE MESH

The **Create Mesh** tool is used to create a mesh of the current model. (You will learn about mesh modeling in Chapter 14 of this book.) The procedure to use this tool is discussed next.

- Click on **Create Mesh** tool of **CREATE** drop-down from **Toolbar**; refer to Figure-109. **Mesh** workspace will be activated.

Figure-109. Create Mesh tool

- Make sure that you have selected the **Mesh Workspace** check box in **Preview** section of **Preferences** dialog box. You can access **Preferences** dialog box by clicking on **Preferences** tool in **User Account** drop-down; refer to Figure-110.

Figure-110. Preferences tool

- Create and modify the desired model as desired in **Mesh Workspace.**
- Click on **FINISH MESH** button from **Toolbar** to exit **Mesh Workspace** and return to **Model Workspace**; refer to Figure-111.

Figure-111. Finish Mesh button

CREATING MESH SECTION SKETCH

The Mesh section sketch is created at the intersection of mesh with selected plane. The procedure to create mesh section sketch is discussed next.

- Click on the **Create Mesh Section Sketch** tool from the **CREATE** drop-down in the **SOLID** tab of **Toolbar**. The **CREATE MESH SECTION SKETCH** dialog box will be displayed; refer to Figure-112.

Figure-112. CREATE MESH SECTION SKETCH dialog box

- Select the desired mesh body. The updated dialog box will be displayed; refer to Figure-113.

Figure-113. Updated CREATE MESH SECTION SKETCH dialog box

- You can select the desired plane for section or you can use dynamic handles to set location for section plane; refer to Figure-114.

Figure-114. Preview of mesh section

- After setting desired parameters, click on the **OK** button from the dialog box to create the section sketch.

CREATE PCB FEATURE

The **Create PCB** tool in **CREATE** drop-down is used to create and modify PCB design in collaboration with **EAGLE** users. (You will learn about PCB design in Chapter 23 of this book.) This tool is available only if the **PCB Feature** check box in **Preview** section of **Preferences** dialog box is selected. You can access **Preferences** dialog box by clicking on **Preferences** tool in **User Account** drop-down. The procedure to use this tool is given next.

- Click on **Create PCB** tool from **CREATE** drop-down in **Toolbar**; refer to Figure-115.

Figure-115. Create PCB tool

- The **PCB Workspace** will be activated and related toolbar will be displayed; refer to Figure-116.

Figure-116. PCB workspace

- Make the desired changes in PCB and then click on the **FINISH PCB** button to return to **Model workspace**; refer to Figure-117.

Figure-117. Finish PCB button

SELF ASSESSMENT

Q1. Which of the following is not the default plane available in Autodesk Fusion 360?

a. Front Plane
b. Right Plane
c. Top Plane
d. Left Plane

Q2. Discuss the procedure of creating multiple holes with example.

Q3. Which of the following tool is not available in **CREATE** drop-down of Autodesk Fusion 360?

a. Thread
b. Box
C. Torus
d. Curve

Q4. **Thicken** tool is used to add thickness and length. (T/F)

Q5. The **Pattern On Path** tool is available in the **CREATE** drop-down. (T/F)

Q6. Discuss the use of **Pipe** tool with examples.

Q7. Discuss the use of **Web** tool with examples.

Q8. Which tool is used to create a solid body connecting two sketch from different planes?

Q9. Discuss the use of **Pattern On Path** tool with examples.

Q10. The --------- tool is used to cut helical thread on cylindrical faces.

FOR STUDENTS NOTES

FOR STUDENTS NOTES

Chapter 5

Practical and
Practice

Topics Covered

The major topics covered in this chapter are:

- *Practical*
- *Practice*

PRACTICAL 1

Create the model as shown in Figure-1. The views of the model with dimension are given in Figure-2.

Figure-1. Model For Practical 1

Figure-2. Views of practical 1

Before we start working on Practical 1, it is important to understand two terms; first angle projection and third angle projection. These are the standards of placing views in the engineering drawings. The views placed in the above figure are using third angle projection. In first angle projection, the top view of model is placed below the front view and right side view is placed at the left of the front view. You will learn more about projection in chapter related to drafting.

Creating the Sketch

- Click on **Center Diameter Circle** tool of **Circle** cascading menu from **CREATE** drop-down in **Toolbar**. You will asked to select a plane for creating sketch.
- Select **Top Plane** from the canvas screen.
- Click at the **Origin** to place the center point of circle. Enter **50** in floating window as diameter of circle and press **ENTER** key.
- Sketch another circle of radius **10** (diameter **20**) taking center point as origin.

How to show radius in place of diameter of circle? Create the circle with diameter value. Right-click on diameter dimension and select **Toggle Radius** button from Marking menu; refer to Figure-3.

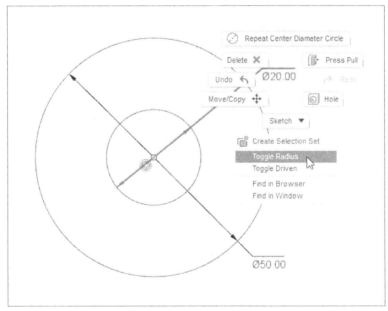

Figure-3. Toggle Radius Option

- Select **Center Rectangle** tool of **Rectangle** cascading menu from **CREATE** drop-down in **Toolbar**.
- Click at **Origin** as center point for rectangle and enter **5** as width & **25** as length in floating window to create a rectangle; refer to Figure-4.

Figure-4. Sketch After Creating Circle And Rectangle

- Select **Trim** tool of **MODIFY** drop-down from **Toolbar** and trim the entities in such a way that the sketch is displayed as shown in Figure-5.

Figure-5. Sketch After Trimming

- Click on **Finish Sketch** button from **Toolbar** to exit the sketch mode.

Creating Extrude Feature

- Click on **Extrude** tool of **CREATE** drop-down from **Toolbar** or press **E** key from keyboard to select **Extrude** tool. The **EXTRUDE** dialog box will be displayed.
- Profile selection is active by default. Select the recently created sketch profile. The updated **EXTRUDE** dialog box will be displayed.

- Specify the height of extrusion as **25** in **Distance** edit box or floating window. The preview of extrusion will be displayed; refer to Figure-6. (You need to rotate the model by using **SHIFT**+Middle Mouse Button to check the preview.)

Figure-6. Preview Of Extrusion

- Click **OK** button from **EXTRUDE** dialog box to complete the process of extrusion. The model will be displayed as shown in Figure-7.
- Save the file and close it.

Figure-7. Final Model Of Practical 1

PRACTICAL 2

Create the model as shown in Figure-8. The dimensions are given in Figure-9. Assume the missing dimensions.

Figure-8. Model For Practical 2

Figure-9. Practical 2 drawing

Creating sketch for model

- Start a new sketch using **Top Plane**.
- Select **Centre Rectangle** tool of **Rectangle** cascading menu from **CREATE** drop-down.
- Click on the origin to specify the centre point of rectangle and enter **60** and **50** in floating window as dimensions of rectangle; refer to Figure-10. Press **TAB** to toggle between edit boxes.

Figure-10. Sketch After Creating Rectangle

- Select **Line** tool from **CREATE** drop-down. Create a line of length as **70** and angle of **80** degree as shown in Figure-11.

Figure-11. Creating Angular Line

- Select **Mirror** tool of **CREATE** drop-down from **Toolbar** and create a mirror copy of recently created line about centerline as shown in Figure-12.

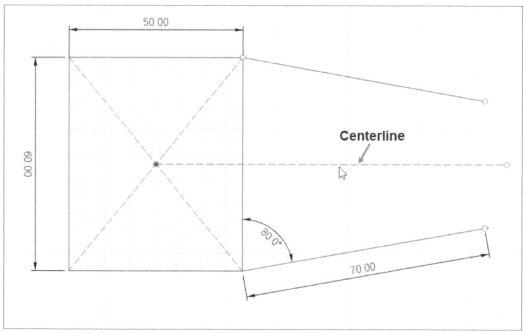

Figure-12. Creating Mirror Copy

- Create a line joining end points of two earlier created lines as shown in Figure-13.

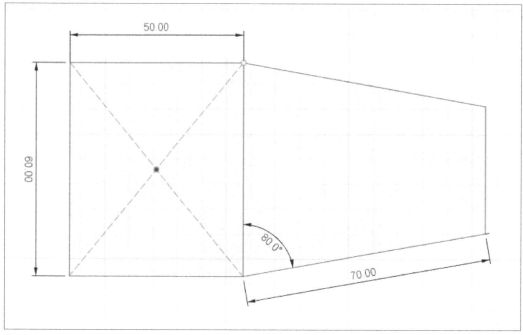

Figure-13. Joining End Points Of Lines

- Select **Center Point Slot** tool of **Slot** cascading menu from **CREATE** drop-down and create a slot of diameter as **15** and length as **8** at a distance of **65** from origin on the centerline; refer to Figure-14.

Figure-14. Creating Slot

- Press **T** from keyboard or click on the **Trim** tool from **MODIFY** drop-down in Toolbar to activate trimming tool. Select the inner lines of rectangle to remove them; refer to Figure-15.

Figure-15. Lines To Be Trimmed

- Click on the **Finish Sketch** button to exit sketch.

Creating Extrude Feature

- Select **Extrude** tool from **CREATE** drop-down or press **E** key. The **EXTRUDE** dialog box is displayed.
- Profile selection is active by default. Click in the sketch outside the slot.
- Specify **10** as height of extrusion in **Distance** edit box of **EXTRUDE** dialog box; refer to Figure-16. (Rotate the model to get clear view.)

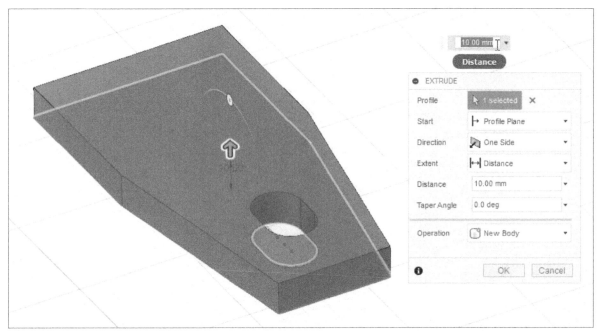

Figure-16. Preview Of Extrusion2

- Click **OK** button from **EXTRUDE** dialog box to complete the process of extrusion.
- Click on the **Create Sketch** tool from **CREATE** cascading menu. You are asked to select the plane to create sketch. Select the side face of model as shown in Figure-17.

Figure-17. Face To Be Select For Sketching

- Select the **2-Point Rectangle** tool from the **Rectangle** cascading menu in the **CREATE** drop-down of **Toolbar**. Create a rectangle of dimensions **25** and **60** with two holes of diameter **10** as shown in Figure-18.

- Create the Click on the **Finish Sketch** button to exit sketching.

Figure-18. Creating the rectangle with holes

- Select **Extrude** tool from **CREATE** drop-down. The **EXTRUDE** dialog box will be displayed.
- Select the upper portion of recently created sketch in **Profiles** selection and enter **-5** as height of extrusion.
- Select **Join** from **Operation** drop-down of **EXTRUDE** dialog box to join the two extrusions.
- Click **OK** button from **EXTRUDE** dialog box to finish this process; refer to Figure-19.

Figure-19. Extrude feature created

Creating Midplane

- Select **Midplane** tool of **CONSTRUCT** drop-down from **Toolbar.** The **MIDPLANE** dialog box will be displayed. You are asked to select the faces between which you want to create a midplane.
- Select both the faces as shown in Figure-20.

Figure-20. Face selection

- The preview of midplane will be displayed. Click **OK** button from the **MIDPLANE** dialog box to complete the process; refer to Figure-21.

Figure-21. Midplane Created

Creating Rib

- Select **Create Sketch** tool from **CREATE** drop-down. You will be asked to select the plane for creating sketch. Select the newly created midplane from **BROWSER**.
- Create a line as shown in Figure-22 with end points coincident to the vertices of model and finish the sketch.

Figure-22. Creating Sketch For Rib

- Select **Rib** tool from **CREATE** drop-down. The **RIB** dialog box will be displayed.
- Select the recently created line for **Curve** section.
- Select **Symmetric** option from **Thickness Options** drop-down.
- Select **To Next** Option from **Depth Options** drop-down.
- Click in **Thickness** edit box and enter **5** as thickness of rib; refer to Figure-23. (You might need to click on the **Flip Direction** button from the dialog box to get desired preview.)

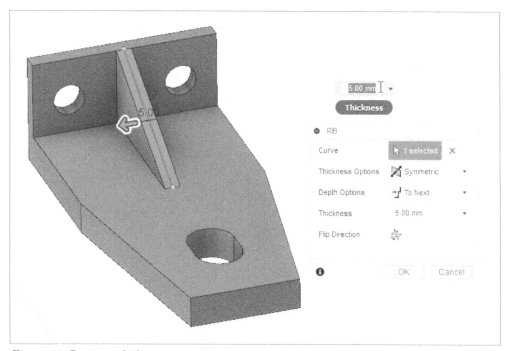

Figure-23. Preview of rib

- Click **OK** button of **RIB** dialog box to finish the process. The model will be displayed as shown in Figure-24.

Figure-24. Final model of Practical 2

PRACTICAL 3

Create the model as shown in Figure-25. The dimensions of the model are given in Figure-26.

Figure-25. Model for Practical 3

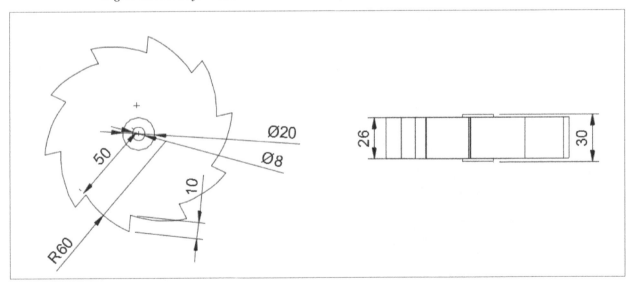

Figure-26. Practical 3 drawing views

Creating sketch for model

- Start a new design file in Autodesk Fusion. Select **Create Sketch** tool from **CREATE** drop-down in the **Toolbar**. You are asked to select sketching plane. Select **Top Plane** to create sketch. Select **Center Diameter Circle** tool of **Circle** cascading menu from **CREATE** drop-down.

- Create three circle of **8**, **20** and **100** as diameter dimension of circles; refer to Figure-27.

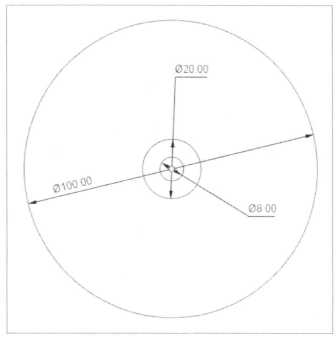

Figure-27. Creating circles

- Press **L** key to select **Line** tool and create a line of length **10**.
- Select **3-Point Arc** tool from **Arc** cascading menu and create an arc of **60** radius and **35** length as shown in Figure-28.

Figure-28. Creating line and arc

Creating Circular Pattern

- Select **Circular Pattern** from **CREATE** drop-down. The **CIRCULAR PATTERN** dialog box will be displayed.
- Objects selection is active by default. Select the recently created line and arc for circular pattern.
- Click on **Select** button of **Center Point** section and select the major circle to define its center as center point for pattern; refer to Figure-29.

Figure-29. Creating circular pattern

- The updated **CIRCULAR PATTERN** dialog box will be displayed. Click in **Quantity** edit box and specify **10** as quantity of circular pattern.
- Click **OK** button from **CIRCULAR PATTERN** dialog box to complete the process.

Trimming

- Select the **Trim** tool from **MODIFY** drop-down and remove all the extra entities from sketch as shown in Figure-30.

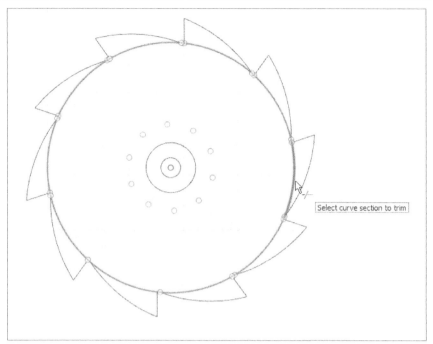

Figure-30. Trimmimg the extra entities

- After removing the extra entities from sketch, the sketch will be displayed as shown in Figure-31.

Figure-31. After removing extra entities

Creating Extrude

- Select **Extrude** tool from **CREATE** drop-down or press **E** key. The **EXTRUDE** dialog box will be displayed.
- Profile selection is active by default. Click between 20 diameter and 8 diameter circle to extrude the middle section.
- Select **Symmetric** button of **Direction** drop-down from **EXTRUDE** dialog box.
- Click in **Distance** edit box of **EXTRUDE** dialog box and specify **15** as height of extrusion. Rotate the model to check preview; refer to Figure-32.

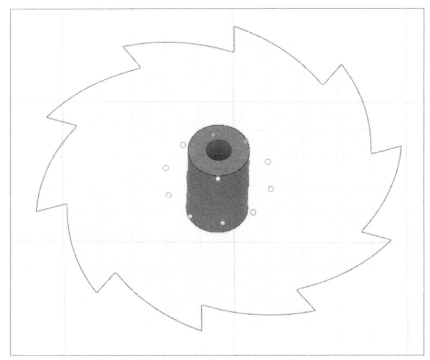

Figure-32. Preview of first extrusion

- Click **OK** button of **EXTRUDE** dialog box to finish this extrusion. The sketch of extrude feature will hide automatically. Click on the crossed eye icon before **Sketch 1** in the **Sketches** node of **BROWSER** to display the sketch again.
- Right-click on the screen and select **Repeat Extrude** button from **Marking Menu**. The **EXTRUDE** dialog box will be displayed.
- Select the area outside the 20 diameter circle earlier created.
- Select **Symmetric** button of **Direction** drop-down from **EXTRUDE** dialog box.
- Click in **Distance** edit box of **EXTRUDE** dialog box and specify **13** as height of extrusion; refer to Figure-33.

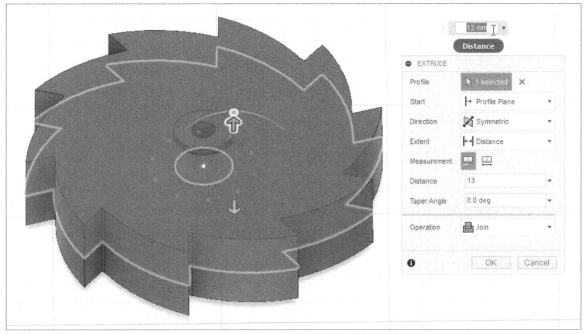

Figure-33. Preview of second extrusion

- Click **OK** button from **EXTRUDE** dialog box to complete the process of extrusion. The model will be displayed as shown in Figure-34.

Figure-34. Final model of Practical 3

You can now hide the sketch and save the file.

PRACTICE 1

Create the model as shown in Figure-35. The dimensions are given in Figure-36.

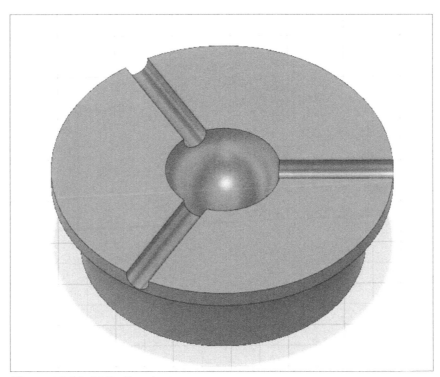

Figure-35. Model For Practice 1

Figure-36. Dimensions For Practice 1

PRACTICE 2

Create the model as shown in Figure-37. The dimensions are given in Figure-38.

Figure-37. Model For Practice 2

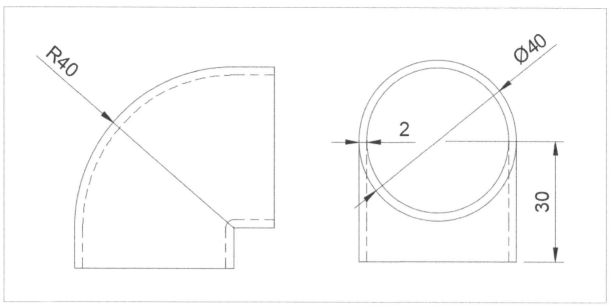

Figure-38. Dimensions For Practice 2

PRACTICE 3

Create the model as shown in Figure-39. The dimensions are given in Figure-40.

Figure-39. Model For Practice 3

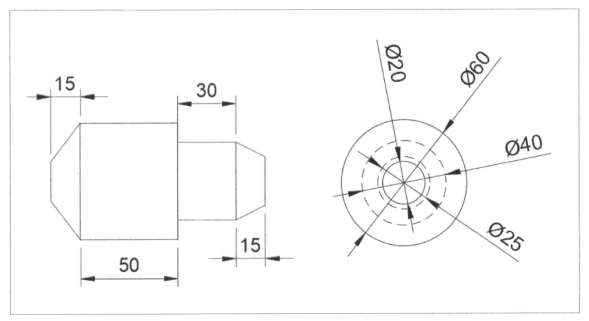

Figure–40. Dimensions For Practice 3

PRACTICE 4

Create the model as shown in Figure-41. The dimensions are given in Figure-42

Figure–41. Model For Practice 4

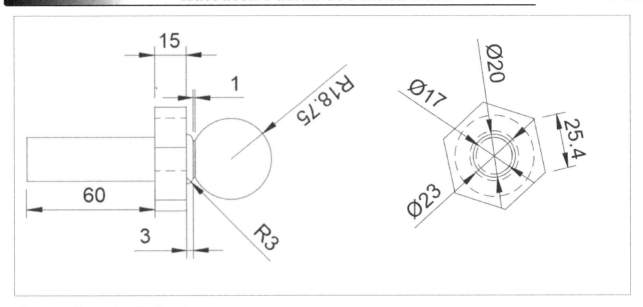

Figure-42. Dimensions For Practice 4

PRACTICE 5

Create the model as shown in Figure-43. The dimensions are given in Figure-44.
(Hint: You will need **Rectangular Pattern** tool and **Move/Copy** tool in this model.)

Figure-43. Model For Practice 5

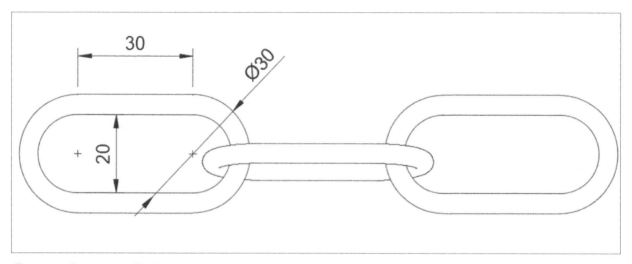

Figure-44. Dimensions For Practice 5

PRACTICE 6

Create the model as shown in Figure-45. The dimensions are given in Figure-46.

Figure-45. Model For Practice 6

Figure–46. Dimensions For Practice 6

PRACTICE 7

Create the model as shown in Figure-47. The dimensions are given in Figure-48.

Figure–47. Model For Practice 7

Figure–48. Dimensions for Practice 7

PRACTICE 8

Create the model as shown in Figure-49. The dimensions are given in Figure-50.

Figure-49. Model For Practice 8

Figure-50. Dimensions For Practice 8

PRACTICE 9

Create the model as shown in Figure-51. The dimensions are given in Figure-52.

Figure-51. Model For Practice 9

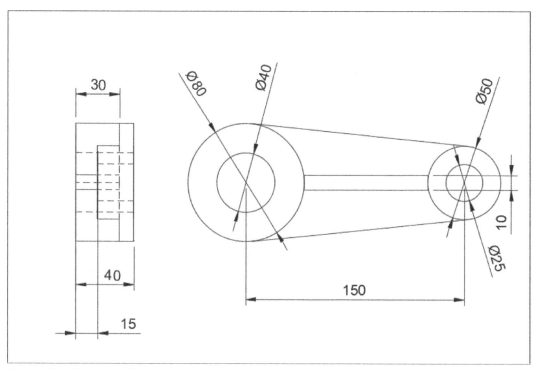

Figure-52. Dimensions For Practice 9

PRACTICE 10

Create the model as shown in Figure-53. The dimensions are given in Figure-54.

Figure-53. Model For Practice 10

Figure-54. Dimensions For Practice 10

FOR STUDENT NOTES

Chapter 6

Solid Editing

Topics Covered

The major topics covered in this chapter are:

- *Press Pull Tool*
- *Fillet Tool*
- *Shell Tool*
- *Combine Tool*
- *Split Body Tool*
- *Align Tool*
- *Physical Material*
- *Appearance*

SOLID EDITING TOOLS

In the previous chapters, we have learned to create solid models and remove materials from them. In this chapter, we will learn to edit the models. Like the other tools, Autodesk Fusion 360 has packed all the editing tools into one drop-down. These tools are available in **MODIFY** drop-down from **Toolbar**; refer to Figure-1. The tools in this drop-down are discussed next.

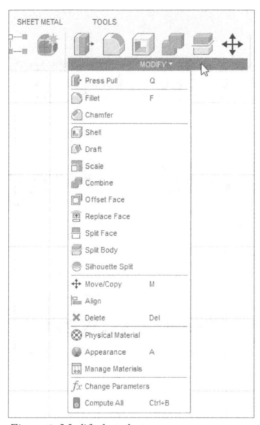

Figure-1. Modify drop down

PRESS PULL

The **Press Pull** tool is used to modify the body by drag and drop methods. The options displayed to perform press pull operations depends on the selected geometry. The procedure to use this tool is discussed next.

*   Select **Press Pull** tool of **MODIFY** drop-down from **Toolbar**; refer to Figure-2. The **PRESS PULL** dialog box will be displayed; refer to Figure-3.

Figure-2. Press Pull tool

Figure-3. PRESS PULL dialog box

- Select a face, if you want to offset or move the face. The **OFFSET FACES** dialog box will be displayed. The **Offset Faces** dialog box will be discussed later.
- Select an edge, if you want to fillet the edge. The **FILLET** dialog box will be displayed. The **Fillet** tool will be discussed later in this unit.
- Select a sketch, if you want to extrude the profile. The **EXTRUDE** dialog box will be displayed. This tool was discussed earlier in this book.

Offset Face

The **Offset Face** tool is used to offset or move the face. The procedure to use this tool is discussed next.

- Select **Press Pull** tool from **MODIFY** drop-down. The **PRESS PULL** dialog box will be displayed. You can also select **Press Pull** tool by pressing **Q** key.
- Click on the face of the model to offset. The **OFFSET FACE** dialog will be displayed; refer to Figure-4.

Figure-4. OFFSET FACE dialog box

- Select **Automatic** button from **Offset Type** drop-down if you do not want to update the sketch or base feature on applying the offset. This action is not added to time line.
- Select **Modify Existing Feature** button from **Offset Type** drop-down if you want to update the sketch or base feature on applying offset. This action is not added to time line.
- Select **New Offset** button from **Offset Type** drop-down if you want to create a new face. This action is added to time line.
- Click in **Distance** edit box of **OFFSET FACE** dialog box or floating window from screen and enter the desired value as the distance for offset. You can also move drag handle to set the distance. The preview of offset face will be displayed; refer to Figure-5.

Figure-5. Preview on applying offset face

- Click **OK** button from **OFFSET FACE** dialog box to complete the process.

FILLET

The **Fillet** tool is used to apply round at the edges. This tool works in the same way as the **Sketch Fillet** do. It is recommended that, apply the fillets after creating all the features required in the model because fillets can increase the processing time during modifications. The procedure to use this tool is given next.

- Select **Fillet** tool of **MODIFY** drop-down from **Toolbar**; refer to Figure-6 or press Q and select an edge. The **FILLET** dialog box will be displayed; refer to Figure-7.

Figure-6. 3D Fillet tool

Figure-7. 3D FILLET dialog box

- **Edges** selection is active by default. Click on the edge(s) from the model to apply fillet. To select multiple edges, hold **CTRL** key while selecting. The updated **FILLET** dialog box will be displayed; refer to Figure-8.

Figure-8. Updated 3D FILLET dialog box

- The options of the updated **FILLET** dialog box are discussed next.

Radius Type Drop-Down

There are three options in **Radius type** drop-down; refer to Figure-9. These options are used to specify the type of round to be created. These options are discussed next.

Figure-9. Fillet Radius Type drop down

Constant Radius

- Select **Constant Radius** button from **Radius Type** drop-down to apply the fillet of fix size on the selected edge.
- Click in the **Radius** edit box of **FILLET** dialog box and enter **10** as the radius of fillet. You can also move the drag-handle from canvas screen to set the radius of fillet; refer to Figure-10.

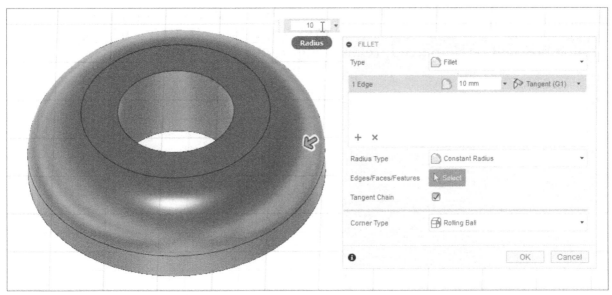

Figure-10. Preview of constant radius fillet

- Select the **Tangent Chain** check box to include tangentially connected edges in fillet.
- Select the **G2** check box if you want to apply the G2 continuity to the selected fillet.
- Select the desired button for **Corner Type** section to define fillet shape at vertex formed by three edges meeting at single point.
- Click **OK** button from **FILLET** dialog box to apply the fillet.

Chord Length

- Select **Chord Length** option of **Type** drop-down from **FILLET** dialog box if you want to specify the chord length to control the size for the fillet.
- Click in the **Chord Length** edit box and enter desired value for fillet. You can also set the value by moving the drag handle. The preview will be displayed; refer to Figure-11.

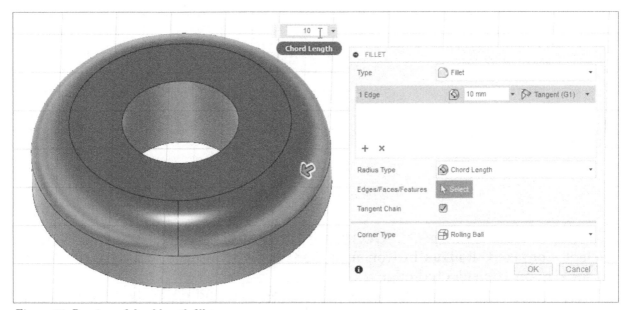

Figure-11. Preview of chord length fillet

- The other parameters are same as discussed in last topic.

Variable Radius

- Select **Variable Radius** option of **Type** drop-down from **FILLET** dialog box if you want to specify radii at selected points along the edge. The updated **FILLET** dialog box will be displayed.
- Click on the edge to create points for applying fillet and specify radius for each point in the dialog box or dynamic input box; refer to Figure-12.

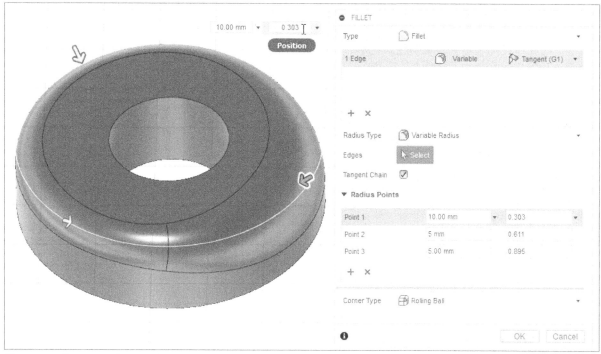

Figure-12. Preview of variable radius fillet

- To delete the created point, select the specific point from the edge and click on the **Remove Selection** button from the **FILLET** dialog box. Point earlier created to apply fillet will be displayed with arrows.
- The other parameters of this dialog box were discussed earlier.
- After specifying the parameters, click on the **OK** button from **FILLET** dialog box to create the fillet.

RULE FILLET

The **Rule Fillet** tool is used to add fillets or rounds to a design based on specified rules. The edges are determined by specified rules rather than selection in the canvas. The procedure to use this tool is discussed next.

- Select **Rule Fillet** tool from **Type** drop down in **FILLET** dialog box; refer to Figure-13. The **RULE FILLET** dialog box will be displayed; refer to Figure-14.

Figure-13. Rule fillet tool in FILLET dialog box

Figure-14. Rule Fillet dialog box

- **Faces/Features** selection is active by default. Select the desired faces/features from model to apply rule fillet.
- Click in the **Radius** edit box and enter the desired value of radius for fillet. The preview of fillet will be displayed; refer to Figure-15. You can also set the radius by moving the drag handle.

Figure-15. Preview of rule fillet

- Select **All Edges** option from **Rule** drop-down if you want to add the fillets to all edges of the input faces/features and select **Between Faces/Features** option if you want to add the fillets at the intersection of the input faces/features. Note that you can also select features from Time line.

- Select **Rounds Only** option from **Rounds/Fillets** drop-down if you want to create only rounds and select the **Fillets Only** option if you want to create only fillets. Selecting the **Rounds And Fillets** option in this drop-down will create both fillets and rounds.

- Click **OK** button from **RULE FILLET** dialog box to finish this process.

CHAMFER

The **Chamfer** tool is used to bevel the sharp edges of the model. The procedure to create chamfer by using this tool is given next.

- Click on the **Chamfer** tool of **MODIFY** drop-down from **Toolbar**; refer to Figure-16. The **CHAMFER** dialog box will be displayed; refer to Figure-17.

Figure-16. Chamfer tool

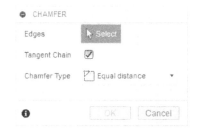

Figure-17. CHAMFER dialog box

- **Edges** selection is active by default. Click on the edge of model to apply chamfer. The updated **CHAMFER** dialog box will be displayed; refer to Figure-18.

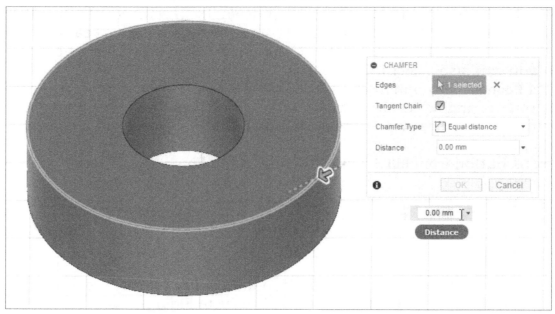

Figure-18. Updated CHAMFER dialog box

- Select the **Tangent Chain** check box to include tangentially connected edges in selection.
- Select **Equal Distance** option of **Chamfer Type** drop-down from **CHAMFER** dialog box if you want to specify a equal distance for both sides of the chamfer.
- Select **Two Distances** option of **Chamfer Type** drop-down from **CHAMFER** dialog box, if you want to specify distance for each side of the chamfer.
- Enter the specific distance for each side in the respective edit box. You can also set the distance by moving the drag handle from canvas screen.
- Select **Distance and angle** option of **Chamfer Type** drop-down if you want to specify a distance and angle to create the chamfer.
- Click in the **Distance** edit box and enter the desired value for distance for chamfer. The preview of chamfer will be displayed; refer to Figure-19.

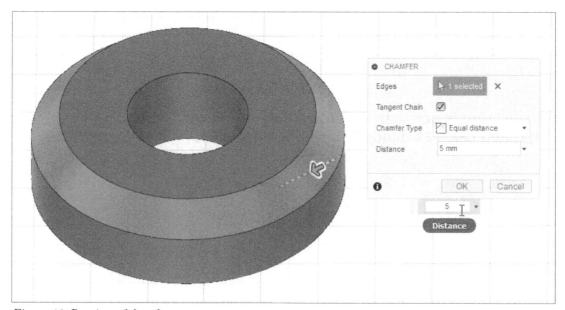

Figure-19. Preview of chamfer

- Click **OK** button of **CHAMFER** dialog box to finish the process.

SHELL

The **Shell** tool is used to make a solid part hollow and remove one or more selected faces. The procedure to use this tool is given next.

- Select **Shell** tool of **MODIFY** drop-down from **Toolbar**; refer to Figure-20. The **SHELL** dialog box will be displayed; refer to Figure-21.

Figure-20. Shell tool

Figure-21. SHELL dialog box

- **Faces/Body** selection is active by default. Click on the face/body of the solid to apply shell. The updated **SHELL** dialog box will be displayed; refer to Figure-22.

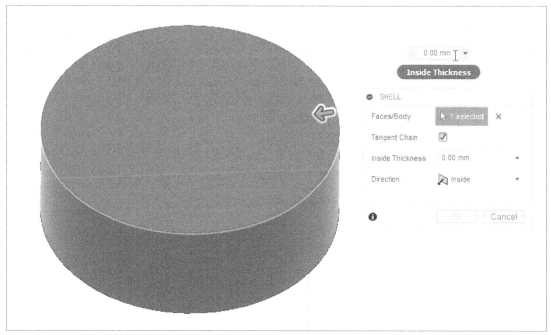

Figure-22. Updated SHELL dialog box

- Select the **Tangent Chain** check box to include tangentially connected edges in selection.
- Click in the **Inside Thickness** edit box and enter the desired value of shell thickness. The preview of shell will be displayed; refer to Figure-23.

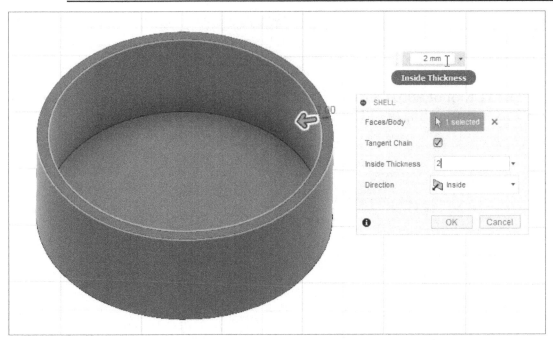

Figure-23. Preview of shell

- Select **Inside** option from **Direction** drop-down if you want to shell the faces toward the interior of the part.
- Select **Outside** option from **Direction** drop-down if you want to shell the faces towards the exterior of the part.
- Select **Both** option from **Direction** drop-down if you want to shell the faces towards the interior and the exterior of the part by equal amount. Click in the specific thickness edit box and enter the specify thickness for shell.
- Click **OK** button from **SHELL** dialog box to complete the process.

DRAFT

The **Draft** tool is used to apply taper to the faces of a solid model. This tool is mainly useful when you are designing components for moulding or casting. **Draft** tool applies taper on the face and this taper allows easy & safe ejection of parts from dies. The procedure to use this tool is discussed next.

- Select **Draft** tool of **MODIFY** drop-down from **Toolbar**; refer to Figure-24. The **DRAFT** dialog box will be displayed; refer to Figure-25.

Figure-24. Draft tool

Figure-25. DRAFT dialog box

- **Plane** selection is active by default. Click on the face or plane of the model which you want to use as fixes reference.
- Click on **Select** button of **Faces** section and select the faces to be tapered.
- Click on the **Flip Direction** button from **DRAFT** dialog box to flip the direction of draft.
- Click in the **Angle** edit box and enter the desired value of angle for draft. The preview of draft will be displayed; refer to Figure-26. You can also set the angle of draft by moving the drag handle.

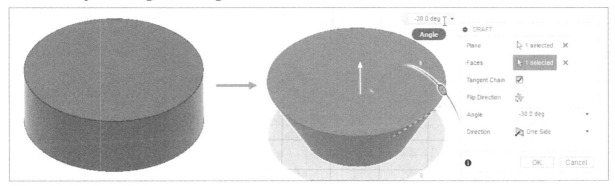

Figure-26. Preview of draft

- The options of **Direction** drop-down were discussed earlier in this book.
- Click **OK** button from **DRAFT** dialog box to finish the process.

SCALE

The **Scale** tool is used to enlarge or reduce selected bodies, sketches, or components based on specified scale factor. The procedure to use this tool is discussed next.

- Select **Scale** tool of **MODIFY** drop-down from **Toolbar**; refer to Figure-27. The **SCALE** dialog box will be displayed; refer to Figure-28.

Figure-27. Scale tool

Figure-28. SCALE dialog box

- **Entities** selection is active by default. Click on the entities to scaled up or down.
- On selecting the entity for scale, point is automatically selected in **Point** section. If you want to use a different point as scale reference then click on the **Select** button for **Point** option in the dialog box and select the desired point.
- Select **Uniform** option from **Scale Type** drop-down if you want to scale the selected entities uniformly in X, Y, and Z direction.
- Select **Non-Uniform** option from **Scale Type** drop-down if you want to scale the entity non-uniformly.
- Click in the **Scale Factor** edit box and enter the desired value for scale. The preview will be displayed; refer to Figure-29.
- Click on **OK** button of **SCALE** dialog box to complete the process.

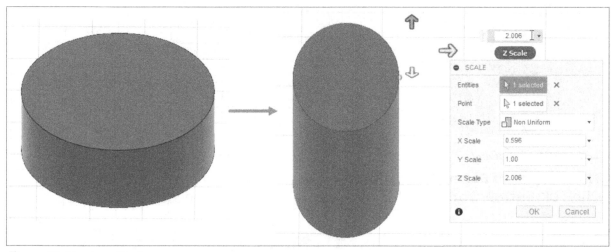

Figure-29. Preview of scale

COMBINE

The **Combine** tool is used to cut, join, and intersect the selected bodies. The procedure to use this tool is discussed next.

- Select **Combine** tool of **MODIFY** drop-down from **Toolbar**; refer to Figure-30. The **COMBINE** dialog box will be displayed; refer to Figure-31.

Figure-30. Combine tool

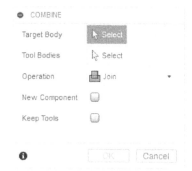

Figure-31. COMBINE dialog box

- **Target Body** selection is active by default. Click on the component from model to be used as a target body.
- Click on other components to select in **Tool Bodies** section. The preview of combine will be displayed; refer to Figure-32.

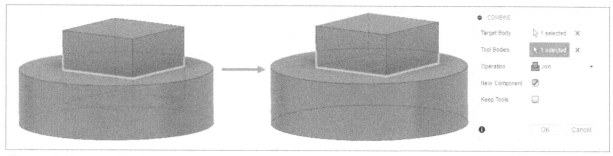

Figure-32. Preview of combine

- The options of **Operations** drop-down were discussed earlier in this book.
- Select the **New Component** check box to create a new component with results.
- Select the **Keep Tools** check box to retain the tool bodies after the combine result.
- Click **OK** button of **COMBINE** dialog box to finish the process.

REPLACE FACE

The **Replace Face** tool is used to replace an existing face with a surface or work plane. The procedure to use this tool is discussed next.

- Select **Replace Face** tool of **MODIFY** drop-down from **Toolbar**; refer to Figure-33. The **REPLACE FACE** dialog box will be displayed; refer to Figure-34.

Figure-33. Replace Face tool

Figure-34. REPLACE FACE dialog box

- **Source Faces** selection is active by default. Click on the component face to select the face.
- Select the **Tangent Chain** check box to include tangentially connected faces in selection.
- Click **Select** button of **Target Faces** options and click on the face or plane to apply this tool. The preview will be displayed; refer to Figure-35.

Figure-35. Preview of replace face

- Click **OK** button of **REPLACE FACE** dialog box to finish the process.

SPLIT FACE

The **Split Face** tool is used to divide faces of a surface or solid to add draft, delete an area, or create features. The procedure to use this tool is discussed next.

- Select **Split Face** tool of **MODIFY** drop-down from **Toolbar**; refer to Figure-36. The **SPLIT FACE** dialog box will be displayed; refer to Figure-37.

Figure-36. Split Face tool

Figure-37. SPLIT FACE dialog box

- **Faces To Split** option is active by default. Click on the model face to be split. You can select multiple faces by holding the **CTRL** key.
- Click on the **Select** button of **Splitting Tool** option and select the face which will split the other faces.
- Select **Split With Surface** option from **Split Type** drop-down, if you want to project the splitting tool face which you had select upon the splitting face.
- Select **Along Vector** option from **Split Type** drop-down, if you want to define the projection direction of splitting face by selecting an face, edge, or axis.
- Select **Closest Point** option from **Split Type** drop-down, if you want to define the direction of projection as the closest distance between the splitting body and target faces.
- Select the **Extend Splitting Tool** check box to extends the tool to completely intersect the target faces.
- After specifying the parameters, click on **OK** button from **SPLIT FACE** dialog box to finish the process; refer to Figure-38.

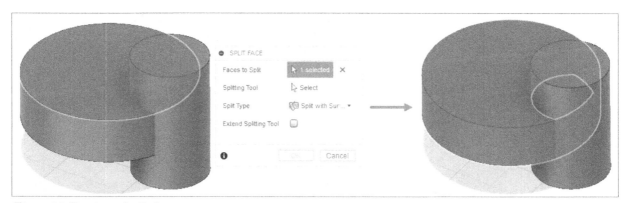

Figure-38. Preview of split face

SPLIT BODY

The **Split Body** tool works similarly to **Split Face** tool but in this tool, component or part is selected in place of faces. The procedure to use this tool is discussed next.

- Select **Split Body** tool of **MODIFY** drop-down from **Toolbar**; refer to Figure-39. The **SPLIT BODY** dialog box will be displayed; refer to Figure-40.

Figure-39. Split Body tool

Figure-40. SPLIT BODY dialog box

- **Body To Split** selection is active by default. Click on the component to be split.
- Click on **Select** button of **Splitting Tool** option and select the body which splitting will be done.
- Select the **Extend Splitting Tool** check box to extends the tool to completely intersect the target faces.
- After specifying the various parameters, click **OK** button of **SPLIT BODY** dialog box to complete the process; refer to Figure-41.

Figure-41. Preview of split body

SILHOUETTE SPLIT

The **Silhouette Split** tool is used to split selected body at the silhouette outline visible from the view direction. The procedure to use this tool is discussed next.

- Select **Silhouette Split** tool of **MODIFY** drop-down from **Toolbar**; refer to Figure-42. The **SILHOUETTE SPLIT** dialog box will be displayed; refer to Figure-43.

Figure-42. Silhouette Split tool

Figure-43. SILHOUETTE
SPLIT dialog box

- **View Direction** selection option is active by default. Click on the plane or face to select the direction to split.
- Click on **Select** button of **Target Body** and select the body which you want to split.
- Select **Split Faces Only** option from **Operation** drop-down, if you want to split the faces of the selected body but keeps it as a single body.
- Select **Split Shelled Body** option from **Operation** drop-down, if you want to split the selected body into two bodies. To use this option , the selected body must be shelled first.
- Select **Split Solid Body** option from **Operation** drop-down, if you want to split the selected body at the parting line. The parting line of the selected body must be planar.
- After specify the parameters, click **OK** button of **SILHOUETTE SPLIT** dialog box to finish the process; refer to Figure-44.

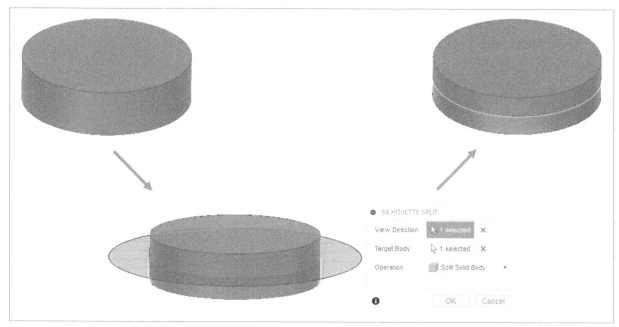

Figure-44. Preview of silhouette split

MOVE/COPY

The **Move/Copy** tool is used to move a face, body, sketch curve, components, or sketch geometry. Using this tool you can also move the whole geometry. The procedure to use this tool is discussed next.

- Select **Move/Copy** tool of **MODIFY** drop-down from **Toolbar**; refer to Figure-45. The **MOVE/COPY** dialog box will be displayed; refer to Figure-46.

Figure-45. Move Copy tool

Figure-46. MOVE COPY dialog box

- Select **Component** option from **Move Object** drop-down, if you want to move a component.
- Select **Bodies** option from **Move Object** drop-down, if you want to move a body.
- Select **Faces** option from **Move Object** drop-down, if you want to move a face.
- Select **Sketch** Objects from **Move Object** drop-down, if you want to move the selected sketch.
- In our case, we are selecting the **Bodies** option from **Move Object** drop-down.
- **Selection** section is active by default. Click on the body to be moved. The updated **MOVE/COPY** dialog box will be displayed.
- Select **Free Move** button from **Move Type** section, if you want to move selected body freely.
- On selecting the **Free Move** button, a Manipulator will be displayed on the selected body. Use the Manipulator to move the body or enter the value in respective field of **MOVE/COPY** dialog box; refer to Figure-47.

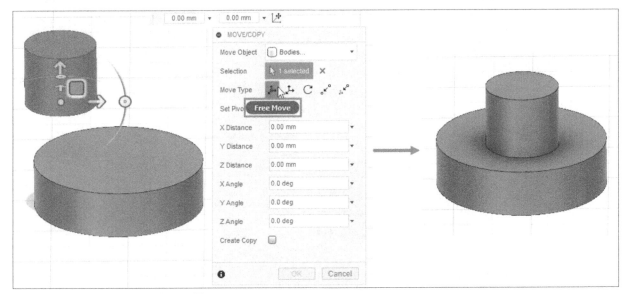

Figure-47. Free Move tool in Move Type section

- Select **Translate** button from **Move Type** section, if you want to move the body along X, Y and Z directions.
- On selecting the **Translate** button, three arrows will be displayed on the entity. Drag the desired arrow to move the body in respective direction. You can also enter the specific value of direction in the respective edit box from **MOVE/COPY** dialog box; refer to Figure-48.

Figure-48. Translate tool in Move Type section

- Select **Rotate** button from **Move Type** section, if you want to rotate the entity.
- On selecting the **Rotate** option, the **Axis** option will be displayed in the **MOVE/COPY** dialog box.
- Click on the **Select** button from **Axis** section of **MOVE/COPY** dialog box and select the axis/edge for rotation of entity. The drag handle will be displayed on the selected face.
- Move the drag handle as required or specify the value in the **Angle** edit box of **MOVE/COPY** dialog box; refer to Figure-49.

Figure-49. Rotate tool in Move Type section

- Select **Point to Point** button from **Move Type** section if you want to move the body from one point to another point.
- Click on the **Select** button of **Origin Point** option from **MOVE/COPY** dialog box and select the start point of body from where you want to move the body.
- Click on the **Select** button of **Target Point** option from **MOVE/COPY** dialog box and select the finish point from model.
- After selecting the points, the preview will be displayed.
- If the preview is as required then click on **OK** button from **MOVE/COPY** dialog box to complete the process; refer to Figure-50.

Figure-50. Point to Point tool in Move Type section

- Select **Point to Position** button from **Move Type** section if you want to move the body by selecting a point and a position from model.
- Select a point of the body. The updated **MOVE/COPY** dialog box will be displayed; refer to Figure-51.

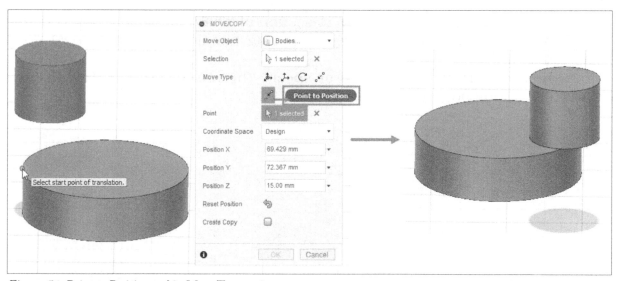

Figure-51. Point to Position tool in Move Type section

- Click in the **Position X** edit box and specify the value. Similarly, specify the value in **Position Y** and **Position Z** edit boxes as required.
- After specifying the parameters click on the **OK** button from **MOVE/COPY** to complete the process.

ALIGN

The **Align** tool is used to align the selected object to another object. The procedure to use this tool is discussed next.

- Click on the **Align** tool of **MODIFY** drop-down from **Toolbar**; refer to Figure-52. The **ALIGN** dialog box will be displayed; refer to Figure-53.

Figure-52. Align tool

Figure-53. ALIGN dialog box

- Select **Bodies** option of **Object** drop-down from **ALIGN** dialog box if you want to select bodies to align.
- Select **Components** option of **Object** drop-down from **ALIGN** dialog box if you want to select components to align.
- In our case, we are selecting **Bodies** option from **Object** drop-down.
- Click on **Select** button of **From** section of **ALIGN** dialog box and select point on the first body from which you want to align that body.
- Click on **Select** button of **To** section of **ALIGN** dialog box and select point on the second body to which the body to be aligned; refer to Figure-54.

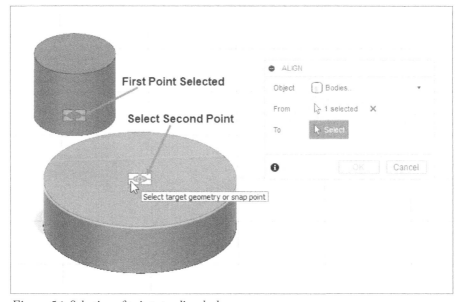

Figure-54. Selection of points to align body

- On selecting the point on second body, the two selected body will align to each other at selected location; refer to Figure-55.

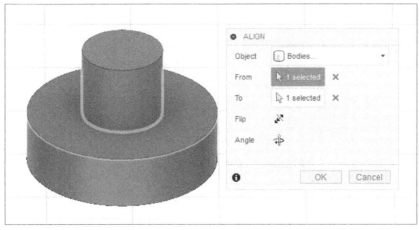

Figure-55. Preview of align

- Click on the **Flip** button, if you want to flip the aligned body.
- Click on **Angle** button if you want to rotate the aligned body.
- After specifying the parameters, click on the **OK** button from **ALIGN** dialog box to finish the process.

DELETE

The **Delete** tool is used to delete the selected object or component. You can also press **DELETE** from keyboard to do the same. The procedure to use this tool is discussed next.

- Click on the **Delete** tool of **MODIFY** drop-down from **Toolbar**; refer to Figure-56. The **DELETE** dialog box will be displayed; refer to Figure-57.

Figure-56. Delete tool

Figure-57. DELETE dialog box

- The **Entities** selection is active by default. Select the entity to be delete from the existing model.
- After selecting the desired entities, click on the **OK** button from **DELETE** dialog box to delete the selected entity; refer to Figure-58.

Figure-58. Entity deleted

PHYSICAL MATERIAL

The **Physical Material** tool is used to apply physical and visual material to the component or body. The procedure to use this tool is discussed next.

* Click on the **Physical Material** tool of **MODIFY** drop-down from **Toolbar**; refer to Figure-59. The **PHYSICAL MATERIAL** dialog box will be displayed; refer to Figure-60.

Figure-59. Physical Material tool

Figure-60. PHYSICAL MATERIAL dialog box

- Select the required option from **Library** drop-down.
- Select the required physical material from **Library** section of **PHYSICAL MATERIAL** dialog box.
- Now, drag the specific material from the **Library** section and drop it to the body or component. The physical material of body/component will be changed; refer to Figure-61.

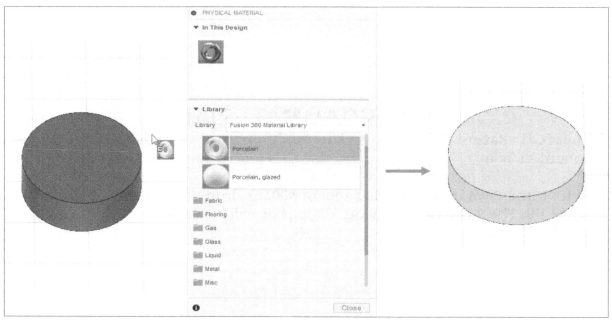

Figure-61. Applying physical material on the body

- After applying material, click on the **Close** button of **PHYSICAL MATERIAL** dialog box to apply changes.

APPEARANCE

The **Appearance** tool is used to change the appearance of body. This tool is generally used to change the color of the body. The procedure to use this tool is discussed next.

- Click on the **Appearance** tool of **MODIFY** drop-down from **Toolbar**; refer to Figure-62. The **APPEARANCE** dialog box will be displayed; refer to Figure-63.

Figure-62. Appearance tool

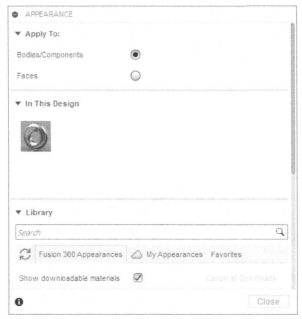

Figure-63. APPEARANCE dialog box

- Select the required radio button of **Apply To** section from **APPEARANCE** dialog box to select bodies/components or faces.
- Drag an appearance and drop it to the body or face; refer to Figure-64.

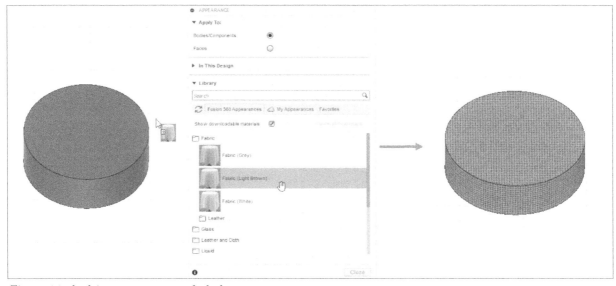

Figure-64. Applying appearance on the body

- After applying the appearance, click on the **Close** button from **APPEARANCE** dialog box to finish the process.

MANAGE MATERIALS

The **Manage Materials** tool is used to define the material properties shown in **PHYSICAL MATERIAL** and **APPEARANCE** dialog boxes discussed earlier. The procedure to use this tool is discussed next.

- Click on the **Manage Materials** tool of **MODIFY** drop-down from **Toolbar**; refer to Figure-65. The **Material Browser** dialog box will be displayed; refer to Figure-66.

Figure-65. Manage Materials tool

Figure-66. Material Browser dialog box

- Click on any material or appearance from list section to check or modify the property of selected material or appearance.
- To edit properties of any material select it from the list and then click on the **Add to Favorites & Edit** button at the bottom-right in the dialog box.
- Change the properties as required using the options displayed in the right area of **Material Browser** dialog box and click on the **OK** button to apply changes.
- Close the dialog box once changes have been applied. Next, when you will be applying material, make sure to select them from favorites list.

CHANGE PARAMETERS

The **Change Parameters** tool is used to change the parameters and apply equations to the model. The procedure to use this tool is discussed next.

- Click on the **Change Parameters** tool of **MODIFY** drop-down from **Toolbar**; refer to Figure-67. The **Parameters** dialog box will be displayed; refer to Figure-68.

Figure-67. Change Parameters tool

Figure-68. Parameters dialog box

- If you want to create some parameters which are to be used later in equation then click on the **User Parameters** button from **Parameters** dialog box. The **Add User Parameter** dialog box will be displayed; refer to Figure-69.

Figure-69. Add User Parameter dialog box

- Click in the **Name** edit box and specify the name of parameter.
- Click on the **Unit** drop-down and select the desired unit of the parameter.
- Click on the **Expression** edit box and enter the desired expression like d1/4. The **Value** will be displayed.
- Click in the **Comment** edit box and enter the required comment.
- After specifying the parameters, click on the **OK** button from **Add User Parameter** dialog box. The user defined parameter will be added in **Parameters** dialog box; refer to Figure-70.

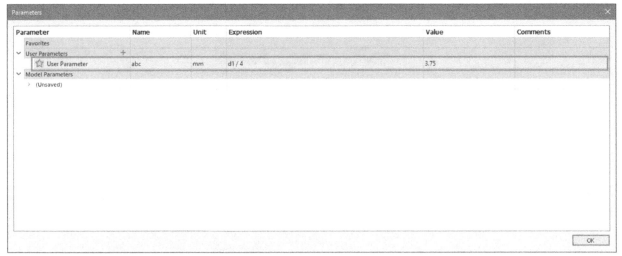

Figure-70. User Parameter added

- Click on the **Model Parameter** node from **Parameters** dialog box, all the model features will be displayed.
- Click on the desired model feature node to check its parameters, the parameters applied in that feature will be displayed; refer to Figure-71.

Figure-71. Parameters applied in the model

- If you want to apply equation in parameters then click on the dimension parameter and enter the desired equation like d1*2; refer to Figure-72. Note that here d1 is dimension number applied automatically to the sketch dimension.

Parameter	Name	Unit	Expression	Value
Favorites				
∨ User Parameters	+			
☆ User Parameter	abc	mm	d1 / 4	3.75
∨ Model Parameters				
∨ Practice v1				
∨ Extrude1				
☆ AlongDistance	d1	mm	15 mm	15.00
☆ TaperAngle	d2	deg	0.0 deg	0.0
∨ Extrude3				
☆ AlongDistance	d6	mm	-50.00 mm	-50.00
☆ TaperAngle	d7	deg	0.0 deg	0.0
∨ Plane2				
☆ AlongDistance	d9	mm	d1 * 2	30.00
∨ Extrude4				
☆ AlongDistance	d10	mm	10.00 mm	10.00
☆ TaperAngle	d11	deg	0.0 deg	0.0

Figure-72. Entering equation

- After specifying the parameters, click on the **OK** button from **Parameters** dialog box
- The equation entered in the **Parameters** dialog box will be applied to the model; refer to Figure-73.

Figure-73. Parameter changed

Click on the **Compute All** tool from the **MODIFY** drop-down to re-calculate all the parameters.

SELF-ASSESSMENT

Q1. Which of the following tools can be used to dynamically use offset face or fillet function depending on the selection?

a. Fillet   b. Offset Face
c. Press Pull   d. Combine

Q2. Which of the following tool is used to apply round at the edges?

a. Fillet   b. Chamfer
c. Draft   d. Shell

Q3. Which of the following tool is used by casting mold designer to allow easy extraction of part from the die?

a. Fillet   b. Draft
c. Shell   d. Chamfer

Q4. Which of the following tool is used to create a body using intersection of two bodies?

a. Combine   b. Shell
c. Split Body   d. Split Face

Q5. The **Move/Copy** tool in Autodesk Fusion **Design** workspace can also be used to rotate the objects. (T/F)

Q6. What is the difference between applications of **Physical Material** tool and **Appearance** tool in **Modify** drop-down of **Design** workspace?

Q7. In Autodesk Fusion 360, you can create a fillet with changing radius at specified points. (T/F)

Q8. Which of the following tools is used to remove material from a solid body and convert it into a thin body of specified thickness?

a. Combine   b. Shell
c. Split Body   d. Split Face

Chapter 7

Assembly Design

Topics Covered

The major topics covered in this chapter are:

- *New Component Tool*
- *Joint Tool*
- *Joint Origin*
- *Rigid Group*
- *Motion Links*
- *Motion Study*

INTRODUCTION

Most of the things you find around you in real-world are assembly of various components; the computer you are working on is an assembly, the automotive you may be driving or sitting in for travelling is an assembly, there are lots of examples. Till this point, we have learned to create solid parts. But most of the time, we need to assemble the parts to get some use of them. In this chapter, we will work on the assembly design of Autodesk Fusion 360 in which we will be assembling two or more components using some assembly constraints.

NEW COMPONENT

The **New Component** tool is used to create an empty component or component from the selected bodies. Note that we need to convert all parts to components before performing their assembly. The procedure to use this tool is discussed next.

*   Click on the **New Component** tool of **ASSEMBLE** drop-down from **Toolbar**; refer to Figure-1. The **NEW COMPONENT** dialog box will be displayed; refer to Figure-2.

Figure-1. New Component tool

Figure-2. NEW COMPONENT dialog box

*   Select the **Empty Component** radio button from **NEW COMPONENT** dialog box, if you want to create an empty component in the assembly structure.
*   Select the **From Bodies** Radio button from **NEW COMPONENT** dialog box, if you want to create a new component from existing body.

Empty Component

In this topic, we will discuss the procedure of creating empty component.

*   Select the **Empty Component** radio button from the **NEW COMPONENT** dialog box if not selected by default.
*   Click in the **Name** edit box of **NEW COMPONENT** dialog box and enter the name of component.

- Click on **Select** button of **Parent** option and select the parent body under which new component will be created.
- Select the **Activate** check box from **New Component** dialog box to activate the new component. Note that all the modeling operations performed after activating the component will become child feature of that component.
- Select the **Sheet Metal Component** check box if you want to create current component as sheet metal part. (You will learn about sheet metal modeling later in this book.)
- After specifying the parameters for empty component, click on the **OK** button from **NEW COMPONENT** dialog box. An empty component will be created; refer to Figure-3.

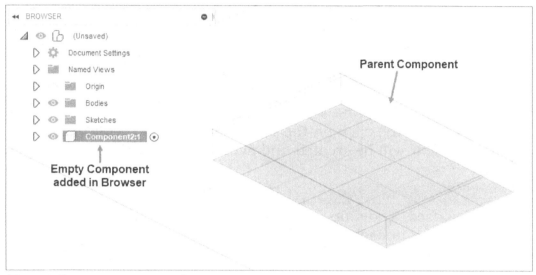

Figure-3. Empty component created

From Bodies

The **From Bodies** radio button is used to create a component from the selected body. The procedure to use this tool is discussed next.

- Select the **From Bodies** radio button from **NEW COMPONENT** dialog box. The updated dialog box will be displayed; refer to Figure-4.

Figure-4. NEW COMPONENT dialog box with From Bodies option

- The **Select** button of **Bodies** option is active by default. Click on the parts/bodies from model to create a new component; refer to Figure-5. You can select multiple bodies by holding the **CTRL** key.

Figure-5. Bodies selected for new component

- After selecting the body, click on the **OK** button from **NEW COMPONENT** dialog box. The new component will be created and action will be displayed in **Timeline**.

JOINT

The **Joint** tool is used to define joints between components to allow movement of components relative to each other. To apply **Joint** tool, you need to create the component of bodies. The procedure to use this tool is discussed next.

The procedure to create apply joint is discussed next.

- Click on the **Joint** tool of **ASSEMBLE** drop-down from **Toolbar**; refer to Figure-6. The **JOINT** dialog box will be displayed; refer to Figure-7.

Figure-6. Joint tool

Figure-7. JOINT dialog box

- **Select** button of **Component1** section is active by default. Click on the first component at desired location to assemble; refer to Figure-8. You will be asked to select a location on second component.

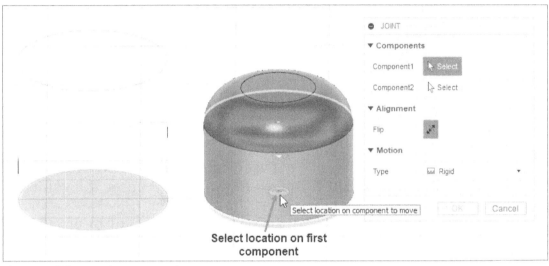

Figure-8. Selection of component1 location

- Click on the second component on mating location to select; refer to Figure-9.

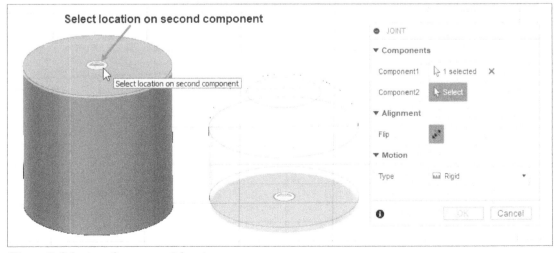

Figure-9. Selection of component2 location

- On selecting the second component, the selected two component will be joined to each other at the locations selected on them and the updated **JOINT** dialog box will be displayed; refer to Figure-10.

Figure-10. Components joined with updated JOINT dialog box

- Click in the **Angle** edit box of **JOINT** dialog box and specify the angle of rotation of component.
- If you want to specify offset distance between components then click in the **Offset X** , **Offset Y**, and **Offset Z** edit boxes as required and enter the value. You can also set the offset distance by moving the drag handles.
- Click on the **Flip** button from **JOINT** dialog box, if you want to flip the direction of second component.

Motion

There are seven motion types in **JOINT** dialog box which we can apply to the component as required; refer to Figure-11. These motion types are described next.

*Figure-11. Types of motion in
JOINT dialog box*

Rigid Motion

- Select the **Rigid** option of **Type** drop-down from **JOINT** dialog box, if you want the joint of two component to be rigid to each other and there should be no motion between the two joined component.

Revolute Motion

- Select the **Revolute** option of **Type** drop-down from **JOINT** dialog box, if you want to revolve the component about other at the joint location. On selecting the **Revolute** option a revolve drag handle will displayed. You can also revolve the component by moving the drag handle; refer to Figure-12.

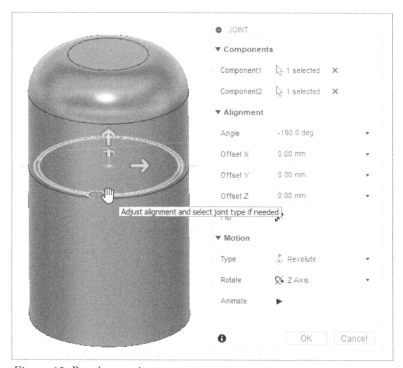

Figure-12. Revolute motion

Slider Motion

- Click on the **Slider** option of **Type** drop-down from **JOINT** dialog box if you want to assemble the component in such a way that selected component can slide over the other; refer to Figure-13.

Figure-13. Slider motion

Cylindrical Motion

- Click on the **Cylindrical** option of **Type** drop-down from **JOINT** dialog box, if you want to assemble the component in such a way that it is free to move along the selected axis and free to rotate about the same selected axis; refer to Figure-14.

Figure-14. Cylindrical motion

Pin-Slot Motion

- Click on the **Pin-Slot** option of **Type** drop-down from **JOINT** dialog box, if you want revolve and slide the component together like in nut & bolt locking-unlocking.

Planar Motion

- Click on the **Planer** option of **Type** drop-down from **JOINT** dialog box, if you want to assemble the component in such a way that the component can move over the selected plane only in defined boundary.

Ball Motion

- Click on the **Ball** option of **Type** drop-down from **JOINT** dialog box, if you want to assemble the component in such a way that the component is free to move 360 degree in 3D space pivoted to a point; refer to Figure-15.

Figure-15. Ball motion

- Click on the **Animate** button from **JOINT** dialog box to watch the applied motion by animating **Component1**. Click the button again to stop the animation.

After specifying the parameters for joint, click on the **OK** button from **JOINT** dialog box to complete the process.

AS-BUILT JOINT

The **As-built Joint** tool allows the joints to be applied to components in their current position as they are built, making it easy to join them in their original orientation. The procedure to use this tool is discussed next.

- Click on the **As-built Joint** tool of **ASSEMBLE** drop-down from **Toolbar**; refer to Figure-16. The **AS-BUILT JOINT** dialog box will be displayed; refer to Figure-17.

Figure-16. As built Joint tool

*Figure-17. AS BUILT JOINT
dialog box*

- Select the components from the canvas.
- Select the required motion from **Type** drop-down. The updated **AS-BUILT JOINT** dialog box will be displayed; refer to Figure-18.

Figure-18. Updated AS BUILT JOINT dialog box

- Select the desired references on the components based on the option selected in **Type** drop-down; refer to Figure-19.

Figure-19. Selecting reference for motion

- After specifying the parameters, click on the **OK** button from **AS-BUILT JOINT** dialog box to complete the process.
- If you want to rotate the component after creating joint then double-click on the flag displayed; refer to Figure-20.

Figure-20. Flag for rotation

- The drag handle will be displayed. Rotate the component as required; refer to Figure-21.

Figure-21. Rotation of component

JOINT ORIGIN

The **Joint Origin** tool is used to define joint origin on a component. The procedure to use this tool is discussed next.

- Click on the **Joint Origin** tool of **ASSEMBLE** drop-down from **Toolbar**; refer to Figure-22. The **JOINT ORIGIN** dialog box will be displayed; refer to Figure-23.

Figure-22. Joint Origin tool

Figure-23. JOINT ORIGIN dialog box

- Select **Simple** option of **Type** drop-down from **JOINT ORIGIN** dialog box, if you want to place the joint origin on a face.
- Select **Between Two Faces** option of **Type** drop-down from **JOINT ORIGIN** dialog box if you want to place the joint origin midway between the faces.
- In our case, we are selecting the **Between Two Faces** option of **Type** drop-down. The updated **JOINT ORIGIN** dialog box will be displayed as shown in Figure-24.

Figure-24. Updated JOINT ORI-GIN dialog box

- The **Select** button of **Plane 1** option is active by default. Click on the first face from model to select; refer to Figure-25.

Figure-25. Selection of first face

- On selecting the first face, the **Select** button of **Plane 2** option will be activated. Similarly, select the second face of the model; refer to Figure-26. The updated **JOINT ORIGIN** dialog box will be displayed.

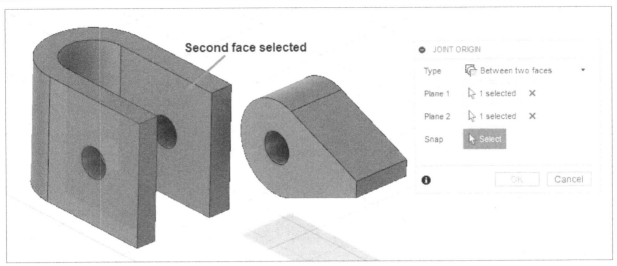

Figure-26. Selection of second face

- The **Select** button of **Snap** option is active by default. Click at desired location to define the snap point; refer to Figure-27.

Figure-27. Selection of snap point

- On selecting the snap point, the **JOINT ORIGIN** dialog box will be updated; refer to Figure-28.

Figure-28. Specifying the location of snap

- If you want to specify the angle of snap then click in the **Angle** edit box of **JOINT ORIGIN** dialog box and specify the angle of rotation of Snap.
- If you want to specify the Offset distance of snap then click on the **Offset X** edit box and enter the value. You can also set the offset distance by moving the drag handle.
- Similarly, set the offset distance in other edit boxes.
- Select the **Flip** check box from **JOINT ORIGIN** dialog box if you want to flip the direction of snap.
- Select the **Reorient** check box from **JOINT ORIGIN** dialog box, if you want to position the axes of origin of geometry.
- After specifying the parameters, click on the **OK** button from **JOINT ORIGIN** dialog box to complete the process.
- Now, you will be able to join the two component with the help of **Joint** tool using newly created joint origin; refer to Figure-29 and Figure-30.

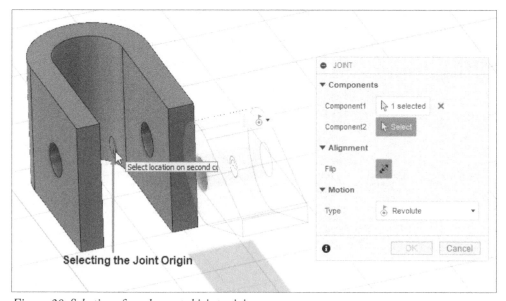

Figure-29. Selection of newly created joint origin

Figure-30. Joint created

RIGID GROUP

The **Rigid Group** tool is used to combine selected components into one group so that the created group act as one object. The procedure to use this tool is discussed next.

- Click on the **Rigid Group** tool of **ASSEMBLE** drop-down from **Toolbar**; refer to Figure-31. The **RIGID GROUP** dialog box will be displayed; refer to Figure-32.

Figure-31. Rigid Group tool

Figure-32. RIGID GROUP dialog box

- The **Select** button of **Components** section is active by default. You need to select the components from the model to create a rigid group.
- Select the **Include Child Components** check box if you want to include the child components into the rigid group.
- Click on **OK** button from **RIGID GROUP** dialog box to complete the process.

DRIVE JOINTS

The **Drive Joints** tool is used to specifying the rotation angle or distance value based on joint's degrees of freedom. The procedure to use this tool is discussed next.

- Click on the **Drive Joints** tool of **ASSEMBLE** drop-down from **Toolbar**; refer to Figure-33. The **DRIVE JOINTS** dialog box will be displayed; refer to Figure-34.

Figure-33. Drive Joints tool

Figure-34. DRIVE JOINTS dialog box

- The **Joint Input** selection is active by default. Click on the joint from model. The updated **DRIVE JOINTS** dialog box will be displayed; refer to Figure-35.

Figure-35. Updated DRIVE JOINTS dialog box

- Click in the **Rotation** edit box and specify the angle of rotation. You can also specify rotation limits by moving the drag handle; refer to Figure-36.

Figure-36. Specifying the rotation limits

- After specifying the parameters, click on the **OK** button from **DRIVE JOINTS** dialog box.

Note that after changing position of joint after driving, the **POSITION** panel is displayed in the **SOLID** tab of **Toolbar**; refer to Figure-37. Select the **Capture Position** tool from the panel if you want to make current position of joint as new start position. Select the **Revert** option from the panel if you want to revert the joint to original position.

Figure-37. POSITION panel

MOTION LINK

The **Motion Link** tool is used to specify the relationship between motion of two selected joints like relation between two gear rotation or related between bolt rotation and translation while fastening. The procedure to use this tool is discussed next.

- Click on the **Motion Link** tool of **ASSEMBLE** drop-down from **Toolbar**; refer to Figure-38. The **MOTION LINK** dialog box will be displayed; refer to Figure-39.

Figure-38. Motion Link tool

Figure-39. MOTION LINK dialog box

- **Joints** selection is active by default. Click on the desired joints. In our case, we are selecting the slider and revolve joints to create a motion of vice.
- On selecting the two joints, the animation of vice will start and the dialog box will be updated; refer to Figure-40.

Figure-40. Selection of joints for Motion Link

- Click in the **Distance** edit box of **MOTION LINK** dialog box and specify the value of distance per revolution.
- Click in the **Angle** edit box of **MOTION LINK** dialog box and specify the value of angle of revolution. The combination of distance and angle value define the range of motion like in our case, for one full rotation of 360 degree by handle, the jaw will move 10 mm of distance.
- Select the **Reverse** check box of **MOTION LINK** dialog box, if you want to reverse the direction of revolution.
- Click on the **Animate** button to watch the animation of joints.
- After specifying the parameters, click on **OK** button of **MOTION LINK** dialog box to complete the process; refer to Figure-41.

Figure-41. Motion Link created between joints

ENABLE CONTACT SETS

The **Enable Contact Sets** tool is used to enable the physical contact conditions. The procedure to use this tool is discussed next.

- Click on the **Enable Contact Sets** tool of **ASSEMBLE** drop-down from **Toolbar**; refer to Figure-42. The tool will be displayed in **BROWSER**; refer to Figure-43.

Figure-42. Enable Contact Sets tool

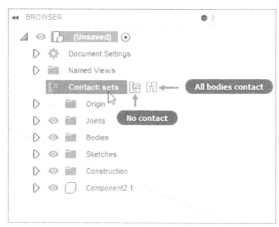

Figure-43. Contact sets

- Click on **All Bodies Contact** button to activate the contact analysis between sets; refer to Figure-44.

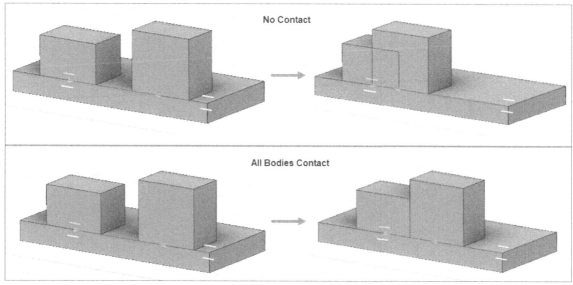

Figure-44. Applying contact sets tool

- Click **No Contact** button to disable the contact between sets.
- In the above figure, the first case is with contact sets not active and the second case is with contact sets active. So, when contact set is active than physical properties of objects are taken into account like one solid object cannot pass through another solid object.

Enable All Contact

The **Enable All Contact** tool is used to enable all contacts which were applied earlier in the part or model.

- To enable contact, click on the **Enable All Contact** tool of **ASSEMBLE** drop-down from **Toolbar**. All contacts will be enabled and the **ASSEMBLE** drop-down will be updated with two new tools which are discussed next.

Disable Contact

The **Disable Contact** tool is used to disable all contacts which were made earlier in the part or model.

- To disable contact, click on the **Disable Contact** tool of **ASSEMBLE** drop-down from **Toolbar**. All contacts will be disabled.

New Contact Set

The **New Contact Set** tool is used to create new contact set between two selected components. These contact sets prevent parts from passing through one another. The procedure to use this tool is discussed next.

- Click on the **New Contact Set** tool of **ASSEMBLE** drop-down from **Toolbar**; refer to Figure-45. The **NEW CONTACT SET** dialog box will be displayed; refer to Figure-46.

Figure-45. New Contact Set tool

Figure-46. NEW CONTACT SET dialog box

- The **Select** button of **Bodies or Components** section is active by default. Select the two component or bodies to create sets and click on **OK** button from **NEW CONTACT SET** dialog box to complete the process.

MOTION STUDY

The **Motion Study** tool is used to perform kinematic motion analysis based on joints. The procedure to use this tool is discussed next.

• Click on the **Motion Study** tool of **ASSEMBLE** drop-down from **Toolbar**; refer to Figure-47. The **Motion Study** dialog box will be displayed; refer to Figure-48.

Figure-47. Motion Study tool

Figure-48. Motion Study dialog box

• You need to select the joint from part or model. Click to select the joint; refer to Figure-49.

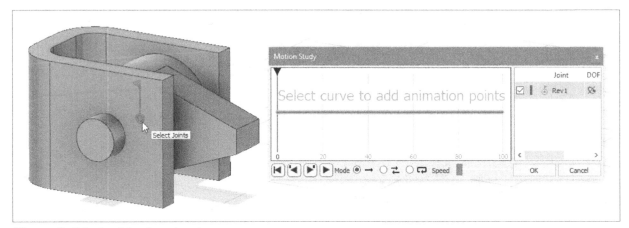

Figure-49. Selecting joint for animation

• After selecting joint, create the points of motion curve as required by clicking in the graph line of motion; refer to Figure-50.

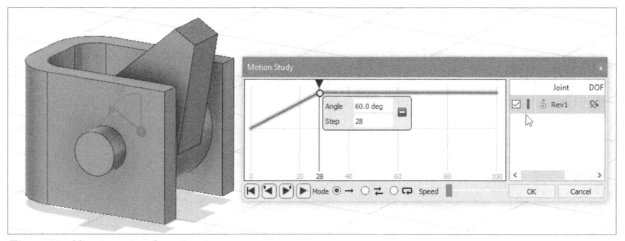

Figure-50. Adjusting points for animation

- Click in the **Angle** edit box and specify the required angle for animation point. Note that the options will be displayed based on selected joint.
- After creating the animation points, set the speed of animation from **Speed** bar.
- Select **Play Once** radio button from **Mode** section to play the animation once.
- Select **Play Forward/Backward** radio button from **Mode** section to play the animation forward and then backward.
- Select **Play Loop** radio button from **Mode** section to play the animation in cycle.
- After specifying the parameters for animation, click on **Play** button to check the animation of selected joint.
- Click on **OK** button from **Motion Study** dialog box to exit the motion study of components.

PRACTICAL 1

Assemble the parts of handle as shown in Figure-51. The exploded view of assembly is displayed as shown in Figure-52.

Figure-51. Assembled handle

Figure-52. Exploded view of handle

All the part files can be downloaded from resource kit of Fusion 360 software, which is provided at **CADCAMCAEWORKS.COM.**

The steps to assemble these parts are given next.

Adding file into Fusion 360

• After downloading the resource kit from CADCAMCAEWORKS.COM, open the **Chapter 7** folder.
• Double-click on **Handle v0.f3d** file. The file will open in **Autodesk Fusion 360** software; refer to Figure-53.

Figure-53. Fusion 360 startup window

Assembling components

- Click on **New Component** tool of **ASSEMBLE** drop-down from **Toolbar**; refer to Figure-54. The **NEW COMPONENT** dialog box will be displayed; refer to Figure-55.

Figure-54. New Component tool 2

Figure-55. New Component dialog box 2

- Select the **From Bodies** radio button from **NEW COMPONENT** dialog box and select all the bodies to make them component; refer to Figure-56.

Figure-56. Selecting bodies to create components

- After selecting the bodies, click on **OK** button from **NEW COMPONENT** dialog box. The components will be created and added in **Timeline**.

- Click on **Joint** tool of **ASSEMBLE** drop-down from **Toolbar.** You can also activate the **Joint** tool by pressing **J** key from keyboard. The **Joint** dialog box will be displayed; refer to Figure-57.

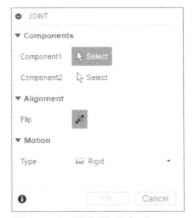

Figure-57. JOINT dialog box

- The **Select** button of **Component 1** is selected by default. Click on the component to join; refer to Figure-58.

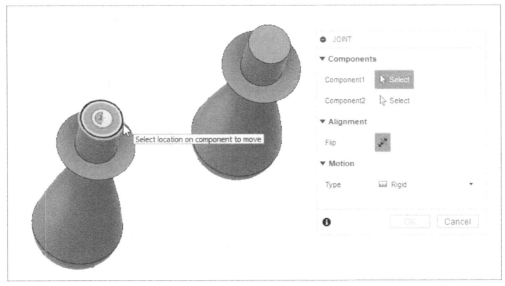

Figure-58. Selection of location on component1

- After selection of first component, select the second component; refer to Figure-59.

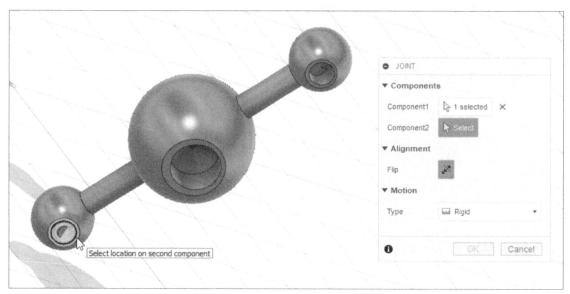

Figure-59. Selection of location on component2

- Select **Rigid** option from **Type** drop-down to create a rigid joint between two component.
- After specifying the parameters, click on **OK** button from **JOINT** dialog box to create a rigid joint.
- Similarly, create another rigid joint between other component.
- After joining these component the assembly will be displayed; as shown in Figure-60.

Figure-60. Final assembly of component

SELF ASSESSMENT

Q1. The .... tool is used to create an empty component or component from the selected bodies.

Q2. Which of the following tool is used to define motion type of a component in an assembly?

a. New Component   b. Joint
c. Rigid Group   d. Drive Joints

Q3. Which of the following motion type is not available to apply joints in assembly of Autodesk Fusion 360?

a. Slider   b. Cylindrical
c. Pin-slot   d. Symmetry

Q4. Which of the following tools is used to combine multiple components to act as a single component?

a. New Component   b. Joint
c. Rigid Group   d. Drive Joints

Q5. Which of the following tools is used to define relation between motion of two components of assembly?

a. Motion Link   b. Joint
c. Rigid Group   d. Drive Joints

PRACTICE 1

Assemble the parts of motor assembly as shown in Figure-61 and Figure-62. The exploded view of assembly is shown in Figure-63. Note that you can open this practice file from the resource kit downloaded for this book.

Figure-61. Assembly view 1

Figure-62. Assembly view 2

Figure-63. Exploded view of assembly

PRACTICE 2

Assemble the parts of crank assembly as shown in Figure-64. The exploded view in which you will get the model is shown in Figure-65.

Figure-64. Assembled crank piston model

Figure-65. Exploded view of crank assembly

FOR STUDENT NOTES

Chapter 8

Importing Files and Inspection

Topics Covered

The major topics covered in this chapter are:

- *Interference Tool*
- *Curvature Comb Analysis*
- *Data Analysis*
- *Section Analysis*
- *Decal tool*
- *Attached Canvas*
- *Insert SVG*
- *Inserting a Manufacturing Part*

INTRODUCTION

In the previous chapter, we have learned about the procedure of creating and assembling component. Till now, we have worked on the components that are/have been created in Autodesk Fusion 360. Now, you will learn to insert external model objects like canvas, decal, dxf, and manufacturer parts. In this chapter, you will learn the procedures of inspecting the part and importing files in **Autodesk Fusion 360** software.

INSERTING FILE

In this section, you will learn the procedure to insert the various types of files in **Autodesk Fusion 360**.

Insert Derive

The **Insert Derive** tool is used to insert components, sketches, parameters, or bodies from another design file into the current model file. Note that before using this tool, you need to save the current model file. The procedure to use this tool is discussed next.

- Click on the **Insert Derive** tool of **INSERT** drop-down from **Toolbar**; refer to Figure-1. The **Select Source** dialog box will be displayed; refer to Figure-2.

Figure-1. Insert Derive tool

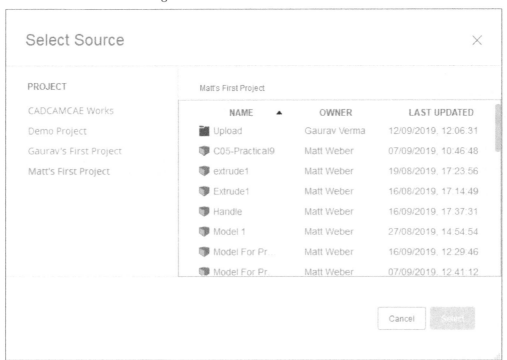

Figure-2. Select Source dialog box

- Select the desired source component and click on the **Select** button from **Select Source** dialog box. The selected component will be inserted in the canvas along with the **DERIVE** dialog box; refer to Figure-3.

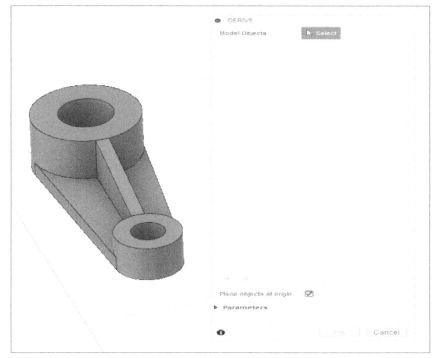

Figure-3. DERIVE dialog box

- The **Select** button of **Model Objects** section is active by default. Click on the inserted component to select the model. The updated **DERIVE** dialog box will be displayed; refer to Figure-4. You can select the sketch and other objects from **BROWSER**.

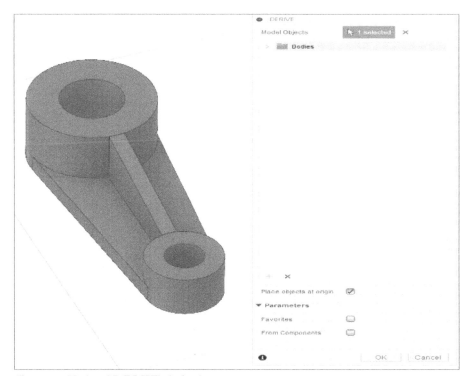

Figure-4. Updated DERIVE dialog box

- Select the **Place objects at origin** check box to place the component origin aligned to model origin.
- Expand the **Parameters** node and select the desired check boxes to include parameters in desired part.
- After specifying all the parameters, click on **OK** button from the **DERIVE** dialog box to complete the process.

Decal

The **Decal** tool is used to place an image on the selected face/plane. The procedure to use this tool is discussed next.

- Click on the **Decal** tool of **INSERT** drop-down from **Toolbar**; refer to Figure-5. The **DECAL** dialog box will be displayed; refer to Figure-6.

Figure-5. Decal tool

Figure-6. DECAL dialog box

- The **Select** button of **Select Face** section is active by default. Click on the face of model to which decal is to be applied.
- Click on **Select Image** button from **DECAL** dialog box. The **Open** dialog box will be displayed; refer to Figure-7.

- Select the required image and click on **Open** button from **Open** dialog box. The updated **DECAL** dialog box will be displayed; refer to Figure-8.

Figure-7. Open dialog box for importing file

Figure-8. Updated DECAL dialog box

- Set the image on the selected face with the help of drag handle displayed on image. You can also set the image by specifying the values in respective edit boxes in the dialog box.
- Click on the **Horizontal Flip** button to flip the image horizontally.
- Click on the **Vertical Flip** button to flip the image vertically.
- Select the **Chain Faces** check box to include tangent faces in selection.
- After specifying the parameters, the preview of model along with image will be displayed; refer to Figure-9.

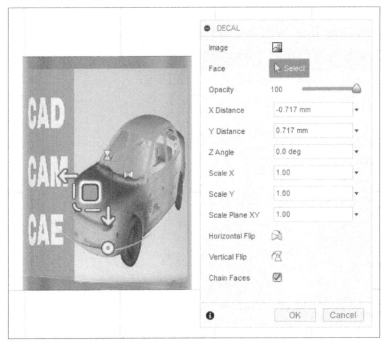

Figure-9. Preview of image on model

If the preview is as desired then click on the **OK** button from the **DECAL** dialog box to complete the process.

Canvas

The **Canvas** tool is used to insert an image on a planer face so that you can create model based on image. The procedure to use this tool is discussed next.

*   Click on the **Canvas** tool of **INSERT** drop-down from **Toolbar**; refer to Figure-10. The **CANVAS** dialog box will be displayed; refer to Figure-11.

Figure-10. Canvas tool

Figure-11. CANVAS dialog box

- The **Select** button of **Face** section is active by default. Click on the face of model/plane where you want to place the canvas image.
- Click on **Select Image** button from **CANVAS** dialog box. The **Open** dialog box will be displayed; refer to Figure-12.
- Select the desired image and click on **Open** button from **Open** dialog box. The updated **CANVAS** dialog box will be displayed; refer to Figure-13.

Figure-12. Open dialog box for attaching canvas

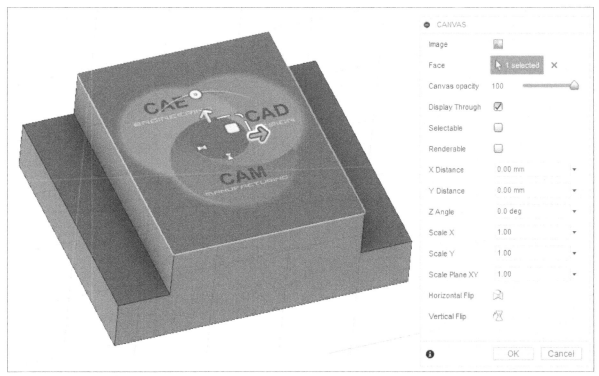

Figure-13. Updated CANVAS dialog box

- Click on **Canvas Opacity** edit box and specify the opacity of image. You an also set the opacity by moving the **Canvas opacity** slider.

- Select the **Display Through** check box if you want to make the image visible through the component.
- Select the **Selectable** check box if you want the image to be selectable.
- Select the **Renderable** check box if you want to include the image in renderings of model.
- Click in the **X Distance** edit box and specify a value of distance to move in X direction.
- Click in the **Y Distance** edit box and specify a value of distance to move in Y direction
- Click in the **Z Angle** edit box and specify a value to rotation around z axis.
- Click in the **Scale X** edit box and specify a scale value in X direction.
- Click in the **Scale Y** edit box and specify a scale value in Y direction.
- Click in the **Scale Plane XY** edit box and specify the value of scale in the XY plane.
- Click on the **Horizontal Flip** button to mirror the image horizontally.
- Click on the **Vertical Flip** button to mirror the image vertically.
- After specifying the parameters, click on the **OK** button from **CANVAS** dialog box to complete the process.

Insert Mesh

The **Insert Mesh** tool is used to insert a mesh file in current model. The procedure to use this tool is discussed next.

- Click on the **Insert Mesh** tool of **INSERT** drop-down from **Toolbar**; refer to Figure-14. The **Open** dialog box will be displayed; refer to Figure-15.

Figure-14. Insert Mesh tool

Figure-15. Open dialog box for inserting file

- Select the file and click on **Open** button of **Open** dialog box. The file will be added in application window along with **INSERT MESH** dialog box; refer to Figure-16.

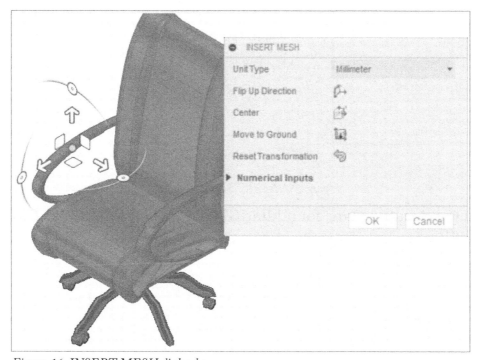

Figure-16. INSERT MESH dialog box

- Click on the **Unit Type** drop-down from **INSERT MESH** dialog box and select the required unit to scale the model.
- Click on **Flip Up Direction** button to flip the direction of model.
- Click on the **Center** button to drag the model to center or coordinate system.
- Click on **Move To Ground** button to move the model to ground plane.
- Click on **Reset Transformation** button to reset the model position to the original state.

- If you want to enter the numerical value to move the model then click on the **Numerical Inputs** section and enter the desired value. You can also move and rotate the model by using drag handles.
- After specifying the parameters, click on the **OK** button from **INSERT MESH** dialog box to complete the process.

Insert SVG

The **Insert SVG** tool is used to insert an SVG file into sketch. The procedure to use this tool is discussed next.

- Click on the **Insert SVG** tool of **INSERT** drop-down from **Toolbar**; refer to Figure-17. The **INSERT SVG** dialog box will be displayed; refer to Figure-18.

Figure-17. Insert SVG tool

Figure-18. INSERT SVG dialog box

- You need to select the plane for adding SVG file. Click on the plane to select; refer to Figure-19.

Figure-19. Selecting face or plane

- On selecting the face or plane, the sketch will be enabled.
- Click on **Select SVG File** button from **INSERT SVG** dialog box the **Open** dialog box will be displayed.

- Select the required file from **Open** dialog box and click on **Open** button. The file will be added in application window along with updated **INSERT SVG** dialog box; refer to Figure-20.

Figure-20. File along with updated INSERT SVG dialog box

- Click in the **X Distance** edit box and specify a value of distance to move in X direction.
- Click in the **Y Distance** edit box and specify a value of distance to move in Y direction.
- Click in the **Z Angle** edit box and specify a value to rotation around z axis.
- Click in the **Scale Plane XY** edit box and specify the value of scale in the XY plane.
- Click on the **Horizontal Flip** button to mirror the image horizontally.
- Click on the **Vertical Flip** button to mirror the image vertically.
- You can also use the drag handle to move or flip the model.
- After specifying the parameters, click on the **OK** button from **INSERT SVG** dialog box to complete the process.

Insert DXF

The **Insert DXF** tool is used to insert a DXF file into the active design. The procedure to use this tool is discussed next.

- Click on the **Insert DXF** tool of **INSERT** drop-down from **Toolbar**; refer to Figure-21. The **INSERT DXF** dialog box will be displayed; refer to Figure-22.

Figure-21. Insert DXF tool

Figure-22. INSERT DXF dialog box

- The **Select** button of **Plane/Sketch** section is active by default. Click on the plane to select.
- Click on **Select DXF File** button from **INSERT DXF** dialog box. The **Open** dialog box will be displayed.
- You need to select the file of .dxf format and click on **Open** button. The preview of DXF file will be displayed along with updated **INSERT DXF** dialog box; refer to Figure-23.

Figure-23. Updated INSERT DXF dialog box

- Click on the **Units** drop-down and select the required unit.

- Select **Single Sketch** option from **Insert Mode** drop-down to insert the layers of selected .DXF file into one sketch.
- Select **One Sketch Per Layer** option from **Insert Mode** drop-down to insert each sketch of DXF file on different layer.
- Click in the **X Distance** edit box and specify a value of distance to move in X direction.
- Click in the **Y Distance** edit box and specify a value of distance to move in Y direction.
- Select the **DXF Layers** check box to list the layers available in the selected DXF file. Select the layers to import.
- After specifying the parameters, click on the **OK** button from **INSERT DXF** dialog box to complete the process.

Insert McMaster-Carr Component

The **Insert McMaster-Carr Component** tool is used to insert 2D or 3D model of various library components provided by McMaster-Carr. The procedure to use this tool is given next.

- Click on the **Insert McMaster-Carr Component** tool from the **INSERT** drop-down in the **Toolbar**; refer to Figure-24. The **INSERT MCMASTER-CARR COMPONENT** window will be displayed; refer to Figure-25.

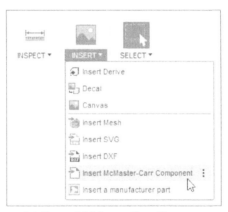

Figure-24. Insert McMaster Carr Component tool

Figure-25. INSERT MCMASTER CARR COMPONENT window

- Select the desired component and its model number from the window. The page in window will be displayed as shown in Figure-26.

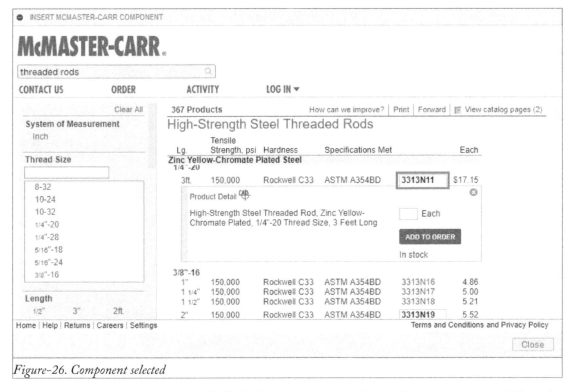

Figure-26. Component selected

- Click on the **Product Detail** link button for selected component. The drawing and model of selected component will be displayed at the bottom in the window; refer to Figure-27.

Figure-27. Model for selected component

- Select the desired format from drop-down above the drawing and click on the **Save** button to save the model in local drive.
- Close the window by selecting **Close** button.

Insert a manufacturer part

The **Insert a manufacturer part** tool is used for inserting a part of manufacturer or supplier in model through parts4cad. The procedure to use this tool is discussed next.

- Click on the **Insert a manufacturer part** tool of **INSERT** drop-down from **Toolbar**; refer to Figure-28. The Part Community web page will be displayed in default web browser; refer to Figure-29.

Figure-28. Insert a manufacturer part tool

Figure-29. AUTODESK FUSION 360 part community window

- Select the part from manufacturer or supplier and open the file in Autodesk Fusion 360.

INSPECT

Till now, we have discussed various tools to insert the objects in Autodesk Fusion 360. Now, we will discuss about measurement and analysis tools available in Autodesk Fusion 360.

Measure

The **Measure** tool is used to measure selected geometry. The procedure to use this tool is discussed next.

- Click on the **Measure** tool of **INSPECT** drop-down from **Toolbar**; refer to Figure-30. The **MEASURE** dialog box will be displayed; refer to Figure-31.

Figure-30. Measure tool

Figure-31. MEASURE dialog box

- Select the **Select Face/Edge/Vertex** button from **Selection Filter** option if you want to select face/edge/vertex for measurement.
- Select the **Select Body** button from **Selection Filter** option if you want to select body for measurement.
- Select the **Select Component** button from **Selection Filter** option if you want to select component for measurement.
- Click on the **Precision** drop-down and select the desired precision option for displaying the required number of decimal places in results.
- Click on the **Restart Selection** button to restart the selection process once you have performed measurement.
- In our case, we are selecting **Select Face/Edge/Vertex** button from **Selection Filter** option. Click on the face to measure; refer Figure-32.

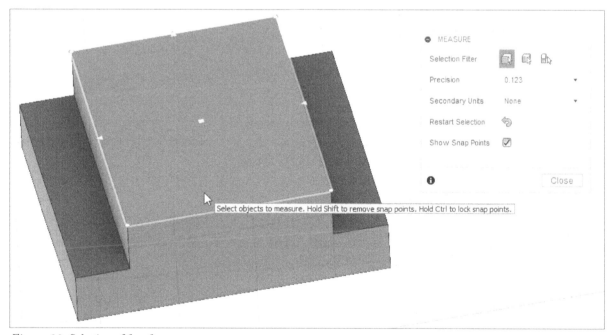

Figure-32. Selection of face for measurement

- On selecting the face, the updated **MEASURE** dialog box will be displayed with the measurement of selected face; refer to Figure-33.

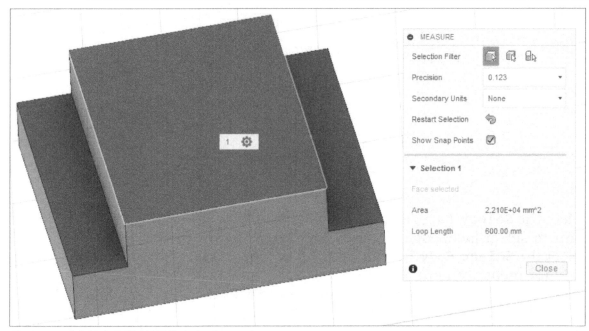

Figure-33. Updated MEASURE dialog box

- If you want to measure the distance between two faces then select the other face.
- Hover the cursor on the respective measurement to copy the value to clipboard; refer to Figure-34.

Figure-34. Copying measurement

- Select the **Show Snap points** check box to display snap points when you hover over your model with the **Measure** tool activated.
- Click on **Close** button of **MEASURE** dialog box to exit the **Measure** tool.

Interference

The **Interference** tool is used to display interference of selected components or bodies. The procedure to use this tool is discussed next.

- Click on the **Interference** tool of **INSPECT** drop-down from **Toolbar**; refer to Figure-35. The **INTERFERENCE** dialog box will be displayed; refer to Figure-36.

Figure-35. Interference tool

Figure-36. INTERFERENCE dialog box

- The **Select** button of **Select** section is active by default. Click on the model to check interference. You can also use window selection.
- Select the **Include Coincident Faces** check box if you want to include the faces in selection which are touching with each other.
- In our case, we are using window selection to select the component; refer to Figure-37.

Figure-37. Selection of component for interference

- After selecting the components, click on **Compute** button to calculate the interference. The **Interference Results** dialog box will be displayed; refer to Figure-38.

Figure-38. Interference Results dialog box

- Click on the **OK** button from **Interference Results** dialog box to exit the **Interference** tool.

Curvature Comb Analysis

The **Curvature Comb Analysis** tool is used to display a curvature comb on the spline or circular edges to determine the change in curvature. The procedure to use this tool is discussed next.

- Click on the **Curvature Comb Analysis** tool of **INSPECT** drop-down from **Toolbar**; refer to Figure-39. The **CURVATURE ANALYSIS** dialog box will be displayed; refer to Figure-40.

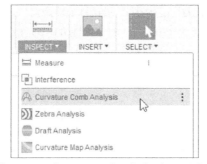

Figure-39. Curvature Comb Analysis tool

Figure-40. CURVATURE ANALYSIS dialog box

- **Edges** selection of **CURVATURE ANALYSIS** dialog box is active by default. Click on the geometry to select the edge. The preview of comb on edge will be displayed; refer to Figure-41.

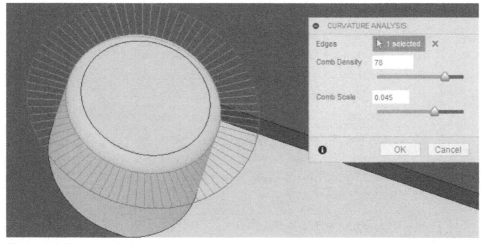

Figure-41. Preview of comb on circular edge

- Click in the **Comb Density** edit box and specify the value. You can also set the comb density by moving the **Comb Density** slider.
- Click in the **Comb Scale** edit box and specify the value. You can also set the comb scale by moving the **Comb Scale** slider.
- After analyzing, click on **OK** button from **CURVATURE ANALYSIS** dialog box to exit the tool.

Zebra Analysis

The **Zebra Analysis** tool is used to analyze continuity between the surfaces of component by displaying strips on model. The procedure to use this tool is discussed next.

- Click on the **Zebra Analysis** tool of **Inspect** drop-down from **Toolbar**; refer to Figure-42. The **ZEBRA ANALYSIS** dialog box will be displayed; refer to Figure-43.

Figure-42. Zebra Analysis tool

Figure-43. ZEBRA ANALYSIS dialog box

- The **Select** button of **Body** selection option is active by default. Click to select the body for analysis.
- On selecting the body, preview of zebra strips will be displayed; refer to Figure-44.

Figure-44. Selection of body for zebra analysis

- Select **Vertical** option from **Direction** drop-down for display of vertical lines on model.
- Select **Horizontal** option from **Direction** drop-down for display of horizontal lines on model.
- Set the number of strips for model from **Repeats** slider.
- Select the **Lock Strips** check box of **ZEBRA ANALYSIS** dialog box to freeze the stripes on body.
- Click on the **Opacity** edit box and enter the value for opacity. You can also set the value of opacity by moving the **Opacity** slider.
- Select the **High Quality** check box of **ZEBRA ANALYSIS** dialog box to increase the display quality of strips.
- After specifying the parameters, click on **OK** button from **ZEBRA ANALYSIS** dialog box. The strips will be displayed on model; refer to Figure-45.

Figure-45. Strips on model

Draft Analysis

The **Draft Analysis** tool is used to display a color gradient on the selected body to evaluate draft angle of various faces of the part. The procedure to use this tool is discussed next.

- Click on the **Draft Analysis** tool of **Inspect** drop-down from **Toolbar**; refer to Figure-46. The **DRAFT ANALYSIS** dialog box will be displayed; refer to Figure-47.

Figure-46. Draft Analysis tool

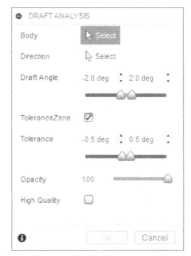

Figure-47. DRAFT ANALYSIS dialog box

- The **Select** button of **Body** section is active by default. Click on the body to perform analysis.
- Click on **Select** button of **Direction** option and select the direction for analysis. On selection, the preview will be displayed; refer to Figure-48.

Figure-48. Preview of draft analysis

- Click in **Draft Angle** edit boxes and specify the range of draft angle for which you want to perform analysis. You can also set the draft angle limits by moving the **Draft angle** slider.
- Select the **ToleranceZone** check box if you want to display a tolerance gradient on the results.
- Click on the **Tolerance** edit box and specify the start and stop angles tolerance. You can also set the tolerance angle by moving the slider.
- Click on the **Opacity** edit box and enter the value for opacity for draft colors. You can also set the value of opacity by moving the **Opacity** slider.
- Select the **High Quality** check box of **DRAFT ANALYSIS** dialog box to increase the display quality of gradient.
- After specifying the parameters for analysis, click on **OK** button from **DRAFT ANALYSIS** dialog box to complete the analysis.

Curvature Map Analysis

The **Curvature Map Analysis** tool is used to displays a color gradient on the faces of selected bodies to evaluate the amount of curvature. The procedure to use this tool is discussed next.

- Click on the **Curvature Map Analysis** tool of **Inspect** drop-down from **Toolbar**; refer to Figure-49. The **CURVATURE MAP ANALYSIS** dialog box will be displayed; refer to Figure-50.

Figure-49. Curvature Map Analysis tool

*Figure-50. CURVATURE MAP
ANALYSIS dialog box*

- The **Select** button of **Body** option is active by default. Click on the body to select for analysis.
- Select **Smooth** option from **Display** drop-down if you want to display a blend of two colors.
- Select **Bands** option from **Display** drop-down if you want to display no transition between colors.
- Select **Gaussian** option from **Type** drop-down if you want to display the gradient as the product of curvature in the U direction and curvature in the V direction.
- Select **Principal Minimum** option from **Type** drop-down if you want to display the gradient highlighting areas of lowest curvature.
- Select **Principal Maximum** option from **Type** drop-down if you want to display the gradient highlighting areas with the highest curvature.
- Click in the **Scale** edit box of **CURVATURE MAP ANALYSIS** dialog box and enter the value. You can also set the value of scale by moving the **Scale** slider.
- Click on the **Opacity** edit box and enter the value for opacity. You can also set the value of opacity by moving the **Opacity** slider.
- Select the **High Quality** check box of **CURVATURE MAP ANALYSIS** dialog box to increase the display quality of gradient.
- After specifying the parameters for analysis, click on **OK** button from **CURVATURE MAP ANALYSIS** dialog box to exit this analysis; refer to Figure-51.

Figure-51. Curvature map analysis of model

Accessibility Analysis

The **Accessibility Analysis** tool is used to determine whether the area of the model is accessible or inaccessible through selected view of the plane. This analysis is used to perform undercut analysis. The procedure to use this tool is discussed next.

- Click on the **Accessibility Analysis** tool of **INSPECT** drop-down from **Toolbar**; refer to Figure-52. The **ACCESSIBILITY ANALYSIS** dialog box will be displayed; refer to Figure-53.

Figure-52. Accessibility Analysis tool

Figure-53. ACCESSIBILITY ANALYSIS dialog box

- The **Select** button of **Body** section is active by default. Click on the face of the body to select; refer to Figure-54. You will be asked to select a direction.

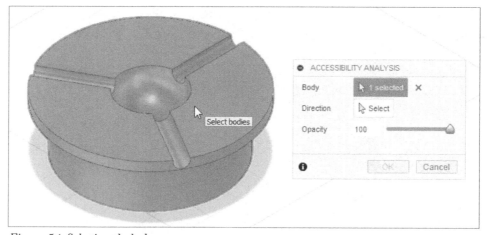

Figure-54. Selecting the body

- Click on the **Select** button of **Direction** section and select the edge, plane or axis of the model to indicate the direction of analysis. The preview of the accessible areas will be displayed along with updated **ACCESSIBILITY ANALYSIS** dialog box; refer to Figure-55.

Figure-55. Updated ACCESSIBILITY ANALYSIS dialog box

- On selecting the direction, the areas that are accessible from selected direction are shaded in green and the areas that are inaccessible are shaded in red.
- You can flip the direction of analysis by clicking on the flip button of **Flip Direction** section.
- You can also set the opacity by sliding the slider button or edit the opacity in edit box of **Opacity** section.
- The visibility of this analysis can be control by expanding the **Analysis** folder in the **BROWSER** and clicking on the eye button to view or hide the analysis; refer to Figure-56.

Figure-56. Visibility of analysis

- After specifying the parameters for analysis, click on **OK** button from **ACCESSIBILITY ANALYSIS** dialog box to exit this analysis.

Minimum Radius Analysis

The **Minimum Radius Analysis** tool is used to highlight the areas of the model which are at or below the minimum radius. It also detects the minimum fit for fillets and holes.

- Click on the **Minimum Radius Analysis** tool of **Inspect** drop-down from **Toolbar**; refer to Figure-57. The **MINIMUM RADIUS ANALYSIS** dialog box will be displayed; refer to Figure-58.

Figure-57. Minimum Radius Analysis tool

Figure-58. MINIMUM RADIUS
ANALYSIS dialog box

- The **Select** button of **Body** section is active by default. Click on the body to select the face. On selecting the desired face, the areas of curvature of the model will be highlighted; refer to Figure-59.

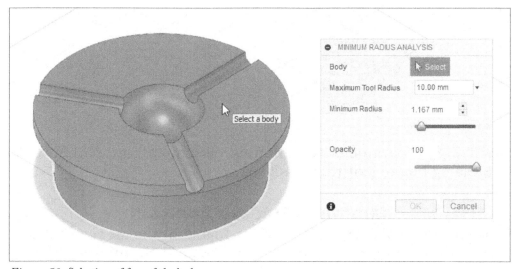

Figure-59. Selection of face of the body

- After selecting the body, set the **Maximum Tool Radius** in the edit box for analysis of the model.
- For tool of **Minimum Radius** 0, the selected parts are all green; refer to Figure-60.

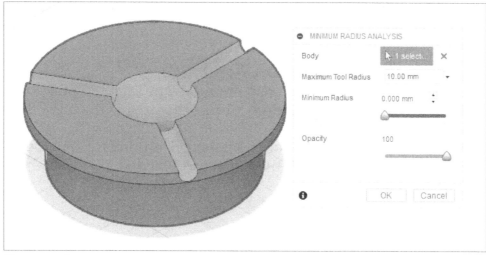

Figure-60. Minimum radius color

- As you increase the minimum radius of the tool, some parts are shaded with red color which indicates that these parts have high curvature to be correctly manufactured by the tool of that radius; refer to Figure-61.

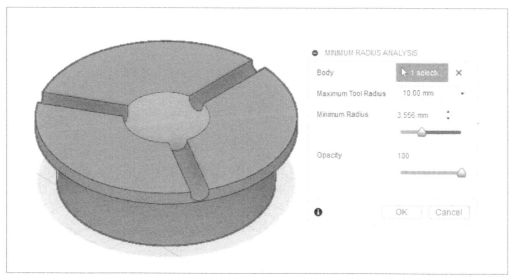

Figure-61. Increasing the tool radius

- Set the opacity of the analysis as you did in the **Accessibility Analysis** tool.
- The visibility of this analysis can be control by expanding the **Analysis** folder in the **BROWSER** and clicking on the eye button to view or hide the analysis; refer to Figure-62.

Figure-62. Visibility of minimum radius analysis

- After specifying all the parameters, click on the **OK** button of **MINIMUM RADIUS ANALYSIS** dialog box to exit this analysis.

Section Analysis

The **Section Analysis** tool is used to cut the model at selected plane reference and check the temporary view. The procedure to use this tool is discussed next.

- Click on the **Section Analysis** tool of **Inspect** drop-down from **Toolbar**; refer to Figure-63. The **SECTION ANALYSIS** dialog box will be displayed; refer to Figure-64.

Figure-63. Section Analysis tool

Figure-64. SECTION ANALYSIS dialog box

- The **Select** button of **Faces** section is active by default. Click on the face to select.
- On selection of face, the dialog box will be updated along with the preview of model; refer to Figure-65.

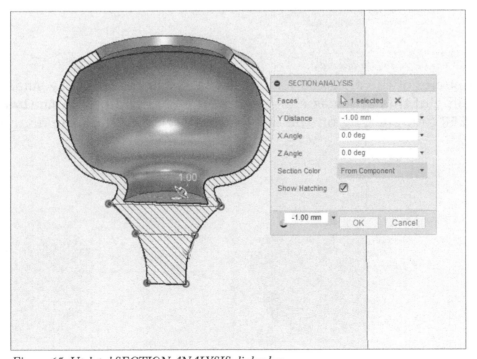

Figure-65. Updated SECTION ANALYSIS dialog box

- Click in the **Y Distance** edit box and specify the location of the section plane along y. You can also set the value by moving the drag handle.
- Click in the **X Angle** edit box and specify the angle of plane about x. You can also set the value by moving the drag handle.
- Click in the **Z Angle** edit box and specify the angle of plane about y. You can also set the value by moving the drag handle.
- Select **From Component** option from **Section Color** section if you want to use the same color as applied to the model.
- Select **Custom** option from **Section Color** section if you want to use the custom color for the section.
- Select the **Show Hatching** check box if you want to show hatching on the section.
- After specifying the parameters for analysis, click on **OK** button from **SECTION ANALYSIS** dialog box to complete the analysis.

Center of Mass

The **Center of Mass** tool is a center point of body use for representing the mean position of matter in a body. The procedure to use this tool is discussed next.

- Click on the **Center of Mass** tool of **INSPECT** drop-down from **Toolbar**; refer to Figure-66. The **CENTER OF MASS** dialog box will be displayed; refer to Figure-67.

Figure-66. Center of Mass tool

Figure-67. CENTER OF MASS dialog box

- You need to select the body and click on **OK** button from **CENTER OF MASS** dialog box. The center of mass of the body will be displayed; refer to Figure-68.

Figure-68. Center of mass of the body

Component Color Cycling Toggle Tool

The **Component Color Cycling Toggle** tool is used to toggle color of various objects in Autodesk Fusion. You can also press **SHIFT+N** to do the same thing.

SELF ASSESSMENT

Q1. Which of the following tools is used for inserting image on the face of a model?

a) Insert Mesh
b) Insert Derive
c) Decal
d) Insert SVG

Q2. What is the use of **Reset Transformation** button in **INSERT MESH** dialog box?

Q3. What is the use of **Insert Mc-Master Carr Component** tool and what is Mc-Master Carr?

Q4. Write down the procedure of inserting manufacturer or supplier part in the model.

Q5. Write down the procedure to measure the distance between two faces.

Q6. Write down the procedure to find interference between two components?

Q7. The **Curvature Comb Analysis** tool is used to display a curvature comb on the spline or circular edges to determine the ....

Q8. The **Zebra Analysis** tool is used to analyze continuity between the surfaces of component by ....on model.

Q9. Write down the procedure to display zebra strips on body.

10. The **Draft Analysis** tool is used to display a color gradient on the selected body to .... of various faces of the part.

11. The .... tool is used to displays a color gradient on the faces of selected bodies to evaluate the amount of curvature.

12. What is the use of **Gaussian** option in Curvature Map Analysis?

13. The **Section Analysis** tool is used to define the view of component from .... side.

14. Which of the following analyses uses **ToleranceZone** option to display a tolerance gradient on the results.

a) Section Analysis
b) Zebra Analysis
c) Curvature Comb Analysis
d) Draft Analysis

FOR STUDENTS NOTES

Chapter 9

Surface

Modeling

Topics Covered

The major topics covered in this chapter are:

- *Surface Tool*
- *Surface Trim Tool*
- *Stitch Tool*
- *Reverse Normal*
- *Practical*
- *Practice*

INTRODUCTION

Surface Designing or surfacing is a technique used to create complex shapes. The most general application of surfacing can be seen in the object that are made with good aerodynamics like car body, aeroplanes, ships, and so on. Sometimes, surface modeling is also used to add complex geometry to the models. The models created by surfacing are called surface models and they do not exist in real world because they have zero thickness. After converting these surfaces to solids, we make real objects.

In Autodesk Fusion 360, there is no separate workspace for creating surface designs. We have all the surfacing tools available in the **SURFACE** tab of **DESIGN** workspace; refer to Figure-1.

Figure-1. SURFACE modeling tools

Note that we have already used many tools of surface design earlier while creating solid models. So, now we will use the surface modeling tools similar to solid modeling.

Extrude

The **Extrude** tool can also be used to create the extruded surfaces. The procedure to use this tool is discussed next.

- Click on the **Extrude** tool of **CREATE** drop-down from **Toolbar** in **SURFACE** tab; refer to Figure-2. The **EXTRUDE** dialog box will be displayed; refer to Figure-3.

Figure-2. Extrude tool

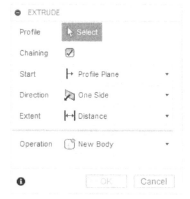

Figure-3. EXTRUDE dialog box

- The **Select** button of **Profile** section is active by default. Click on the profile to select. The updated **EXTRUDE** dialog box will be displayed; refer to Figure-4.

Note that you can select open as well as closed sketch for profile selection to extrude.

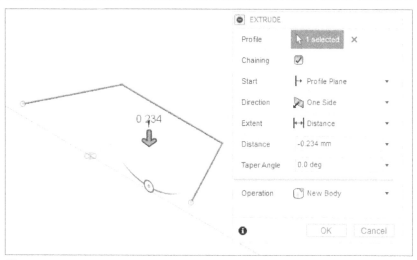

Figure-4. Updated EXTRUDE dialog box

- Select the **Chaining** check box if you want to select all the sketch entities in chain.
- The other options of **Extrude** dialog box are same as discussed earlier for solid modeling.
- After specifying the parameters, preview of extrude will be displayed; refer to Figure-5.

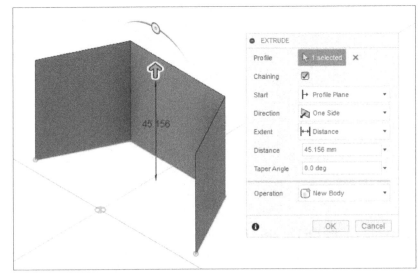

Figure-5. Preview of Extrude

- If the preview of extrude is as required then click on **OK** button from **EXTRUDE** dialog box. The extruded surface will be created.

You can use the **Revolve**, **Sweep**, and **Loft** tools in the same way as discussed in previous chapters.

Patch

The **Patch** tool is used to create a surface by connecting edges/curves. The procedure to use this tool is discussed next.

- Click on the **Patch** tool of **CREATE** drop-down from **Toolbar**; refer to Figure-6. The **PATCH** dialog box will be displayed; refer to Figure-7.

Figure-6. Patch tool

Figure-7. PATCH dialog box

- The **Select** button of **Boundary Edges** section is active by default. Click on the edges/curves forming close loop.
- Select the **Group Edges** check box if you want to select all the edges in a group.
- Select the **Enable Chaining** check box if you want to select all the adjacent edges when clicking on one edge.
- Select **Connected** from **Continuity** drop-down if you want to create a surface with G0 edges (connected at an angle).
- Select **Tangent** option from **Continuity** drop-down if you want to create a surface with G1 edges (tangential).
- Select **Curvature** option from **Continuity** drop-down, if you want to creates a surface with G2 edges (blended with continuous curvature).
- Click on the **Select** button for **Interior Rails/Points** selection and select the curves/points to be used as guide rails/points.
- After specifying the parameters, the preview of patch will be displayed; refer to Figure-8.

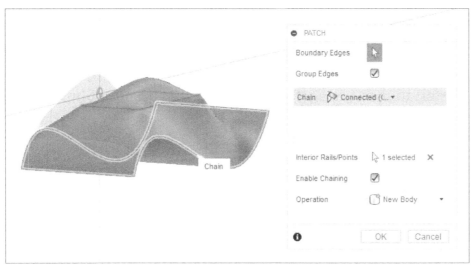

Figure-8. Preview of Patch

- Click on **OK** button from **PATCH** dialog box to complete the process.

Other Solid Modeling Tools For Surfacing

The other tools in the **CREATE** drop-down can be used in the same way as discussed in **Chapter 4: Advanced 3D Modeling** of the book. You can now create surfaces by using **Offset**, **Pattern**, **Mirror**, **Thicken**, and **Boundary Fill** tools by following the procedure discussed earlier.

EDITING TOOLS

In the previous section, we have learned about different surface creation tools used in surface modeling. In this section, we will discuss the surface editing tools.

Trim

The **Trim** tool is used to trim the surface using selected trimming object as cutting tool. The procedure to use this tool is discussed next.

- Click on the **Trim** tool of **Modify** drop-down from **Toolbar**; refer to Figure-9. The **TRIM** dialog box will be displayed; refer to Figure-10.

Figure-9. Trim tool

Figure-10. TRIM dialog box

- The **Select** button of **Trim Tool** option is active by default. You need to select an existing sketch to trim the surface. You can also select a plane/face intersecting with the surface as trim tool; refer to Figure-11.

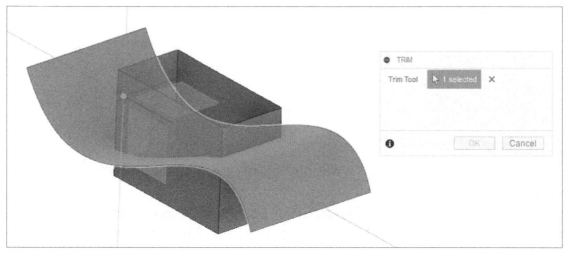

Figure-11. Selection of face as trim tool

- Now, you need to select the area to be removed. Click on the desired area of sketch to trim; refer to Figure-12.

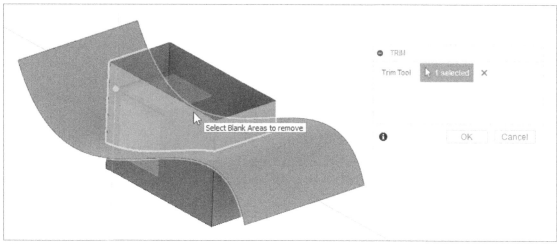

Figure-12. Selection of area to trim

- Click on the **OK** button from **TRIM** dialog box to trim the selected area; refer to Figure-13.

Figure-13. Selected area trimmed

Extend

The **Extend** tool is used to extend the surface edge. The procedure to use this tool is discussed next.

- Click on the **Extend** tool of **MODIFY** drop-down from **Toolbar**; refer to Figure-14. The **EXTEND** dialog box will be displayed; refer to Figure-15.

Figure-14. Extend tool

Figure-15. EXTEND dialog box

- The **Select** button of **Edges** section is active by default. You need to select the edge to extend. The updated **EXTEND** dialog box will be displayed; refer to Figure-16.

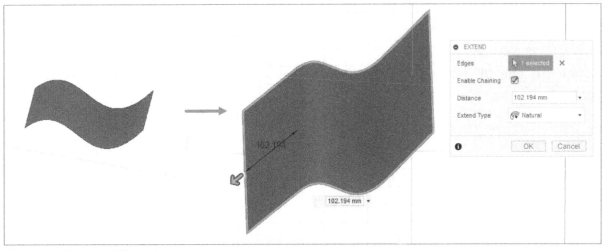

Figure-16. Preview of Extend

- Select the **Enable Chaining** dialog box if you want to select all tangent or adjacent faces on selection of single face.
- Click in the **Distance** edit box and specify the distance for extend. You can also set the distance by moving the manipulator.
- Select **Natural** option from **Extend Type** drop-down if you want to extend the surface naturally.
- Select **Perpendicular** option from **Extend Type** drop-down if you want to extend the selected edge perpendicularly.
- Select **Tangent** option from **Extend Type** drop-down if you want to extend the selected edge tangentially.
- After specifying the parameters, click on **OK** button from **EXTEND** dialog box.

Stitch

The **Stitch** tool is used to combine the surface into one body. The procedure to use this tool is discussed next.

- Click on the **Stitch** tool of **MODIFY** drop-down from **Toolbar**; refer to Figure-17. The **STITCH** dialog box will be displayed; refer to Figure-18.

Figure-17. Stitch tool

Figure-18. STITCH dialog box

- The **Select** button of **Stitch Surfaces** section is active by default. You need to select the surfaces of model to be stitched; refer to Figure-19.

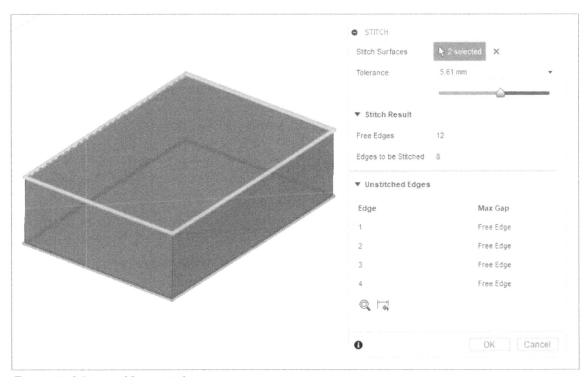

Figure-19. Selection of face to stitch

- The green line on the model shows the stitched surface and red line shows the loose surface connection.
- You need to increase the tolerance from **Tolerance** edit box or **Tolerance** slider to stitch the remaining surfaces which have higher gap between consecutive edges.

- You can also check the result of stitched and unstitched edge from **Stitch Result** section.
- After specifying the parameters, click on the **OK** button from **STITCH** dialog box to complete the process.

Unstitch

The **Unstitch** tool is used to unstitch the earlier stitched surface from model. The procedure to use this tool is discussed next.

- Click on the **Unstitch** tool of **MODIFY** drop-down from **Toolbar**; refer to Figure-20. The **UNSTITCH** dialog box will be displayed; refer to Figure-21.

Figure-20. Unstitch tool

Figure-21. UNSTITCH dialog box

- The **Select** button of **Faces/Bodies** section is active by default. You need to select the surface or body to be unstitched.
- Select the **Chain Selection** check box to select the adjacent surface of the selected surface.
- After selecting the surfaces, click on **OK** button from **UNSTITCH** dialog box to unstitch the selected surface.

Reverse Normal

The **Reverse Normal** tool is used to flip the normal direction of selected surfaces. When modifying the body or model, some of the surfaces of model may have unexpected normal directions. To reverse their normal direction, this tool is used. The procedure to use this tool is discussed next.

- Click on the **Reverse Normal** tool of **Modify** drop-down from **Toolbar**; refer to Figure-22. The **REVERSE NORMAL** dialog box will be displayed; refer to Figure-23.

Figure-22. Reverse Normal tool

Figure-23. REVERSE NORMAL dialog box

- The **Select** button of **Faces** section is active by default. You need to select the face to flip; refer to Figure-24.

Figure-24. Selection of surface to flip

- After selection of surfaces, click on the **OK** button from **REVERSE NORMAL** dialog box. The selected surfaces will be flipped; refer to Figure-25.

Figure-25. Flipped surface

The other tools of **SURFACE** tab have been discussed earlier in this book.

PRACTICAL 1

Create the model of aircraft toy as shown in Figure-26. (This is an open dimension problem, you need to get the shape of an aircraft using surfaces.)

Figure-26. Practical 1 model

Creating first sketch

- Click on the **SURFACE** tab from **Toolbar**; refer to Figure-27. The tools to create surface will be activated.

Figure-27. Tools to create surface

- Create the sketch on Top plane using **Ellipse**, **Line**, and **Trim** tools; refer to Figure-28.

Figure-28. First sketch

Creating Surface

- Click on **Revolve** tool of **CREATE** drop-down from **Toolbar**. The **REVOLVE** dialog box will be displayed; refer to Figure-29.

Figure-29. REVOLVE dialog box

- You need to select the sketch and axis of sketch to apply the revolve feature; refer to Figure-30.

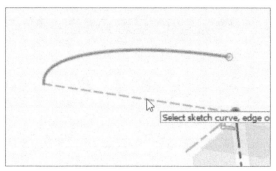

Figure-30. Selecting sketch and axis

- Revolve the sketch to 360 degree to create the nose of aircraft.
- Start a new sketch and project the round edge of nose on Right plane as shown in Figure-31. Exit the sketching environment.

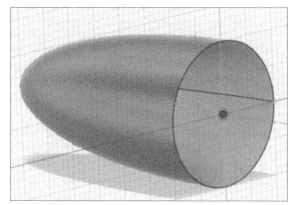

Figure-31. Edge projected on plane

- Click on **Extrude** tool of **CREATE** drop-down from **Toolbar**. The **EXTRUDE** dialog box will be displayed.
- Select the sketch as displayed to extrude; refer to Figure-32.

Figure-32. Selecting sketch to extrude

- Click in the **Distance** edit box and enter the value as **90**.
- After specifying the parameters, click on **OK** button from **EXTRUDE** dialog box to complete the extrude process.
- Click on **Offset Plane** tool of **Construct** drop-down from **Toolbar**. The **OFFSET PLANE** dialog box will be displayed.

- Select the YZ plane as shown in Figure-33.

Figure-33. Creating offset plane

- Click in the **Distance** edit box of **OFFSET PLANE** dialog box and enter the value as **125**.
- After specifying the parameters, click on **OK** button from **OFFSET PLANE** dialog box to create the plane.
- Start a new sketch using newly created plane and click on the **Center Diameter Circle** tool from **CREATE** drop-down.
- Create the circle as shown in Figure-34.

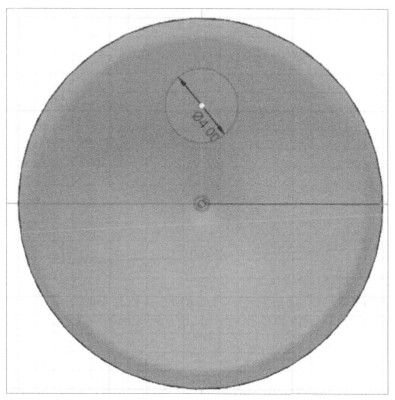

Figure-34. Creating circle

- After creating the sketch, click on **Finish Sketch** button from **Toolbar**.
- Click on **Loft** tool of **CREATE** drop-down from **Toolbar**. The **LOFT** dialog box will be displayed.

- You need to select the two sketch to create loft feature; refer to Figure-35.

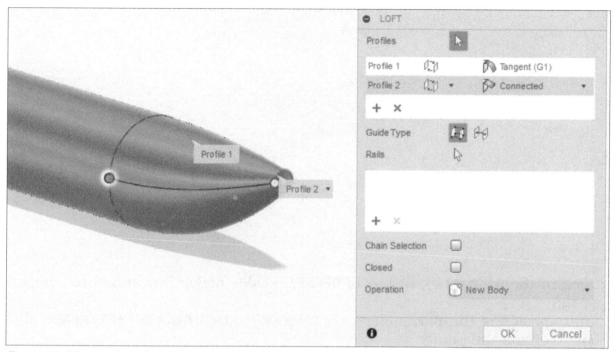

Figure-35. Selecting sketch for loft feature

- Specify the parameters as desired and click on **OK** button from **LOFT** dialog box to complete the process.
- Click on the **Create Sketch** tool and select the XZ plane as sketching plane. Create the sketch with the help of **Ellipse** and **Line** tool as shown in Figure-36.

Figure-36. Sketch for wing

- After creating the sketch, click on **Finish Sketch** button from **Toolbar**.
- Now, create the offset plane at a distance of **75** from the XZ plane; refer to Figure-37.

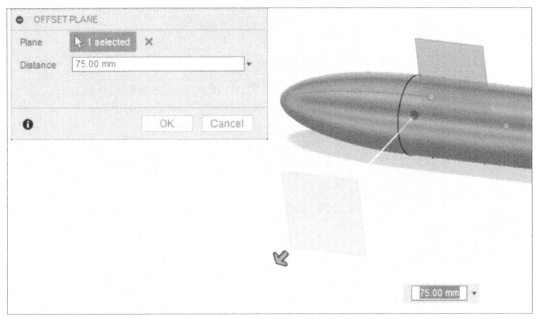

Figure-37. Creating third offset plane

- Click on the **Ellipse** tool from **CREATE** drop-down and select the recently created plane.
- Create the ellipse current plane as shown in Figure-38.

Figure-38. Creating ellipse

- Click on the **Finish Sketch** tool from **Toolbar**.
- Click on the **Loft** tool from **CREATE** drop-down. The **LOFT** dialog box will be displayed.
- Select the recently created sketches (ellipse forms) and create the loft; refer to Figure-39. Make sure the **Chain Selection** check box is selected.

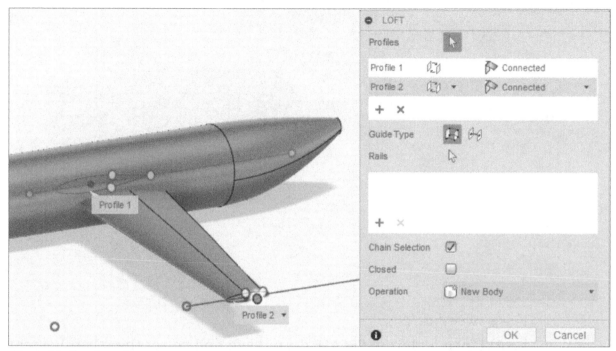

Figure-39. Creating wing

- After selection of profiles for loft, click on the **OK** button from **LOFT** dialog box to complete the loft process.
- Click on **Mirror** tool of **CREATE** drop-down from **Toolbar**. The **MIRROR** dialog box will be displayed; refer to Figure-40.

Figure-40. MIRROR dialog box

- Click on **Pattern Type** drop-down from **MIRROR** dialog box and select **Bodies** option.
- Click on **Select** button of **Objects** section and select the recently created wing.
- Click on **Select** button of **Mirror Plane** option and select the **XZ** plane; refer to Figure-41.

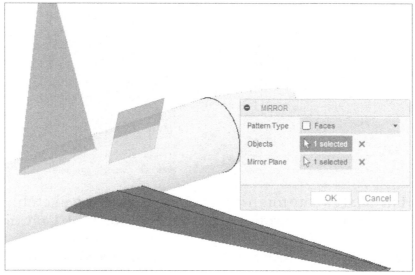

Figure-41. Creating Mirror copy of wing

- Click on **OK** button from **MIRROR** dialog box to complete the process.
- Click on the **Offset Plane** tool of **CONSTRUCT** drop-down from **Toolbar**. The **OFFSET PLANE** dialog box will be displayed.
- Create an offset plane at distance of 23 mm from XZ plane as shown in Figure-42.

Figure-42. Creating fourth offset plane

- Create an ellipse on the XZ plane using **Ellipse** tool as shown in Figure-43.

Figure-43. Creating sketch for rear wing

- After creating sketch, click on **Finish Sketch** button from **Toolbar**.
- Create another ellipse on the newly created offset plane as shown in Figure-44.

Figure-44. Sketch for rear wing

- Click on **Finish Sketch** button from **Toolbar** to exit the sketch.
- Click on **Loft** tool of **CREATE** drop-down from **Toolbar**. The **Loft** dialog box will be displayed.
- You need to select two recently created sketch in **Profiles** section of **LOFT** dialog box; refer to Figure-45.

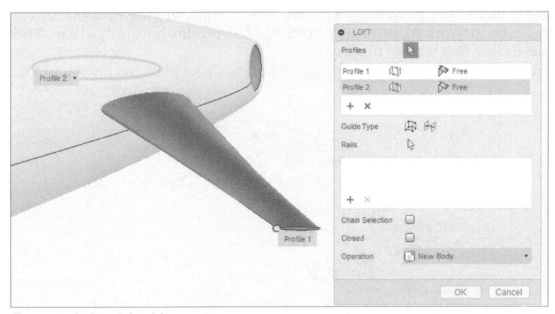

Figure-45. Applying loft tool for rear wing

- After specifying the parameters, click on **OK** button from **LOFT** dialog box to complete the process.
- To fill the open ends of wings, we need to apply the **Patch** tool.
- Click on the **Patch** tool of **CREATE** drop-down from **Toolbar**. The **PATCH** dialog box will be displayed; refer to Figure-46.

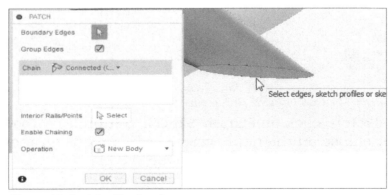

Figure-46. Applying Patch tool

- The **Select** button of **Selection** option is active by default. Click on the area displayed in the above figure.
- Click on the **Continuity** drop-down and select **Connected** option.
- After specifying the parameters, click on the **OK** button from **PATCH** dialog box to complete the process.
- To create other rear wing, click on **Mirror** tool of **CREATE** drop-down from **Toolbar**. The **MIRROR** dialog box will be displayed.
- Select the recently created wing in **Objects** section of **MIRROR** dialog box.
- Click on **Select** button of **Mirror Plane** option of **MIRROR** dialog box and select the **XY** plane as reference; refer to Figure-47.

Figure-47. Creating other rear wing

- Click on **OK** button from **MIRROR** dialog box to create the copy.
- Click on **Create Sketch** tool of **CREATE** drop-down and select the **XY** plane for creation of sketch. Create the ellipse as shown in Figure-48.

Figure-48. Creating sketch for third wing

- After creating the sketch, click on **Finish Sketch** button from **Toolbar**.
- Click on **Offset Plane** tool from **CONSTRUCT** drop-down and create a plane with XY plane as reference; refer to Figure-49.

Figure-49. Creating offset plane for third rear wing

- Click on the **Create Sketch** tool of **CREATE** drop-down and select the recently created plane for sketch.
- Create the sketch as shown in Figure-50.

Figure-50. Creating another sketch for rear wing

- Click on **Finish Sketch** button from **Toolbar** to exit the sketch.
- Click on **Loft** tool from **CREATE** drop-down and select the recently created sketch under **Profiles** section; refer to Figure-51.

Figure-51. Applying Loft feature

- Click in the **Takeoff Weight** edit box and enter the value as **0.10**.
- Click in the **Takeoff Angle** edit box and enter the value as **165**.
- After specifying the parameters for loft feature, click on the **OK** button from **LOFT** dialog box. The third arm of air craft will be created.
- Click on **Patch** tool of **CREATE** drop-down in **SURFACE** tab from **Toolbar**. The **PATCH** dialog box will be displayed; refer to Figure-52.

Figure-52. Applying patch on wing

- Select the open edge and click on **OK** button from **PATCH** dialog box to complete the process.
- Similarly, apply the patch tool to all wings and back of aircraft body.
- Click on **Reverse Normal** tool of **MODIFY** drop-down from **Toolbar**. The **REVERSE NORMAL** dialog box will be displayed.

- The **Select** button of **Faces** option is active by default. Click on the faces with wrong normal; refer to Figure-53.

Figure-53. Applying Reverse Normal tool

- Click on the **OK** button from **Reverse Normal** dialog box to complete the process.
- Click on **Center Rectangle** tool of **CREATE** drop-down and select the YZ plane for sketch; refer to Figure-54.

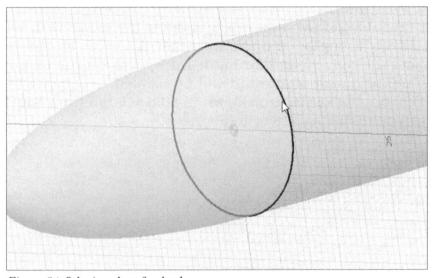

Figure-54. Selecting plane for sketch

- Create a rectangle on the selected plane as shown in Figure-55.

Figure-55. Sketch for windshield

- Click on **Finish Sketch** button from **Toolbar** to exit the sketch.
- Click on **Trim** tool of **MODIFY** drop-down from **Toolbar**. The **TRIM** dialog box will be displayed.

- The **Select** button of **Trim Tool** option is active by default. Select the recently created rectangular sketch and click on the inner area of trim preview; refer to Figure-56.

Figure-56. Selection of area for trim

- After selecting, click on the **OK** button of **TRIM** dialog box to exit the **Trim** tool.
- Click on **Loft** tool from **CREATE** drop-down. The **LOFT** dialog box will be displayed.
- Select the area in **Profiles** section as displayed in Figure-57.

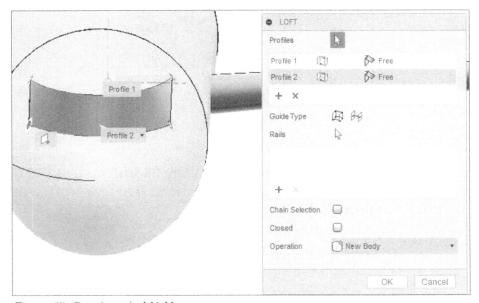

Figure-57. Creating windshield

- Click on the **OK** button from **LOFT** dialog box to complete the process.

Removing extra material

- Click on the **Trim** tool from **MODIFY** drop-down. The **TRIM** dialog box will be displayed; refer to Figure-58.

Figure-58. TRIM dialog box

- The **Select** button for **Trim Tool** selection is active by default. Click on the extra material to remove; refer to Figure-59.

Figure-59. Removing extra material

- After selection of material to remove, click on the **OK** button from **TRIM** dialog box.
- After applying all the tools from above section. The aircraft will be created completely; refer to Figure-60.

Figure-60. Front view of aircraft

PRACTICAL 2

Create the model of Jug as shown in Figure-61 and Figure-62.

Figure-61. Model of Jug

Figure-62. Another view of Jug

Starting Autodesk Fusion 360

- Double-click on the **Autodesk Fusion 360** software icon from desktop if the software has not started yet.
- Click on the **SURFACE** tab from **Toolbar** in **DESIGN** workspace. The tools to create surface will be activated.

Creating Sketch

The first step to create jug is to create sketches. The procedure is discussed next.

- Click on the **Create Sketch** tool of **CREATE** drop-down from **Toolbar** and select the **Top** plane as reference for sketch.
- Create the sketch as shown in Figure-63. Click on the **Finish Sketch** tool to exit.

Figure-63. Creating base sketch

- Click on **Offset Plane** tool of **CONSTRUCT** drop-down from **Toolbar**. The **OFFSET PLANE** dialog box will be displayed.
- The **Select** button of **Plane** option is active by default. Select the **Top** plane as reference.
- Click in the **Distance** edit box and enter the value as **2**; refer to Figure-64.

Figure-64. Creating first offset plane

- After specifying the parameters, click on the **OK** button from **OFFSET PLANE** dialog box to complete the process of creating plane.
- Create a center diameter circle on recently created offset plane; refer to Figure-65.

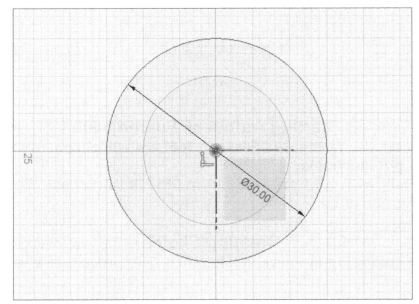

Figure-65. Creating second sketch

- Click on the **Patch** button from **CREATE** drop-down. The **PATCH** dialog box will be displayed.
- The **Select** button of **Selection** option from **PATCH** dialog box is active by default. You need to select the first sketch to patch.
- After specifying the parameters, click on the **OK** button from **PATCH** dialog box to complete the process; refer to Figure-66.

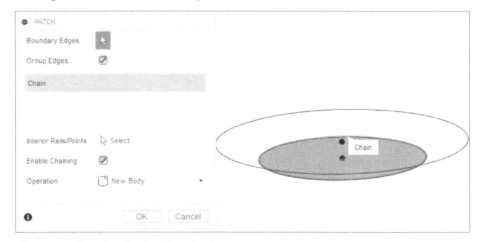

Figure-66. Creating Patch of first sketch

- Click on the **Offset Plane** tool of **CONSTRUCT** drop-down from **Toolbar**. The **OFFSET PLANE** dialog box will be displayed.
- The **Select** button of **Plane** option is active by default. Select the first offset plane as reference.
- Click in the **Distance** edit box and enter the value as **22**; refer to Figure-67.

Figure-67. Creating third offset plane

- After specifying the parameter, click on the **OK** button from **OFFSET PLANE** dialog box to create the plane.
- Create the sketch as shown in Figure-68 on newly created offset plane.

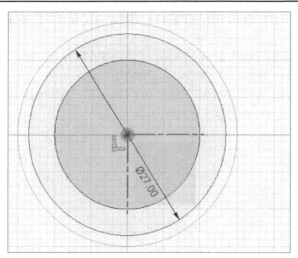

Figure-68. Creating third sketch

- Click on **Finish Sketch** button from **Toolbar** to exit the sketch.
- Click on the **Offset Plane** tool of **CONSTRUCT** drop-down from **Toolbar**. The **OFFSET PLANE** dialog box will be displayed.
- The **Select** button of **Plane** option is active by default. Select the second offset plane as reference.
- Click in the **Distance** edit box and enter the value as **7**; refer to Figure-69. You can also set the distance by moving the drag handle.

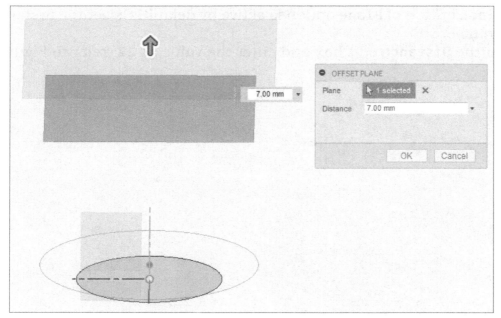

Figure-69. Creation of third offset Plane

- After specifying the parameter, click on the **OK** button from **OFFSET PLANE** dialog box to create the plane.
- Create the sketch as shown in Figure-70 on newly created offset plane.

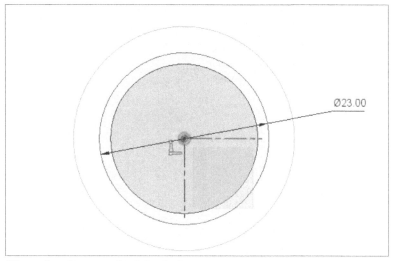

Figure-70. Creating third sketch of jug

- Click on the **Offset Plane** tool of **CONSTRUCT** drop-down from **Toolbar**. The **OFFSET PLANE** dialog box will be displayed.
- The **Select** button of **Plane** option is active by default. Select the third offset plane as reference.
- Click in the **Distance** edit box and enter the value as **8**; refer to Figure-71. You can also set the distance by moving the drag handle.

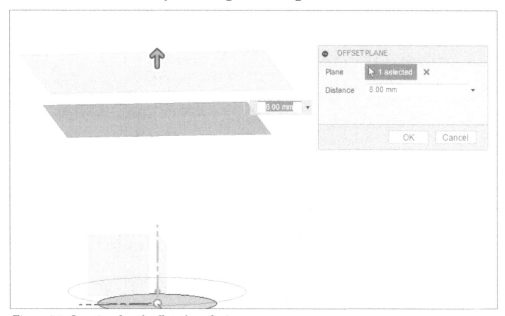

Figure-71. Creating fourth offset plane for jug

- After specifying the parameter, click on the **OK** button from **OFFSET PLANE** dialog box to create the plane.
- Create the sketch as shown in Figure-72 on newly created offset plane.

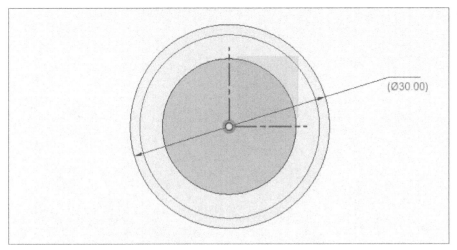

Figure-72. Creating fifth sketch for Jug

- Click on the **Offset Plane** tool of **CONSTRUCT** drop-down from **Toolbar**. The **OFFSET PLANE** dialog box will be displayed.
- The **Select** button of **Plane** option is active by default. Select the third offset plane as reference.
- Click in the **Distance** edit box and enter the value as **8**; refer to Figure-73. You can also set the distance by moving the drag handle.

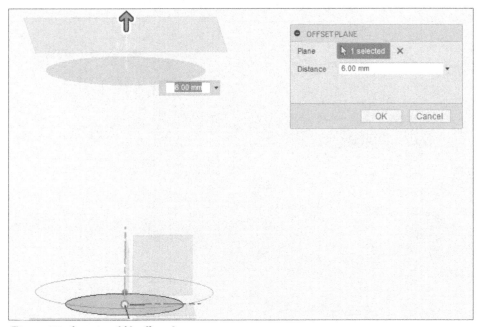

Figure-73. Creating fifth offset plane

- After specifying the parameter, click on the **OK** button from **OFFSET PLANE** dialog box to create the plane.
- Click on the **Circle** tool of **CREATE** drop-down from **Toolbar** and select the recently created plane as reference.
- Create the sketch as shown in Figure-74 with the help of **Circle**, **Trim**, and **Arc** tool.

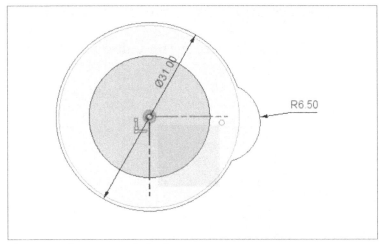

Figure-74. Creating sixth sketch

Creating Loft feature

Till now we have created the sketch for jug. Now, we will apply the loft feature to join all the sketches. The procedure is discussed next.

* Click on the **Loft** tool of **CREATE** drop-down from **Toolbar**. The **LOFT** dialog box will be displayed.
* You need to select all the sketch from bottom to top in **Profiles** section of **LOFT** dialog box; refer to Figure-75.

Figure-75. Creating loft feature of jug

* After selecting the profiles, click on the **OK** button from **LOFT** dialog box to complete the loft feature.

Here loft feature is completed. Now, we will create the handle of jug.

* Click on the **Offset Plane** tool of **CONSTRUCT** drop-down from **Toolbar**. The **OFFSET PLANE** dialog box will be displayed.

- The **Select** button of **Plane** option is active by default. Select the YZ plane as reference.
- Click in the **Distance** edit box and enter the value as **-10** ; refer to Figure-76.

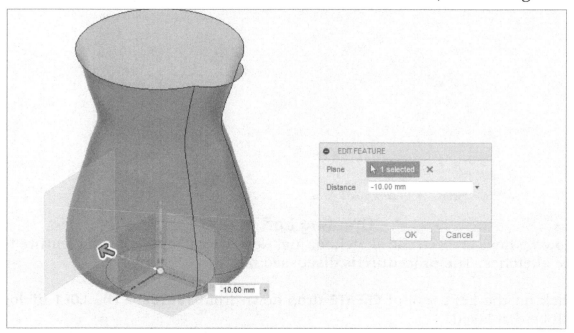

Figure-76. Creating sixth offset plane

- After specifying the parameter, click on the **OK** button from **OFFSET PLANE** dialog box to create the plane.
- Create the sketch as shown in Figure-77 on newly offset plane.

Figure-77. Creating seventh sketch

- Click on the **Create Sketch** tool from **CREATE** drop-down and select the **XZ** plane.
- Create the sketch as shown in Figure-78.

Figure-78. Creating eighth sketch

Creating Sweep feature

- Click on the **Sweep** tool from **CREATE** drop-down. The **SWEEP** dialog box will be displayed; refer to Figure-79.

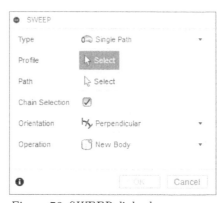

Figure-79. SWEEP dialog box

- The **Select** button of **Profile** option is active by default. You need to select the recently created rectangular sketch.
- Click on the **Select** button of **Path** option and select the recently created arc; refer to Figure-80.

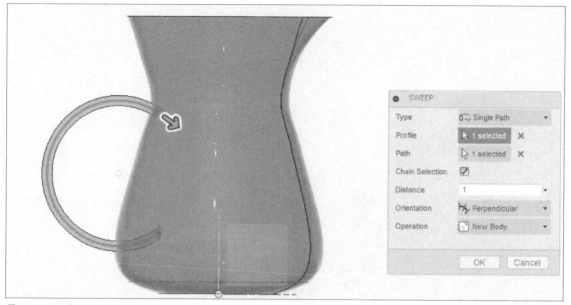

Figure-80. Creating sweep feature for jug

- Click on the **Orientation** drop-down of **SWEEP** dialog box and select the Perpendicular option.
- After specifying the parameters, click on the **OK** button from **SWEEP** dialog box to complete the feature.

Till here, we have created the model of jug but we need to apply the trim tool on the jug to remove the unwanted parts.

Trimming Extra Entities

- Click on the **Trim** tool of **MODIFY** drop-down from **Toolbar**. The **TRIM** dialog box will be displayed.
- The **Select** button of **Trim Tool** is active by default. Click on the interior of jug and select the unwanted parts; refer to Figure-81.

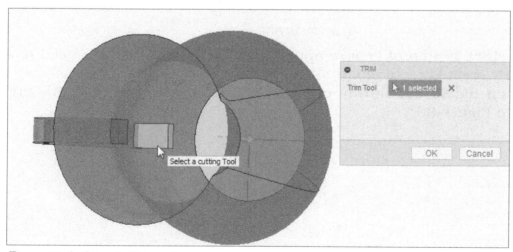

Figure-81. Applying the Trim tool

- After selecting, click on the **OK** button from **Trim** dialog box to trim the material.
- The model of jug is created successfully; refer to Figure-82.

Figure-82. Model of Jug created

- You can apply the physical material or appearance as required to the jug.
- You can also create the model of jug with the help of **Revolve** tool in place of **Loft** tool.

SELF ASSESSMENT

Q1. What is Surfacing? Explain in brief.

Q2. Why surface models can not exist in real world ? And how it can be made real?

Q3. Explain the creation of surface with G0 edges, G1 edges and G2 edges.

Q4. How can you perform an extrude protrusion of an open sketch?

Q5. What is the use of Reverse Normal tool?

6. The .... tool is used to combine the surface into one body.

PRACTICE 1

Create the model of mouse as shown in Figure-83 and Figure-84.

Figure-83. Model of mouse

Figure-84. Right view of mouse

PRACTICE 2

Create the model of water bottle as shown in Figure-85 and Figure-86. The drawing view of water bottle is shown in Figure-87. (You are free to apply your artistic mind for improving design of bottle)

Figure-85. Model of Water Bottle

Figure-86. Top view of water bottle

Figure-87. Dimensions of Water Bottle

FOR STUDENTS NOTES

Chapter 10

Rendering and
Animation

Topics Covered

The major topics covered in this chapter are:

- *Environment Library Tab*
- *Texture Map Control*
- *In-Canvas Render Setting*
- *Render*
- *Animation Workspace*
- *Transform Components*
- *Manual Explode*

INTRODUCTION

When a designer is working on a 3D Model, the model he/she creates is generally a mathematical representation of points and surfaces in three-dimensions. Sometimes, a realistic 2D image of 3D model is required for presentation to the client. The conversion of 3D model with specified environmental scenario through mathematical approximation to a finalized 2D image is known as Rendering. During this process, the entire scene's textural and lighting information are combined to determine the color value of each pixel in the finalized image.

INTRODUCTION TO RENDER WORKSPACE

The tools in **Render Workspace** are used to create the photo-realistic image from a scene of model. There are various tools used for rendering process which are discussed next.

Appearance Tool

The **Appearance** tool is used to apply different materials to selected bodies/ components/faces. The procedure to use this tool has been discussed earlier in the book. So we are not repeating the tool here.

Scene Settings

The **Scene Settings** tool is used to control the lighting, background color, ground effects, and camera rendering. The procedure to use this tool is discussed next.

- Click on the **Scene Settings** tool of **SETUP** panel from **Toolbar**; refer to Figure-1. The **SCENE SETTINGS** dialog box will be displayed; refer to Figure-2.

Figure-1. Scene Settings tool

Figure-2. SCENE SETTINGS dialog box

Environment section

- Click on the **Brightness** edit box and specify the value of brightness for model. You can also move the **Brightness** slider to adjust the brightness for the model.
- If you want to control the position and rotation of lights then click on the **Position** button of **Environment** section from **Settings** tab. The drag handle along with some tools will be displayed on the canvas screen; refer to Figure-3.

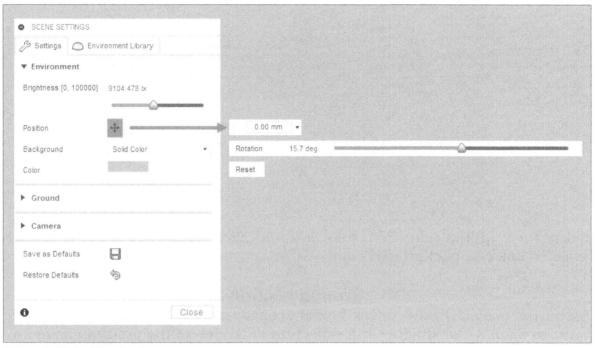

Figure-3. Tools of Position button

- Click in the floating window and enter the position of lights. You can also set the position by moving the drag handle from model.
- Click in the **Rotation** edit box and enter the value of rotation of lights. You can also adjust the value by moving the **Rotation** slider.
- If you want to reset all the changed settings then, click on the **Reset** button from rotation tools.
- Select **Environment** option from **Background** drop-down if you want to use environment image. The environments are available in **Environment Library** tab of this dialog box.
- Select **Solid Color** option from **Background** drop-down if you want to set a particular color to the background.
- To select a solid color, click on the **Color** button. A color box will be displayed; refer to Figure-4.

Figure-4. Color box

- Select the required color from color box and click on the **Apply** button to set the selected color as background color.

Ground section

- Select the **Ground Plane** check box of **Ground** section from **Settings** tab if you want to display the shadow and reflection of model on the ground canvas.
- Select the **Flatten Ground** check box of **Ground** section from **Settings** tab if you want to enable a "textured" ground plane where the environment image is mapped as a texture.
- Select the **Reflections** check box of **Ground** section from **Settings** tab if you want to display the reflection of model on the ground.
- Click in the **Roughness** edit box and enter the value of sharpness of reflection. You can also set the sharpness of reflection by moving the **Roughness** slider.

Camera section

- Select **Orthographic** option of **Camera** drop-down from **Camera** section if you want to set the orthographic view of model.
- Select the **Perspective** option of **Camera** drop-down from **Camera** section if you want to set the perspective view of model.
- Select the **Perspective with Ortho Faces** option from **Camera** drop-down if you want to set the perspective view of model with ortho faces.
- Click in the **Exposure** edit box of **Camera** section from **Settings** tab and enter the value of camera exposure. You can also set the camera exposure by moving the **Exposure** slider.
- Select the **Depth of Field** check box if you want to apply depth of field effect. Depth of field is used to focus on specific area of the model. This effect is only enabled when **Ray Tracing** is enabled. On selecting the **Depth of Field** check box, the dialog box will be updated; refer to Figure-5.

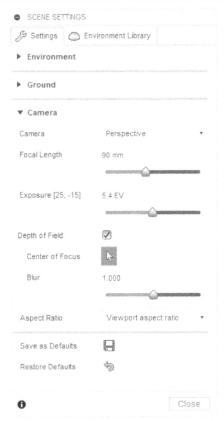

Figure-5. Updated dialog box on selecting Depth of Field check box

- The **Center of Focus** selection is active by default. You need to select a location on model for focusing.
- Click in the **Blur** edit box and enter the value of blur the model except the selected center of focus. You can also set the value of blur by moving the **Blur** slider.
- Click on the **Aspect Ratio** drop-down and select the required aspect ratio of canvas screen.
- Click on **Save as Defaults** button to save the setting as default setting.
- Click on the **Restore Defaults** button to restore the changed settings to default.

Environment Library tab

- Click on the **Environment Library** tab from **SCENE SETTINGS** dialog box. The tab will be displayed; refer to Figure-6.

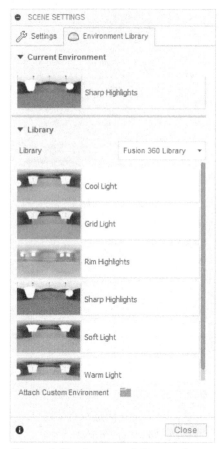

Figure-6. Environment Library tab

- The **Current Environment** section shows the applied environment on the current model.
- If you want to change the environment of the model then drag a specific environment from **Library** section and drop it to the current model or in the **Current Environment** section. You can download the environments in library by using the **Download** button next to them in the list.
- If you want to apply the custom environment for model then click on the **Attach Custom Environment** button of **Environment Library** tab from **SCENE SETTINGS** dialog box. The **Open** dialog box will be displayed; refer to Figure-7.

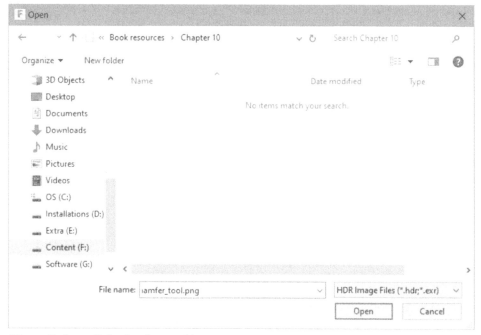

Figure-7. Open dialog box for attaching custom environment

- Select the required file and click on **Open** button. The environment will be applied to model.
- After selecting the required environment from **Environment Library** tab, click on **Close** button to exit the **Scene Settings** tool.

Note- There is no **Timeline** in the **Render** workspace. The tools applied in the **RENDER** workspace will not be recorded.

Decal tool has been discussed earlier in the book.

Texture Map Controls

The **Texture Map Control** tool is used to set the orientation of the texture applied to the face or model. The procedure to use this tool is discussed next.

- Click on the **Texture Map Control** tool of **SETUP** panel from **Toolbar**; refer to Figure-8. The **TEXTURE MAP CONTROLS** dialog box will be displayed; refer to Figure-9.

Figure-8. Texture Map Controls tool

Figure-9. TEXTURE MAP
CONTROLS dialog box

- The **Select** button of **Selection** option is selected by default. You need to select the texture of model. The updated **TEXTURE MAP CONTROLS** dialog box will be displayed; refer to Figure-10.

Figure-10. Updated TEXTURE
MAP CONTROLS dialog box

Automatic

- Select the **Automatic** option from **Projection Type** drop-down if you want to adjust the texture on the model using model topology.

Planer

- Select the **Planer** option from **Projection Type** drop-down if you want to map the image or texture on the model as projection.
- On selecting the **Planer** option, you need to select the axis for adjusting the texture. On selecting the texture the dialog box will be updated; refer to Figure-11.

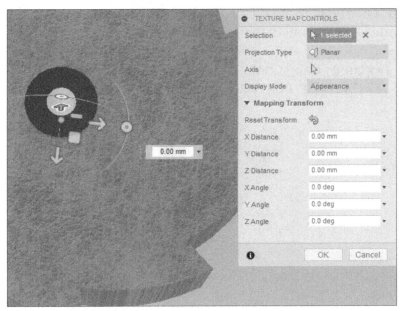

Figure-11. Updated dialog box after selecting axis

- Adjust the image or texture by moving the manipulator or by entering the values in specific edit box from **TEXTURE MAP CONTROLS** dialog box.

- After adjusting the texture, click on the **OK** button from **TEXTURE MAP CONTROLS** dialog box.

Box

- Click on the **Box** option from **Projection Type** drop-down if you want to map the image on model into box like objects.
- On selecting the **Box** option, the manipulator and updated dialog box will be displayed; refer to Figure-12.

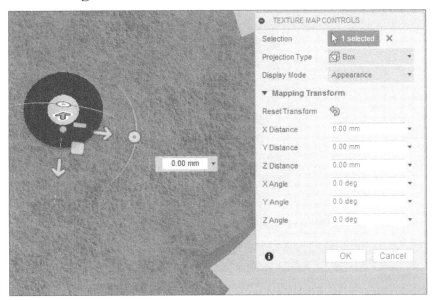

Figure-12. Dialog box on selecting Box-option

- Click in the specific edit box and enter the desired value. You can also set the value by moving the arrow of manipulator.
- If you want to reset the values of **Mapping Transform** or manipulator then click on the **Reset Transform** button.

Spherical

- Select the **Spherical** option from **Projection Type** drop-down if you want to map texture into a spherical object.
- On selecting the **Spherical** option, the manipulator along with updated dialog box will be displayed.
- The options were discussed in last topic.

Cylindrical

- Select the **Cylindrical** option from **Projection Type** drop-down if you want to map texture into a cylindrical object.
- On selecting the **Cylindrical** option, the manipulator along with updated dialog box will be displayed.
- The options were discussed in last topic.
- After specifying the parameters, click on the **OK** button from **TEXTURE MAP CONTROLS** dialog box to exit the tool.

In-canvas Render

The **In-canvas Render** button is used to start and stop the In-canvas rendering process. The procedure to use this tool is discussed next.

- Click on the **In-canvas Render** button from **IN-CANVAS RENDER** drop-down; refer to Figure-13. The render quality slider will be displayed to display at the bottom right area of canvas screen; refer to Figure-14.

Figure-13. In-canvas Render tool

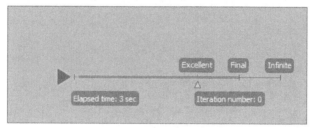

Figure-14. Render quality slider

- The current scene of the model will be changed into the photo-realistic 2D image.
- Clicking again on the **In-canvas Render** button will stops the rendering process.

In-Canvas Render Setting

The **In-canvas Render Setting** tool is used to change the setting of rendering process. The procedure to use this tool is discussed next.

- Click on the **In-Canvas Render Settings** tool from **In-Canvas Render** panel; refer to Figure-15. The **IN-CANVAS RENDER SETTINGS** dialog box will be displayed; refer to Figure-16.

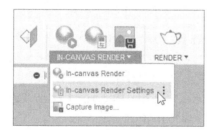

Figure-15. In-canvas Render Settings tool

Figure-16. IN-CANVAS RENDER SETTINGS dialog box

- Set the quality of rendering by adjusting the **Limit Resolution to** slider. The higher quality rendering takes more time to calculate rendering process and lower quality rendering takes less time to calculate the rendering process.
- Select the **Lock View** check box to lock the current view of model otherwise clear the check box.
- After specifying the parameters, click on the **OK** button from **IN-CANVAS RENDER SETTINGS** dialog box.

Capture Image

The **Capture Image** tool is used to capture the current canvas as an image. The procedure to use this tool is discussed next.

- Click on the **Capture Image** tool of **IN-CANVAS RENDER** panel in Toolbar; refer to Figure-17. The **Image Options** dialog box will be displayed; refer to Figure-18.

Figure-17. Capture Image tool

Figure-18. Image Options dialog box

- Click on the **Image Resolution** drop-down and select the required resolution of image.
- Select the **Transparent Background** check box if you want to set the transparent background of model.
- Select the **Enable Anti-Aliasing** check box if you want to activate the anti-aliasing property.
- After specifying the parameters, click on the **OK** button from **Image Options** dialog box. The **Save As** dialog box will be displayed; refer to Figure-19.

Figure-19. Save As dialog box

- Click in the **Name** edit box of **Save As** dialog box and enter the specific name for image.
- Click on the **Type** drop-down and select the required format of image file.
- Click on the **Location** drop-down button and select the location of saving image.
- Select the **Save to my computer** check box if you want to save the file to computer.
- Select the **Save to a project in the cloud** check box to save the image file on cloud.
- After specifying the parameters for image, click on the **Save** button from **Save As** dialog box. The image will be saved to the specified location.

Render

The **Render** tool is used to create a high quality rendered image of the current scene. The procedure to use this tool is discussed next.

- Click on the **Render** tool from **Toolbar**; refer to Figure-20. The **RENDER SETTINGS** dialog box will be displayed; refer to Figure-21.

Figure-20. Render tool

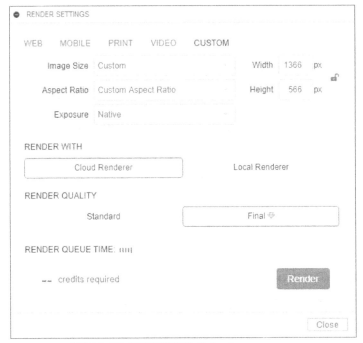

Figure-21. RENDER SETTINGS dialog box

WEB

*   Click on the **WEB** tab of **RENDER SETTINGS** dialog box. Various options under **WEB** tab will be displayed; refer to Figure-22.

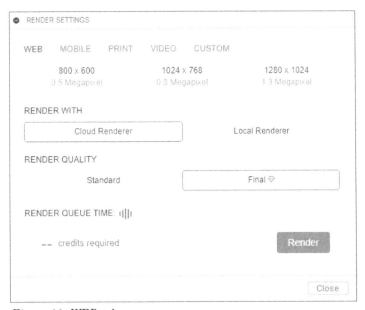

Figure-22. WEB tab

- Three highlighted options are the size of image in which your rendered file will be saved. Click on the required size.
- Click on the **Cloud Renderer** option from **RENDER WITH** section, if you want to render the file from Autodesk cloud. On selecting the **Cloud Renderer** button the dialog box will be updated; refer to Figure-23.

Figure-23. Updated WEB tab

- With **Local Renderer** option selected, click on the **Advanced settings** toggle button from **WEB** tab to manually set the render quality value. The **RENDER QUALITY** slider will be displayed; refer to Figure-24.

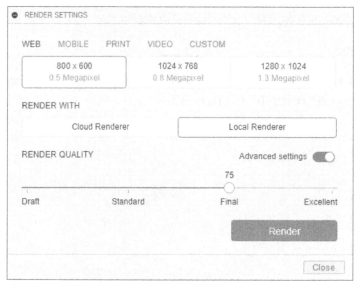

Figure-24. RENDER QUALITY slider in WEB tab

- Set the value of quality from slider as required. If you want to automatically set the quality of render then again click on the **Advanced Settings** toggle button. The **Standard(50)** and **Final(75)** option will be displayed.
- Click on the required option from **RENDER QUALITY** section and click on the **Render** button from **WEB** tab. The rendering process will start.

- The completed rendered file will be saved in **RENDERING GALLERY**; refer to Figure-25.

Figure-25. RENDERING GALLERY

Render Gallery

- To view the enlarged size of rendered image, click on that particular image. The image will be displayed in **RENDERING GALLERY** dialog box; refer to Figure-26.

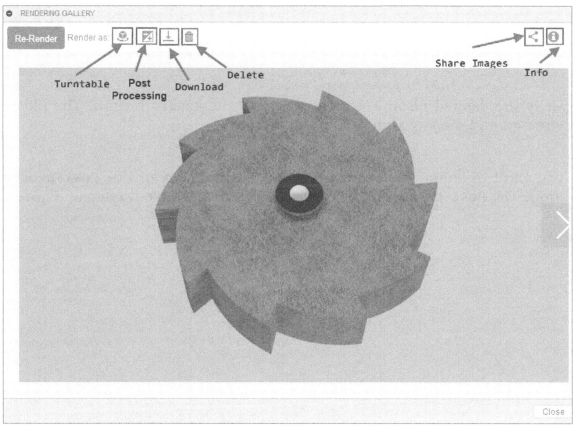

Figure-26. RENDERING GALLERY dialog box

- If you want to create a video of the rotating model then click on the **Turntable** button from **RENDERING GALLERY** dialog box. The **Render Settings - Turntable** box will be displayed; refer to Figure-27.

Figure-27. Render Settings-Turntable dialog box

- Specify the desired parameters and click on the **Render** button. The file will be re-created and displayed in **RENDERING GALLERY**.

Post Processing

- If you want to adjust the exposure of model then click on the **Post-processing** button. The **Post-processing** dialog box will be displayed; refer to Figure-28.

Figure-28. Post-processing dialog box

- The value of exposure can be adjusted by using the slider for Exposure Value.
- Select the desired option from the **Preset** drop-down. The options in the dialog box will be automatically adjusted presentation settings for rendering.
- Similarly, you can set the other parameters in the dialog box. After setting the parameters, click on the **Apply** button.

Downloading Render Image File

- If you want to download the current file then click on the **Download** button from **RENDERING GALLERY** dialog box. The drop-down will be displayed as shown in Figure-29.

Figure-29. Download drop-down

- Select the **Transparent Background** toggle button if you want to make background of model transparent. On selecting this toggle button, you will be able to save the image file in PNG or TIFF format only.
- Select the desired **Download image as...** button. The **Save File** dialog box will be displayed; refer to Figure-30.

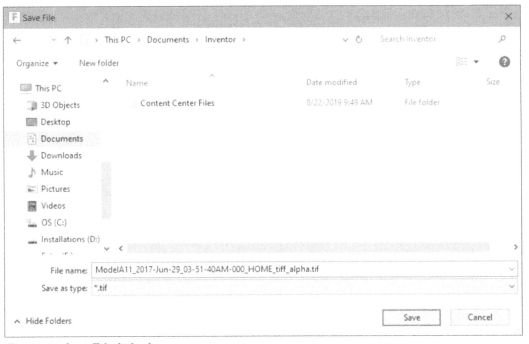

Figure-30. Save File dialog box

- Select the location for saving file and click on the **Save** button from the dialog box to save the file.
- If you want to delete the current file from **RENDERING GALLERY** then click on the **Delete** button from **RENDERING GALLERY** dialog box. The **Delete Image** dialog box will be displayed; refer to Figure-31.

Figure-31. Delete Image dialog box

- If you are sure about deleting the particular file then click on the **Delete** button from **Delete Image** dialog box otherwise click on **Cancel** button.

- If you want to share the image to Fusion 360 Gallery or A360 then click on the **Share Images** button at the top right in **RENDERING GALLERY** dialog box and select the respective option.
- If you want to see the information of the current file then click on the **Info** button from **RENDERING GALLERY** dialog box.
- After rendering the file, click on the **Close** button from **RENDERING GALLERY** dialog box to exit the rendering process.

ANIMATION

The **Animation** workspace is used to animate the joints of assembly. This workspace is also used to create exploded view of assembly. You can create the exploded view automatically as well as manually in this workspace. To activate the workspace, click on the **ANIMATION** option from the **Workspace** drop-down. The tools to perform animation will be displayed.

New Storyboard

A storyboard is automatically generated for each model when you switch to **ANIMATION** workspace. In the process of creating animation, additional storyboard can be added at any time as well. Each new storyboard has a default name "Storyboardx" where x is a number. You can edit this name by double-clicking on it at the bottom in application window. Storyboard acts as base for animation. To create different animations of same assembly, you can create different storyboards. The procedure to create new storyboard is discussed next.

- Click on the **New Storyboard** tool from **STORYBOARD** drop-down of **Toolbar** in **ANIMATION** workspace; refer to Figure-32. The **NEW STORYBOARD** dialog box will be displayed; refer to Figure-33.

Figure-32. New Storyboard tool

Figure-33. NEW STORYBOARD dialog box

- Select the **Clean** option from **Storyboard Type** drop-down if you want to delete all previous actions of animation and want to create a new storyboard.
- Select the **Start from end of previous** option from **Storyboard Type** drop-down if you want to use position of components at the end of previous animation as the starting position for the new animation.
- After setting desired options, click on the **OK** button from the dialog box. The created storyboard will be added at the bottom of **ANIMATION TIMELINE**; refer to Figure-34.

Figure-34. ANIMATION TIMELINE

Transform Components

The **Transform Components** tool is used to move and rotate the component. Note that the movement and rotation performed in this workspace will be recorded in animation. The procedure to use this tool is discussed next.

- Click on the **Transform Components** tool of **TRANSFORM** drop-down; refer to Figure-35. The **TRANSFORM COMPONENTS** dialog box will be displayed; refer to Figure-36.

Figure-35. Transform Components tool

Figure-36. TRANSFORM COMPONENTS dialog box

- The **Select** button of **Components** option is selected by default. Click on the component that you want to move or rotate. On selection of component, a manipulator will be displayed on the selected component along with updated **TRANSFORM COMPONENTS** dialog box; refer to Figure-37.

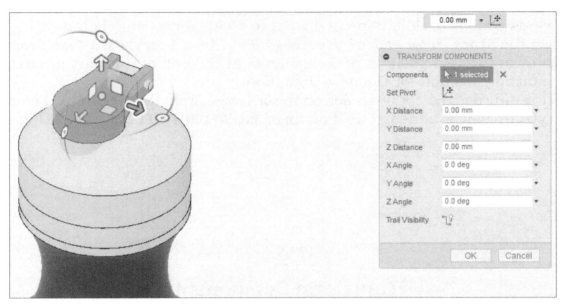

Figure-37. Manipulator on selected component

- The actions like moving or rotating the components are registered as animation in storyboard. To register the movement, drag the playhead in **ANIMATION TIMELINE** area to time value upto which the selected transformation operation will be completed. For example, if you want to move the component shown in figure by 60 mm in 2 seconds then first move the playhead of timeline to 2 seconds and then move the component by 60 mm; refer to Figure-38.

Figure-38. Registering movement of component in timeline

- You can specify the desired values for movement in the TRANSFORM COMPONENTS dialog box or you can set the parameters by moving the manipulator.
- After specifying the parameters, click on the **OK** button from **TRANSFORM COMPONENTS** dialog box to add the action in animation timeline.
- To play the animation, you need to click on the **Play** button from **ANIMATION TIMELINE.**

Restore Home

The **Restore Home** tool is used to restore the model position as it is at the end of animation.

• Click on the **Restore Home** tool from **TRANSFORM** drop-down; refer to Figure-39. The position of model will be restored.

Figure-39. Restore Home tool

Auto Explode: One Level

The **Auto Explode: One Level** tool is used to automatically separate all selected components down to one level in hierarchy. The procedure to use this tool is discussed next.

• Select the parts of assembly to be exploded (separated from each other) while holding the **CTRL** key. You can also select all components using window selection; refer to Figure-40.

Figure-40. Window selection of component

• Click on the **Auto Explode: One Level** tool from **TRANSFORM** drop-down; refer to Figure-41. The components will be separated on the canvas screen; refer to Figure-42.

Figure-41. Auto Explode One Level tool

Figure-42. Preview of Auto Explode One Level

- By moving the highlighted slider (**Explosion Scale**), you can set the distance between component.
- After adjusting the space between components, click on the **OK** button from slider.

Auto Explode: All Levels

The **Auto Explode: All Levels** tool is used to automatically separate all selected components down to all levels in component hierarchy (including sub-assemblies). The procedure to use this tool is discussed next.

- Select the parts of components to separate by holding the **CTRL** key. You can also select the components using window selection.
- Click on the **Auto Explode: All Levels** tool from **TRANSFORM** drop-down; refer to Figure-43. The components of selected model will be separated.

Figure-43. Auto Explode All Levels tool

- Click on the screen to view the separated component properly; refer to Figure-44.

Figure-44. Preview of Explode

- Move the slider to adjust the distance between separated components of model.
- After adjusting the components, click on the ✔ **OK** button. The exploded view of assembly will be displayed; refer to Figure-45.

Figure-45. Exploded view of water bottle assembly

Manual Explode

The **Manual Explode** tool is used to manually separate the selected component. The procedure to use this tool is discussed next.

- Click on the **Manual Explode** tool of **Transform** drop-down from **Toolbar**; refer to Figure-46.

Figure-46. Manual Explode tool

- You are asked to select the components to be moved during exploding. Click on the component to separate; refer to Figure-47.

Figure-47. Separating component manually

- On selecting a component, number of arrows will be displayed on the selected component. You need to click on the arrow of direction in which you want to move the selected component.
- Move the **Explosion Scale** slider to separate the selected component from remaining model; refer to Figure-48.

Figure-48. Separating the selected component

Show/Hide

The **Show/Hide** tool is used to show or hide the selected component. The procedure to use this tool is discussed next.

- Click on the desired component from model to show or hide.
- Now, click on the **Show/Hide** tool from **TRANSFORM** drop-down; refer to Figure-49. The selected component will be shown or hidden based on its condition.

Figure-49. Show/Hide tool

- To display the hidden component, click on the crossed eye button from **Browser**; refer to Figure-50.

Figure-50. Viewing the hidden component

Create Callout

The **Create Callout** tool is used to add annotation to the animation. The procedure to use this tool is discussed next.

- Click on the **Create Callout** tool from **ANNOTATION** panel; refer to Figure-51. The callout symbol will be attached to the cursor.

Figure-51. Create Callout tool

- Click on the component to add the callout. A text box will be displayed; refer to Figure-52.

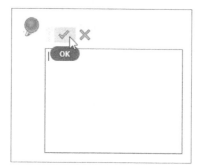

Figure-52. Callout text box

- Type the desired text in the text box and click on **OK** button. The annotation callout will be added to the selected component.

View

The **View** tool is used to start and stop the recording of the actions or commands occurring on the model or component. When **View** tool is activated then it captures the actions like move for animation and when the **View** tool is deactivated it does not record the process; refer to Figure-53.

Figure-53. View tool

Publish Video

The **Publish Video** tool is used to publish the video. The procedure to use this tool is discussed next.

- Click on the **Publish Video** tool from the **PUBLISH** panel in the **Toolbar**; refer to Figure-54. The **Video Options** dialog box will be displayed; refer to Figure-55.

Figure-54. Publish Video tool

Figure-55. Video Options dialog box

- Select **Current Storyboards** option from **Video Scope** section if you want to create a video of current storyboard animation only.
- Select **All Storyboards** option from **Video Scope** section if you want to create a video of all storyboard animations combined.
- Click on the **Current Document Window Size** drop-down from **Video Resolution** section or select the required video resolution.
- After specifying the parameters, click on the **OK** button from **Video Options** dialog box. The **Save As** dialog box will be displayed; refer to Figure-56.

Figure-56. Save As dialog box for Pubish Video tool

- Click in the **Name** edit box and specify the name of file.
- Select the **Save to a project in the cloud** check box if you want to save the file online or in your Autodesk account.

- Select the **Save to my computer** check box if you want to save the file in your computer.
- After specifying the parameters, click on the **Save** button from **Save As** dialog box. The **Publish Video** progress dialog box will be displayed which tells about the progress of publishing video; refer to Figure-57.

Figure-57. Publish Video progress dialog box

The video will be published online and saved to the computer at preferred location.

SELF ASSESSMENT

Q1. What is Rendering?

Q2. The .... is used to create the photo-realistic image from a scene of model.

Q3. The .... tool is used to control the lighting, background color, ground effects, and camera rendering.

Q4. From where can you get the environments for background as well as for model?

Q5. How can you display the shadow and reflections of model on ground canvas?

Q6. A textured ground plane where the environment image is mapped as a texture can be enable by selecting **Ground Plane** check box. (T/F)

Q7. The reflection of model on the ground can be display by selecting the **Reflections** check box. (T/F)

Q8. What is Depth of Field? And how it can be enable?

Q9. If you want to change the environment of the model then drag a specific environment from .... section and drop it to the current model or in the Current Environment section.

Q10. The **Appearance** tool is used to set the orientation of the texture applied to the face or model. (T/F)

Q11. What is the use of **Reset Transform** button in **Box** dialog box?

Q12. What happens when **In-canvas Render** button is selected?

Q13. The value of exposure can be adjusted between   to   .

Q14. What is use of Animation Workspace?

Q16. Which tool is used to add annotation to the animation?

FOR STUDENT NOTES

FOR STUDENT NOTES

FOR STUDENT NOTES

Chapter 11

Drawing

Topics Covered

The major topics covered in this chapter are:

- *Drawing View*
- *Projected view*
- *Section View*
- *Detail View*
- *Center line*
- *Datum Identifier*
- *Spline Balloon*
- *Output DWG, CSV, and PDF*

INTRODUCTION

Drawing is the engineering representation of a model on the paper. For manufacturing a model in the real world, we need some means by which we can tell the manufacturer what to manufacture. For this purpose, we create drawings from the models. These drawings have information like dimensions, material, tolerances, objective, precautions, and so on.

STARTING DRAWING WORKSPACE

In Autodesk Fusion 360, we create drawings in the **Drawing** workspace. The procedure to open a file in **DRAWING** workspace is discussed next.

*   Open the desired model from **Data Panel** or saved directory.
*   Click on **From Design** option from **DRAWING** cascading menu in **Change Workspace** drop-down. The **CREATE DRAWING** dialog box will be displayed along with the model; refer to Figure-1.

Figure-1. CREATE DRAWING dialog box

*   Select the **Full Assembly** check box from **CREATE DRAWING** dialog box if you want to create drawing using whole assembly. Clear the check box if you want to select the component of a model.
*   Click on the **Standard** drop-down from **CREATE DRAWING** dialog box and select the standard for the drawing. **ASME** option can use the third angle projection as well as first angle projection but **ISO** option uses first angle projection for placing views. There are also many other differences between two standards which you can find better in related books. Note that these projections are default settings but you can override them using **Preferences** dialog box.
*   Click on the **Units** drop-down from **CREATE DRAWING** dialog box and select the unit for drawing.
*   Click on the **Sheet Size** drop-down from **CREATE DRAWING** dialog box and select the size of sheet for drawing.

- After specifying the parameters, click on the **OK** button from **CREATE DRAWING** dialog box. The **DRAWING** workspace will be activated along with **DRAWING VIEW** dialog box in a new drawing file; refer to Figure-2.
- The model will be attached to the cursor. Click on the drawing sheet to place the base view.

Figure-2. DRAWING workspace

Parameters in DRAWING VIEW dialog box

- Click on the **Orientation** drop-down and select the base view of model. Here **Front** view is default option. When you change the view from **Front** to **Top**, the view of model will automatically changed.
- Select the style of model from the **Style** section.
- Click in the **Scale** drop-down and select the required scaling factor for model.
- Select the required option from **Tangent Edges** options to apply the edges with the selected view.
- Select the **Interference Edges** check box if you want to keep interfering edges within the selected view.
- Select the **Thread Edges** check box if you want to keep the threads within the selected view.
- After specifying the parameters in **DRAWING VIEW** dialog box, click on **OK** button. The selected view of model will be placed; refer to Figure-3.

Figure-3. Top view of model

SPECIFYING DRAWING PREFERENCES

- Click on the **Preferences** option from the **Autodesk Account** drop-down. The **Preferences** dialog box will be displayed.
- Select the **Drawing** option from the **General** node at the left in the dialog box. The options will be displayed as shown in Figure-4.

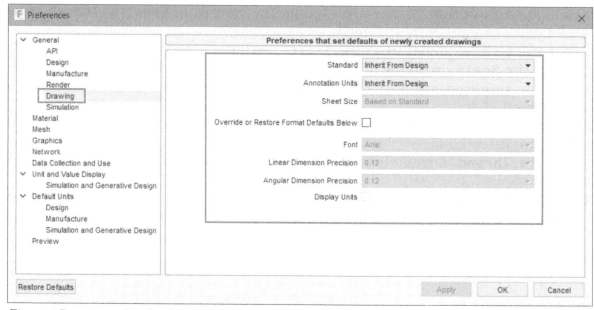

Figure-4. Drawing node in Preferences dialog box

- Select the desired option from the **Standard** drop-down to define which standard to use for drafting. You can select **ASME** or **ISO** option from the drop-down to set it default for drafting or you can select the **Inherit From Design** to define the standard by 3D Model.

- Select the desired unit of length from the **Annotation Units** drop-down. You can select inch or mm as unit.
- Select the desired default size of sheet from the **Sheet Size** drop-down.
- Select the **Override or Restore Format Defaults Below** check box if you want to use parameters different from selected standard. The options below this check box will be activated; refer to Figure-5.

Figure-5. Override options

- Select the desired option from the **Projection Angle** drop-down to define the view projection method for drawing.
- Set the other parameters like font, height, precision, units displayed, and so on.
- Click on the **OK** button from the **Preferences** dialog box.

CREATING BASE VIEW

The **Base View** tool is used to create base view derived directly from a 3D model. You can create various views of your model using this view. Note that you should have only one base view and other views should be projection of that view. The procedure to use this tool is discussed next.

- Click on the **Base View** tool from **DRAWING VIEWS** panel; refer to Figure-6. The **DRAWING VIEW** dialog box will be displayed.

Figure-6. Base View tool

- Click at desired location to place the view and specify desired parameters in the dialog box. The options of **DRAWING VIEW** dialog box have been discussed earlier.
- Click on the **OK** button from the dialog box to generate the view.

CREATING PROJECTED VIEW

The **Projected View** tool is used to create drawing views generated from an existing base or drawing view. The procedure to use this tool is discussed next.

- Click on the **Projected View** tool from **DRAWING VIEWS** panel in the **Toolbar**; refer to Figure-7. The tool will be activated.

Figure-7. Projected View tool

- Click on the pre-existing base view from drawing sheet to select the view as parent view; refer to Figure-8. The projected view will be attached to the cursor; refer to Figure-9.

Figure-8. Selecting parent view

Figure-9. Placing projected view

- Place the projected views of model at desired locations and press **ENTER**. The projected view(s) are created on drawing sheet; refer to Figure-10.

Figure-10. Projected views created

CREATING SECTION VIEW

The **Section View** tool is used to create full, half, offset, or aligned section views. The procedure to use this tool is discussed next.

- Click on the **Section View** tool from **DRAWING VIEWS** panel; refer to Figure-11. The tool will be activated.

Figure-11. Section View tool

- Click on the projected or base view from drawing sheet to be used for section view. The **DRAWING VIEW** dialog box will be displayed.
- You need to divide the selected parent view into two parts to create half section; refer to Figure-12.

Figure-12. Creating section view

- Click on the parent view to specify the start point and end point. You can create different shape of section line to create desired type of section. Note that you can use snap point in right-click shortcut menu to select points for section line; refer to Figure-13. After specifying the start point, intermediate points, and end point, click on **ENTER** key. The section view will be created and attached to the cursor; refer to Figure-14.

Figure-13. Shortcut menu for snap points

Figure-14. Section view attached to the cursor

- Place the section view at desired location and click on **OK** button from **DRAWING VIEW** dialog box. The section view will be created on drawing sheet; refer to Figure-15.

Figure-15. Section View created

- Note that the hatching is created automatically in the section view. To edit hatching double-click on it. The **HATCH** dialog box will be displayed. Specify the desired values and click on the **Close** button.
- If you want to edit the section annotation then double-click on it. The **TEXT** dialog box will be displayed; refer to Figure-16.

Figure-16. TEXT dialog box for annotation

- Click on the **Font** drop-down and select the required font from the list.
- Click in the **Height** edit box and specify the height of text and select the writing style of text from **TEXT** dialog box.
- Click on the desired text alignment from **Justification** section.
- If you want to insert any special symbol then click on it from **Symbols** section of the dialog box.
- After specifying the parameters for the text, click in the text box from drawing sheet and enter the required text.
- Click on the **Close** button from **TEXT** dialog box to complete the process. The text will be modified according to parameters specified.

CREATING DETAIL VIEW

The **Detail View** tool is used to create detail view from any projected or base view. The procedure to use this tool is discussed next.

- Click on the **Detail View** tool of **DRAWING VIEWS** panel; refer to Figure-17. The tool will be activated and you will be asked to select a view whose selected section is to be included in detail view.

Figure-17. Detail View tool

- Select the desired view from drawing sheet; refer to Figure-18. The **DRAWING VIEW** dialog box will be displayed.

Figure-18. Selecting parent view for detail view

- Click at the desired location to specify the center point for boundaries of detail view; refer to Figure-19.
- Create the boundary on parent view as required; refer to Figure-20.

Figure-19. Specifying center point for boundary

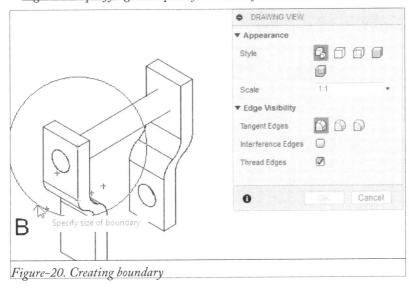

Figure-20. Creating boundary

- On creating the circular boundary, the detail view of model will be attached to the cursor; refer to Figure-21. Place it as desired.

Figure-21. Placing detail view

- After placing the view, set the parameters of detail view in **DRAWING VIEW** dialog box and click on **OK** button. The detailed view will be created; refer to Figure-22.

Figure-22. Detailed view created

MOVING VIEWS

The **Move** tool is used to move selected view from one place to another. The procedure to use this tool is discussed next.

- Click on the **Move** tool from **MODIFY** drop-down; refer to Figure-23. The **MOVE** dialog box will be displayed; refer to Figure-24.

Figure-23. Move tool

Figure-24. MOVE dialog box

- The **Select** button of **Selection** option in **MOVE** dialog box is active by default. Click on the view to select the view to be moved. The updated **MOVE** dialog box will be displayed; refer to Figure-25.
- Click on **Transform** button from **MOVE** dialog box and select a base point from the selected view. The selected view will get attached to the cursor to move the view from one place to another; refer to Figure-26.

Figure-25. Updated MOVE dialog box

Figure-26. Specifying second point

- Click on the sheet to place the view. The view will be moved from previous position to new position.
- Click on the **OK** button from **MOVE** dialog box to complete the process.

ROTATING VIEWS

The **Rotate** tool is used to rotate the selected view as desired. The procedure to use this tool is discussed next.

- Click on the **Rotate** tool from **MODIFY** panel; refer to Figure-27. The **ROTATE** dialog box will be displayed; refer to Figure-28.

Figure-27. Rotate tool

Figure-28. ROTATE dialog box

- The **Select** button of **Selection** option in **ROTATE** dialog box is active by default. Click on the view to be rotated.
- Click on **Transform** button from **ROTATE** dialog box and select the base point from selected view. The view will be attached to the cursor; refer to Figure-29.

Figure-29. Rotating view

- You can adjust the angle of rotation of view by moving the cursor around parent view and place as required. If you want to specify the value of rotation then click in the **Angle** edit box of **ROTATE** dialog box and specify the value.
- You can also set the reference for rotation by clicking on **Select** button of **Reference** section and selecting the reference point from parent view.
- After specifying the parameters, click on **OK** button from **ROTATE** dialog box to complete the process.

CREATING CENTERLINE

The **Centerline** tool is used to create centre line. The procedure to use this tool is discussed next.

- Click on the **Centerline** tool from **GEOMETRY** panel; refer to Figure-30. The tool will be activated.

Figure-30. Centerline tool

- You need to select parallel edges from a view to create a center line. Click on the desired edge to select; refer to Figure-31. You will be asked to select the second edge.

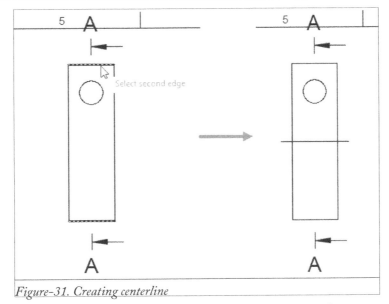

Figure-31. Creating centerline

- On selecting second edge, the center line will be created.

CREATING CENTER MARK

The **Center Mark** tool is used to create center mark for rounds and circles. The procedure to use this tool is discussed next.

- Click on the **Center Mark** tool from **GEOMETRY** panel; refer to Figure-32. The tool will be activated. You need to select a round edge from any view.

Figure-32. Center Mark tool

- On selecting the edge, the center mark will be created for selected round edge; refer to Figure-33.

Figure-33. Creating center mark

CREATING CENTER MARK PATTERN

The **Center Mark Pattern** tool is used to generate pattern of center marks in the drawing view. The procedure to use this tool is given next.

- Click on the **Center Mark Pattern** tool from the **GEOMETRY** panel of **Toolbar**; refer to Figure-34. The **CENTER MARK PATTERN** dialog box will be displayed; refer to Figure-35. You will be asked to select a hole or round edge whose center mark is to be created.

Figure-34. Center Mark Pattern tool

Figure-35. CENTER MARK PATTERN dialog box

- Click on the desired holes one by one. If the holes are in circular pattern then the dialog box will be displayed as shown in Figure-36. Select the **Center Mark** check box to generate center mark for pitch circle. Click on the **OK** button to generate center marks.

Figure-36. Holes selected in circular pattern

- In cases where you want to specify the PCD reference manually, click on the **Reference Edge** selection button after selecting holes and then select the reference edge; refer to Figure-37.

Figure-37. Selecting reference edge

- In case of selecting holes in linear direction, you can select maximum 3 holes for center mark.

EDGE EXTENSION

The **Edge Extension** tool is used to create an extension of associative edge for two intersecting (unequal) edges within an existing drawing view. The procedure to use this tool is discussed next.

- Click on the **Edge Extension** tool from **GEOMETRY** panel; refer to Figure-38. The tool will be activated.

Figure-38. Edge Extension tool

- You need to select the two non-parallel (going to intersect) edges to create the extension. Click on the edge to select; refer to Figure-39.

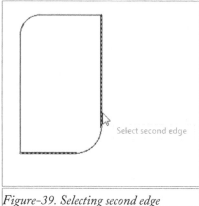

Figure-39. Selecting second edge

- On selecting the second edge, the extended edge will be displayed; refer to Figure-40.

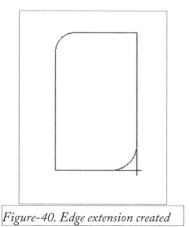

Figure-40. Edge extension created

DIMENSIONING

The **Dimension** tool is used to apply dimension to model. The procedure to use this tool is discussed next.

- Click on the **Dimension** tool from **DIMENSIONS** panel; refer to Figure-41. The tool will be activated.

Figure-41. Dimension tool

- When you hover the cursor over on any geometry, the measurement of that dimension will be displayed; refer to Figure-42.

Figure-42. Checking dimension

- If you want to mention that dimension then click on the line. The dimension will attached to the cursor.
- Place the dimension at desired distance by clicking.

Ordinate Dimensioning

The **Ordinate Dimension** tool is used to apply ordinate dimensioning. The procedure to use this tool is discussed next.

- Click on the **Ordinate Dimension** tool from **DIMENSIONS** panel; refer to Figure-43. The tool will be activated and you will be asked to specify origin for ordinate dimensioning.

Figure-43. Ordinate Dimension tool

- Click at the desired location to place origin of ordinate dimensioning. The ordinate dimension will be attached to the cursor; refer to Figure-44.

Figure-44. Calculating ordinate dimension

- Click at the desired location to place dimension text. Similarly, you can dimension horizontally/vertically.

Creating Linear Dimension

The **Linear Dimension** tool is used to create linear dimensions in horizontal/vertical directions. The procedure to use this tool is given next.

- Click on the **Linear Dimension** tool from the **DIMENSIONS** panel in the **Toolbar**; refer to Figure-45. You will be asked to select points.

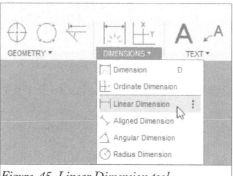

Figure-45. Linear Dimension tool

- Select the two points one by one to create horizontal/vertical distance dimension. The dimension will get attached to cursor.
- Move the cursor in desired direction to create vertical or horizontal dimension if the two points are not in aligned vertically/horizontally; refer to Figure-46.

Figure-46. Creating linear dimension

- Click at the desired location to place the dimension.

Creating Aligned Dimension

The **Aligned Dimension** tool is used to create aligned dimension between two selected points. The procedure is given next.

- Click on the **Aligned Dimension** tool from **DIMENSIONS** panel in the **Toolbar**; refer to Figure-47. You will be asked to select points.

Figure-47. Aligned Dimension tool

- Click at the desired two points. The distance dimension between two selected points will get attached to cursor; refer to Figure-48.

Figure-48. Placing Aligned dimension

- Click at desired location to place the dimension.

Creating Angular Dimension

The **Angular Dimension** tool is used to create angle dimension between two selected lines/edges. If you select an arc then its angular span is created as dimension. The procedure to use this tool is given next.

- Click on the **Angular Dimension** tool from the **DIMENSIONS** panel in the **Toolbar**; refer to Figure-49. You will be asked to select entities.

Figure-49. Angular Dimension tool

- Select two lines between which you want to create angular dimension or select an arc whose angular dimension is to be created. The dimension will get attached to cursor; refer to Figure-50.

Figure-50. Creating angular dimension

- Click at desired location to place the dimension.

Creating Radius Dimension

The **Radius Dimension** tool is used to apply radius dimension to selected arc, circle, and circular edges. The procedure to use this tool is given next.

- Click on the **Radius Dimension** tool in **DIMENSIONS** panel of **Toolbar**; refer to Figure-51. You will be asked to select circular edge or circle in the drawing.

Figure-51. Radius Dimension tool

- Click at the desired entity. The radius dimension will get attached to cursor; refer to Figure-52.

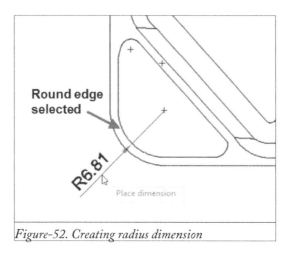

Figure-52. Creating radius dimension

- Click at desired location to place the dimension.

Creating Diameter Dimension

The **Diameter Dimension** tool is used to create diameter dimension for selected round edges, circles, and fillets in the drawing; refer to Figure-53. The procedure to use this tool is similar to **Radius Dimension** tool.

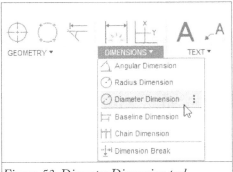
Figure-53. Diameter Dimension tool

Baseline Dimensioning

The baseline dimensioning is performed when you want to create linear dimensions with respect to one common base reference. The procedure to create baseline dimensions is given next.

- Click on the **Linear Dimension** tool from the **DIMENSIONS** panel of **Toolbar**; refer to Figure-54, and create a linear dimension which will be used as base line; refer to Figure-55.

Figure-54. Linear Dimension tool

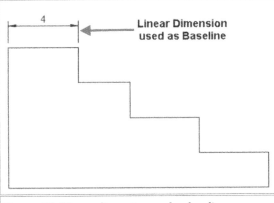
Figure-55. Linear dimension used as baseline

- Click on the **Baseline Dimension** tool from the **DIMENSIONS** panel of the **Toolbar**; refer to Figure-56, and select one of the leg of base dimension.

Figure-56. Baseline Dimension tool

- A new dimension will be generated with one end point fixed to selected leg and other end point of dimension attached to cursor; refer to Figure-57.

Figure-57. Placing baseline dimension

- Select the desired point of sketch to create the dimension. You will be asked to specify end point for another dimension. Select the desired points to create required dimensions. Once you have created required dimensions, press **ENTER** from keyboard to complete the process. The dimensions will be generated; refer to Figure-58.

Figure-58. Baseline dimension created

Chain Dimensioning

In chain dimensioning, all the linear dimensions are placed side by side. The procedure to use this tool is given next.

- Create a linear dimension to used as reference for chain dimensioning as discussed in previous section for baseline dimensioning.
- Click on the **Chain Dimension** tool from the **DIMENSIONS** panel of the **Toolbar**; refer to Figure-59, and select the base dimension. You will be asked to specify end point of new dimension; refer to Figure-60.

Figure-59. Chain Dimension tool

Figure-60. Placing chain dimensions

- Click at desired location to specify end point. You will be asked to specify end point of another dimension.
- Click at desired locations to create required dimensions and then press **ENTER** to exit. The dimensions will be created; refer to Figure-61.

Figure-61. Chain dimensions created

Dimension Break

The **Dimension Break** tool is used to resolve intersecting dimensions in the drawing. This tool adds/removes break in selected dimension. The procedure to use this tool is given next.

- Click on the **Dimension Break** tool from the **DIMENSIONS** panel of the **Toolbar**; refer to Figure-62. The **DIMENSION BREAK** dialog box will be displayed; refer to Figure-63, and you will be asked to select the dimension to add or remove break.

Figure-62. Dimension Break tool

Figure-63. DIMENSION BREAK dialog box

- Select the desired dimension and then select the **Add Break** or **Remove Break** option from the **Operation** drop-down to perform respective action. In our case, we are selecting **Add Break** option from the drop-down to add break in intersecting dimension.
- Click on the **OK** button from the dialog box. The selected operation will be performed on the dimension; refer to Figure-64.

Figure-64. Dimension after applying Add Break

ANNOTATION SETTINGS

There are various options available in **Annotation Settings** flyout to change annotation text, font, precision, and so on; refer to Figure-65. Various options of this flyout are discussed next.

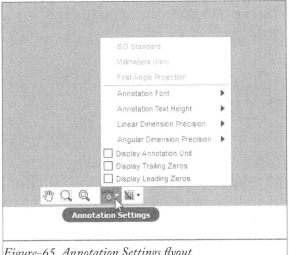

Figure-65. Annotation Settings flyout

- The top three options in the flyout are fixed and they give information about Drafting standard, unit, and projection type used in the drawing.
- Select the desired font from **Annotation Font** cascading menu of the flyout to define font of all the annotations in drawing area.
- Select the desired value for height of annotations in **Annotation Text Height** cascading menu of the flyout
- Select the desired precision level for linear and angular dimensions in the **Linear Dimension Precision** and **Angular Dimension Precision** cascading menus respectively.
- Select the **Display Annotation Unit** check box to display unit of annotation in drawing.
- Select the **Display Trailing Zeros** check box to display zeros after decimal places if the dimension is not up to specified precision level.
- Select the **Display Leading Zeros** check box if you want to display zeros before the dimension values in the annotations.

EDITING DIMENSIONS

Once you have generated dimensions, there are some cases where you need to provide special symbols with dimensions or you want to modify the value of dimension. The procedure to edit dimension is given next.

- Double-click on the dimension in drawing that you want to edit. The **DIMENSION** dialog box will be displayed; refer to Figure-66.

Figure-66. DIMENSION dialog box

- Select the desired precision level from **Primary Precision** drop-down.
- Select the **Alternate Units** check box to also display dimensions in inches if they are in mm and vice-versa; refer to Figure-67.

Figure-67. Alternate units

- Click at the desired place in dimension box and select the desired symbol to be inserted. The symbol will be added to dimension; refer to Figure-68.

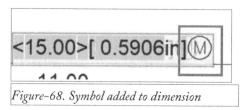

Figure-68. Symbol added to dimension

- Select the desired type of tolerance from the **Type** drop-down in **Tolerance** section to apply tolerance to dimension. Select the **Symmetrical** option from the **Type** drop-down if tolerance is equal in both negative and positive directions. Select the **Deviation** option from the **Type** drop-down if tolerance is different in positive and negative directions. Select the **Limit** option from the **Type** drop-down if you want to display upper and lower limit of dimension; refer to Figure-69.

Figure-69. Tolerance types

- After selecting the desired option from drop-down, specify desired value of tolerance in edit boxes below it in **Tolerance** section.
- Expand the **Representation** node and select the desired button to make the dimension as reference dimension, not to scale, and theoretically exact; refer to Figure-70.

Figure-70. Representation options

- Similarly, expand the **Inspection** node and set the desired parameters if you want to define inspection rate of current dimension.
- After specifying parameters, click on the **Close** button or click anywhere in blank space of drawing to exit the tool.

CREATING TEXT

The **Text** tool is used to insert text into the active drawing. The procedure to use this tool is discussed next.

- Click on the **Text** tool from **TEXT** panel; refer to Figure-71. The **Text** tool is activated and you will be asked to draw a text box.

Figure-71. Text tool

- Click to specify the first corner.
- After specifying the first corner, click on the screen to specify the second corner; refer to Figure-72. The **TEXT** dialog box will be displayed; refer to Figure-73.

Figure-72. Specifying second corner

Figure-73. TEXT dialog box displayed

- Click on the **Font** drop-down and select the required font for text.
- Click in the **Height** edit box and specify the height of text.
- Set the other parameters as required and type the desired text in the Text box.
- Click on **Close** button. The text will be added in drawing sheet.

CREATING LEADERS

The **Leader** tool is similar to **Text** tool but these notes are intended to be associated with a specific component. The procedure to use this tool is discussed next.

- Click on the **Leader** tool from **TEXT** panel; refer to Figure-74. The tool will be activated.

Figure-74. Leader tool

- Click on the drawing to select the start point. An arrow will be attached to the cursor.
- Click on the screen to place text box. The text box will be displayed along with **TEXT** dialog box; refer to Figure-75.

Figure-75. Leader text box

- Set the desired parameter from **TEXT** dialog box and type the text in text box.

- After specifying the parameters, click on **Close** button from **TEXT** dialog box.

APPLYING SURFACE TEXTURE SYMBOL

The **Surface Texture** tool is used to apply surface finish symbol to objects in drawing. The procedure to use this tool is discussed next.

- Click on the **Surface Texture** tool from **SYMBOLS** panel of **Toolbar;** refer to Figure-76. The tool will be activated.

Figure-76. Surface Texture tool

- Click on the model in a drawing view to select object. An arrow will be displayed on the selected part.
- Click to select the second point for leader or press **ENTER** key to place the symbol directly on selected face. The **SURFACE TEXTURE** dialog box will be displayed; refer to Figure-77.

Figure-77. SURFACE TEXTURE dialog box

- Select the desired surface finish symbol button from **Symbol Type** section.
- Select the **All Around** check box from **SURFACE TEXTURE** dialog box if you want to apply surface finish to all the surfaces in current view.
- Click in the **First Requirement** edit box of **SURFACE TEXTURE** dialog box and enter the first parameter of surface finish symbol. Similarly, specify the other parameters in the edit boxes of the dialog box.
- Select the lay direction button as desired from **Direction of Lay** section.
- After specifying the parameters, click on the **OK** button from **SURFACE TEXTURE** dialog box; refer to Figure-78.

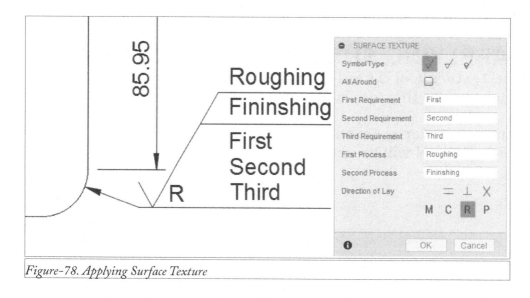

Figure-78. Applying Surface Texture

Surface Texture Symbols or Surface Roughness Symbols

CREATING FEATURE CONTROL FRAME

The **Feature Control Frame** contains data for controlled specifications. It shows the characteristics symbol, datum reference, and tolerance value. It is a rectangular frame which is divided into two or more sections. The feature control frame is also known as GD&T box in laymen's language. The method to insert Feature Control Frame in drawing is same as discussed for **Surface Texture** symbol. In GD&T, a feature control frame is required to describe the conditions and tolerances of a geometric control on a part's feature. The feature control frame consists of four pieces of information:

1. GD&T symbol or control symbol
2. Tolerance zone type and dimensions
3. Tolerance zone modifiers: features of size, projections...
4. Datum references (if required by the GD&T symbol)

This information provides everything you need to know about geometry of part like what geometrical tolerance needs to be on the part and how to measure or determine if the part is in specification; refer to Figure-79. The common elements of feature control frame are discussed next.

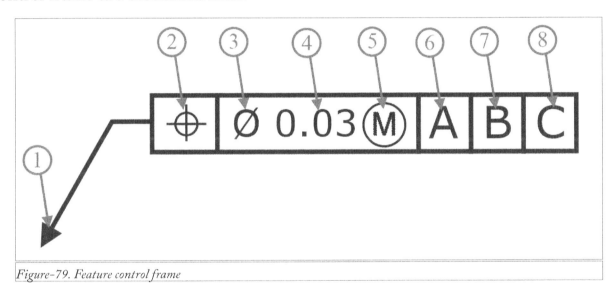

Figure-79. Feature control frame

1. **Leader Arrow** – This arrow points to the feature that the geometric control is placed on. If the arrow points to a surface than the surface is controlled by the GD&T. If it points to a diametric dimension, then the axis is controlled by GD&T. The arrow is optional but helps clarify the feature being controlled.
2. **Geometric Symbol** – This is where your geometric control is specified.
3. **Diameter Symbol (if required)** – If the geometric control is a diametrical tolerance then the diameter symbol (Ø) will be in front of the tolerance value.
4. **Tolerance Value** – If the tolerance is a diameter you will see the Ø symbol next to the dimension signifying a diametric tolerance zone. The tolerance of the GD&T is in same unit of measure that the drawing is written in.
5. **Feature of Size or Tolerance Modifiers (if required)** – This is where you call out max material condition or a projected tolerance in the feature control frame.

6. **Primary Datum (if required)** – If a datum is required, this is the main datum used for the GD&T control. The letter corresponds to a feature somewhere on the part which will be marked with the same letter. This is the datum that must be constrained first when measuring the part. Note: The order of the datum is important for measurement of the part. The primary datum is usually held in three places to fix 3 degrees of freedom

7. **Secondary Datum (if required)** – If a secondary datum is required, it will be to the right of the primary datum. This letter corresponds to a feature somewhere on the part which will be marked with the same letter. During measurement, this is the datum fixated after the primary datum.

8. **Tertiary Datum (if required)** – If a third datum is required, it will be to the right of the secondary datum. This letter corresponds to a feature somewhere on the part which will be marked with the same letter. During measurement, this is the datum fixated last.

Reading Feature Control Frame

The feature control frame forms a kind of sentence when you read it. Below is how you would read the frame in order to describe the feature.

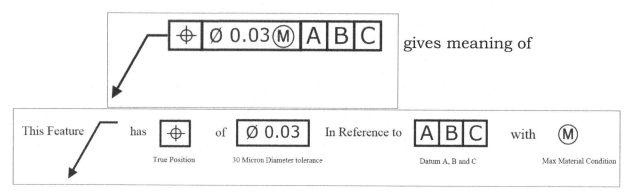

Meaning of various geometric symbols are given in Figure-80.

SYMBOL	CHARACTERISTICS	CATEGORY
—	Straightness	Form
▱	Flatness	
○	Circulatity	
⌭	Cylindricity	
⌒	Profile of a Line	Profile
⌓	Profile of Surface	
∠	Angularity	Orientation
⊥	Perpendicularity	
//	Parallelism	
⊕	Position	Location
◎	Concentricity	
⩶	Symmetry	
↗	Circular Runout	Runout
↗↗	Total Runout	

Figure-80. Geometric Symbols

Figure-81 and Figure-82 shows the use of geometric tolerances in real-world.

Figure-81. Use of geometric tolerance 1

Figure-82. Use of geometric tolerance 2

Note that in applying most of the geometrical tolerances, you need to define a datum plane like in Perpendicularity, Parallelism, and so on. There are a few dimensioning symbols also used in geometric dimensioning and tolerances, which are given in Figure-83.

Symbol	Meaning	Symbol	Meaning
Ⓛ	LMC – Least Material Condition	◄─⊕	Dimension Origin
Ⓜ	MMC – Maximum Material Condition	⊔	Counterbore
Ⓣ	Tangent Plane	∨	Countersink
Ⓟ	Projected Tolerance Zone	⊽	Depth
Ⓕ	Free State	⌀	All Around
∅	Diameter	◄─►	Between
R	Radius	✕	Target Point
SR	Spherical Radius	▷	Conical Taper
S∅	Spherical Diameter	◁	Slope
CR	Controlled Radius	☐	Square
ⓈⓉ	Statistical Tolerance		
77	Basic Dimension		
(77)	Reference Dimension		
5X	Places		

Figure-83. Dimensioning symbols

The procedure to use this tool is discussed next.

- Click on the **Feature Control Frame** tool from **SYMBOLS** panel of **Toolbar**; refer to Figure-84. The tool will be activated.

Figure-84. Feature Control Frame tool

- Click on the drawing to select the object. An arrow will be attached to the cursor; refer to Figure-85.

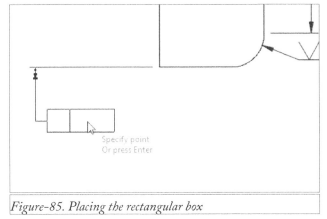

Figure-85. Placing the rectangular box

- Click on the screen to place the rectangular box and press **ENTER** key. The **FEATURE CONTROL FRAME** dialog box will be displayed; refer to Figure-86.

Figure-86. FEATURE CONTROL FRAME dialog box

- Click in the **Top Note** edit box and enter the note. If you want to add any symbol then click on the drop-down button. A list of symbols will be displayed; refer to Figure-87.

Figure-87. Adding symbols

- Click on the required symbol. The selected symbol will be added over the feature control frame box. Similarly, you can set the symbol for **Bottom Note** edit box.
- Similarly, select the required symbol for **Geometric Symbol** section. The selected symbol will be displayed in the feature frame rectangular box.
- Click in the **First Tolerance** edit box and enter the value of tolerance. You can also add the required symbol; refer to Figure-88.

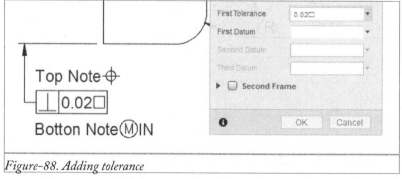

Figure-88. Adding tolerance

- Click on the **First Datum** edit box and enter the value of datum as required; refer to Figure-89.

Figure-89. Specifying datum value

- Similarly enter the remaining parameters in respective edit box.
- Select the **Second Frame** check box of **FEATURE CONTROL FRAME** dialog box if you want to add second frame for the drawing. Feature Control frames with two frames is also called Composite Feature Control Frame.

- After specifying the parameters, click on the **OK** button from **FEATURE CONTROL FRAME** dialog box to complete the process.

CREATING DATUM IDENTIFIER

The **Datum Identifier** tool identifies a datum feature for a feature control frame symbol. Datum identifier are circular frames divided in two parts by a horizontal line. The lower half represents the datum feature, and the upper half is for additional information, such as dimensions of the datum target area; refer to Figure-90.

Figure-90. Datum target area

The procedure to use this tool is discussed next.

- Click on the **Datum Identifier** tool from **SYMBOLS** panel of **Toolbar**; refer to Figure-91. The tool will be activated.

Figure-91. Datum Identifier tool

- Click on the drawing to select object. An arrow will be attached to the cursor.
- Specify the point and press **ENTER** key. The datum ID symbol will be displayed along with **DATUM IDENTIFIER** dialog box; refer to Figure-92.

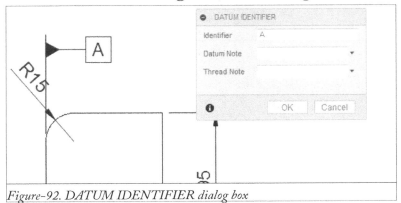

Figure-92. DATUM IDENTIFIER dialog box

- Click in the **Datum Note** edit box and enter the desired note.
- Click in the **Thread Note** edit box and enter the desired text. You can also add the required symbol from **Symbol** drop-down.
- After specifying the parameters, click on the **OK** button from **DATUM IDENTIFIER** dialog box; refer to Figure-93.

Figure-93. Updated DATUM IDENTIFIER dialog box

GENERATING TABLES

The **Table** tool is used to generate a parts list of the assembly model linked with drawing. The procedure to use this tool is discussed next.

- Click on the **Table** tool from **TABLES** drop-down in the **Toolbar**; refer to Figure-94. The **TABLE** dialog box will be displayed along with attached parts list; refer to Figure-95.

Figure-94. Table tool

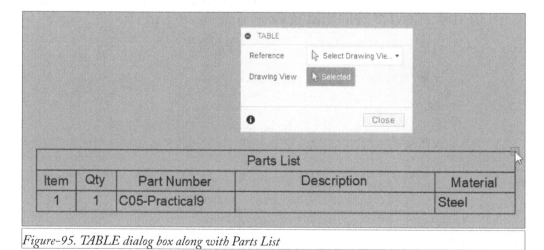

Figure-95. TABLE dialog box along with Parts List

- Select the file name option from **Reference** drop-down if you want to create a parts list of particular file.

- Click on **Select Drawing View** option from **Reference** drop-down if you want to select a view manually which should be used to create part list.
- Click at desired location in the drawing to place the parts list. Parts list will be generated with balloons; refer to Figure-96.

Item	Qty	Part Number	Description	Material
1	1	Component1		Brass
2	1	Component2		Brass
3	1	Component3		Copper
4	1	Component4		Steel, Paint Finish, Blue
5	1	Component5		Steel, Paint Finish, Blue
6	1	Component6		Steel

Figure-96. Parts List of assembly

GENERATING BALLOON

The **Balloon** tool is used to generate balloons for components in drawing. The procedure to use this tool is discussed next.

- Click on the **Balloon** tool from **TABLES** drop-down; refer to Figure-97. The **BALLOON** dialog box will be displayed; refer to Figure-98 and you will be asked to select the component.

Figure-97. Balloon tool

Figure-98. BALLOON dialog box

- By default, the **Standard** option is selected in the dialog box so straight lines are created with balloon. If you want to create spline attached to balloon in place of line then select the **Patent** option from the **Type** drop-down.

- Click on desired edge of component. On selection of edge, an arrow will be attached to the cursor.
- Click at desired location to place the balloon; refer to Figure-99 and Figure-100.

Figure-99. Placing balloon with Standard option

Figure-100. Placing balloon with Patent option

BEND IDENTIFIER AND TABLE

The **Table** tool discussed earlier works in a different way for sheet metal component. If you are generating drawing for a sheetmetal part then **Table** tool will generate bend table for the part and like balloons in assembly, bend identifiers are used to identify bends as per the table. The process is given next.

- After starting drawing environment using flat pattern of a sheet metal part, click on the **Bend Identifier** tool from the **TABLES** drop-down in the **Toolbar**; refer to Figure-101. You will be asked to select the bends in flat pattern.

Figure-101. Bend Identifier tool

- Click on the sheet metal bends in drawing one by one. Bend identifiers will be assigned to the bends; refer to Figure-102.

Figure-102. Bend identifier assigned

- Press **ESC** to exit the tool.
- Click on the **Table** tool from **TABLES** drop-down in the **Toolbar** and place the bend table at desired location; refer to Figure-103.

Figure-103. Flat pattern with bend table

RENUMBERING BALLOONS

The **Renumber** tool is used to renumber the existing balloons. The procedure to use this tool is discussed next.

- Click on the **Renumber** tool from **TABLES** drop-down in the **Toolbar**; refer to Figure-104. The **RENUMBER** dialog box will be displayed; refer to Figure-105.

Figure-104. Renumber tool

Figure-105. RENUMBER dialog box

- Click in the **Starting Number** edit box and enter the desired number.
- Click on **Select** button from **Selection** section and click on the balloons as per their sequences to renumber them. The balloon numbers will be changed; refer to Figure-106.

Figure-106. Changed balloon number

- After specifying the parameters, click on **OK** button from **RENUMBER** dialog box to complete the process.

ALIGNING BALLOONS

The **Align Balloons** tool is used to align all the pre-existing balloons. The procedure to use this tool is discussed next.

- Click on the **Align Balloons** tool from **TABLES** drop-down in **Toolbar**; refer to Figure-107. The tool will be activated.

Figure-107. Align Balloons tool

- Click to select all the balloons to align; refer to Figure-108 and press **ENTER**.

Figure-108. Selection of balloons for allignment

- Click on the screen to specify the start point. All balloons will be attached to cursor.
- Click on the screen to align as desired; refer to Figure-109.

Figure-109. Performing alignment process

GENERATING PDF

The **Output PDF** tool is used to output the drawing in PDF format. The procedure to use this tool is discussed next.

- Click on the **Output PDF** tool from **OUTPUT** drop-down in **Toolbar**; refer to Figure-110. The **OUTPUT PDF** dialog box will be displayed; refer to Figure-111.

Figure-110. Output PDF tool

Figure-111. OUTPUT PDF dialog box

- Click on the **Sheets** drop-down from **OUTPUT PDF** dialog box and select the required sheet for output. You can also use **SHIFT** key or **CTRL** key to select multiple sheets.
- Select the **Open PDF** check box if you want to open the output PDF file.
- Select the **Lineweights** check box if you want to make bold lines of drawing otherwise clear it.
- After specifying the parameters, click on the **OK** button from **OUTPUT PDF** dialog box. The **Output PDF** dialog box will be displayed to save the file; refer to Figure-112.

Figure-112. Output PDF dialog box for saving file

- Click in the **File name** edit box and enter the desired text.
- Select the saving location of file and click on the **Save** button. The PDF file will be created and opened if you had selected the **Open PDF** check box from **OUTPUT PDF** dialog box.

GENERATING DWG

The **Output DWG** tool is used to create an output file of drawing in DWG format. The procedure to use this tool is discussed next.

- Click on the **Output DWG** tool from **OUTPUT** drop-down in the **Toolbar**; refer to Figure-113. The **Output DWG** dialog box will be displayed to save the file; refer to Figure-114.

Figure-113. Output DWG tool

Figure-114. Output DWG dialog box for saving the file

- Select the desired location to save the file.
- After specifying the parameter, click on the **Save** button from **Output DWG** dialog box to save the file.

GENERATING CSV FILE

The **Output CSV** tool is used to create the output of the current file in CSV format. CSV is a format used by database management software. The procedure to use this tool is discussed next.

- Click on the **Output CSV** tool from **OUTPUT** drop-down in the **Toolbar**; refer to Figure-115. The **Output Table** dialog box will be displayed; refer to Figure-116.

Figure-115. Output CSV tool

Figure-116. Output Parts List or Table dialog box

- Select the location of file and enter the desired name in **File Name** edit box.
- After specifying the parameters, click on the **Save** button to save the file.

PRACTICAL 1

Generating part drawing for the model as shown in Figure-117.

Figure-117. Practical 1 Drawing

Starting a New Drawing using Part

- Set the parameters as shown in Figure-118 for preference.

Figure-118. Specifying drawing preferences

- Open the model file for Practical 1 of Chapter 11 in the resource kit. The model will be displayed in the canvas.
- Click on the **From Design** option from **New Drawing** cascading menu of the **File** menu; refer to Figure-119. The **CREATE DRAWING** dialog box will be displayed.

Figure-119. Starting new drawing

- Make sure **ASME** is selected in the **Standard** drop-down and click on the **OK** button. The **DRAWING VIEW** dialog box will be displayed with preview of drawing view; refer to Figure-120.

Figure-120. Preview of drawing view

Placing Views

- Select the **Top** option from the **Orientation** drop-down, **Visible and Hidden Edges** button from **Style** section, and **1:1** in **Scale** drop-down from the dialog box.
- Click at desired location to place the view; refer to Figure-121.

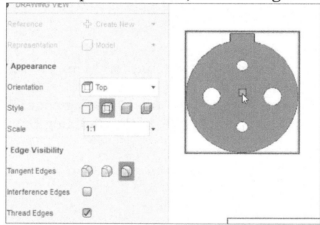
Figure-121. Placing base view

- Click on the **OK** button from the dialog box to create the view.
- Click on the **Projected View** tool from the **DRAWING VIEWS** panel in the **Toolbar**. You will be asked to select the base view.
- Select the view earlier placed and move the cursor towards right. The view will get attached to the cursor; refer to Figure-122.

Figure-122. Projected view attached to cursor

- Click at desired location to place the view and press **ESC** to exit.

Applying Annotations

- Click on the **Center Mark Pattern** tool from the **GEOMETRY** drop-down in the **Toolbar**. The **CENTER MARK PATTERN** dialog box will be displayed.
- Click on one of the holes in the base view and select the **Center Mark** check box. The preview of center mark pattern will be displayed; refer to Figure-123.

Figure-123. Preview of center mark pattern

- Click on the **OK** button from the dialog box.
- Click on the **Dimension** tool from the **DIMENSIONS** panel in the **Toolbar** and apply dimensions as shown in Figure-124.

Figure-124. Applying dimensions

- Click on the **Datum Identifier** tool from the **SYMBOLS** panel in the **Toolbar** and place the datum identifiers as shown in Figure-125.

Figure-125. Applying datum identifier

Adding Tolerances to Dimension

• Double-click on the dimension with **10** value. The **DIMENSION** dialog box will be displayed; refer to Figure-126.

Figure-126. DIMENSION dialog box

• Select the **Symmetrical** option from the **Type** drop-down in **Tolerance** node of dialog box and specify the value as **1** in **Tolerance** edit box. Click on the **Close** button to exit the dialog box.

• Similarly, set the tolerances for other dimensions; refer to Figure-127.

Figure-127. Applying tolerances

• Click on the **Feature Control Frame** tool from the **SYMBOLS** panel in the **Toolbar** and select the hole of diameter **6**. The control frame will get attached to cursor.

• Click at desired location to place the control frame and press **ENTER**. The **FEATURE CONTROL FRAME** dialog box will be displayed; refer to Figure-128.

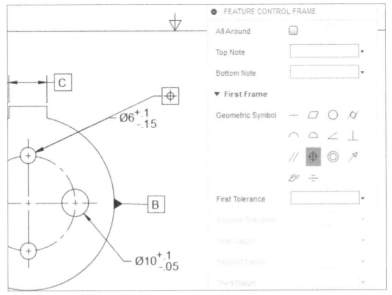

Figure-128. Placing feature control frame

• Specify the parameters as shown in Figure-129 and click on the **Close** button.

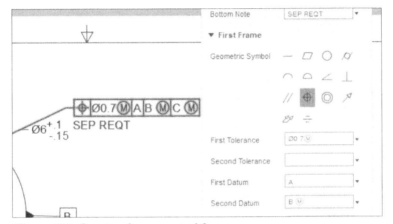

Figure-129. Creating feature control frame

Similarly, define position feature control frame for other hole and place another base view as 3D NE Isometric view; refer to Figure-130.

Figure-130. Completed drawing

SELF ASSESSMENT

Q1. The .... tool is used to create drawing views generated from an existing base or drawing view.

Q2. What is the difference between **ASME** and **ISO** option in **CREATE DRAWING** dialog box?

Q3. In which view of drawing, hatching is automatically created?

Q4. Text can be aligned by Justification section. (T/F)

Q5. The drawing view can be move from one place to another with the help of Move button. (T/F)

Q6. What is the use of Edge extension tool?

Q7. Two parallel edges should be selected to create the extension. (T/F)

Q8. When is the baseline dimensioning required?

Q9. What is Feature Control Frame?

Q10. What is the use of Datum Identifier tool?

Q11. The .... tool is used to create an output file of drawing in DWG format.

Index

Ethics of an Engineer

- Engineers shall hold paramount the safety, health and welfare of the public and shall strive to comply with the principles of sustainable development in the performance of their professional duties.

- Engineers shall perform services only in areas of their competence.

- Engineers shall issue public statements only in an objective and truthful manner.

- Engineers shall act in professional manners for each employer or client as faithful agents or trustees, and shall avoid conflicts of interest.

- Engineers shall build their professional reputation on the merit of their services and shall not compete unfairly with others.

- Engineers shall act in such a manner as to uphold and enhance the honor, integrity, and dignity of the engineering profession and shall act with zero-tolerance for bribery, fraud, and corruption.

- Engineers shall continue their professional development throughout their careers, and shall provide opportunities for the professional development of those engineers under their supervision.

OTHER BOOKS BY CADCAMCAE WORKS

Autodesk Inventor 2020 Black Book

Autodesk Fusion 360 Black Book (V 2.0.6508)

AutoCAD Electrical 2017 Black Book
AutoCAD Electrical 2018 Black Book
AutoCAD Electrical 2020 Black Book

SolidWorks 2017 Black Book
SolidWorks 2018 Black Book
SolidWorks 2019 Black Book

SolidWorks Simulation 2017 Black Book
SolidWorks Simulation 2018 Black Book
SolidWorks Simulation 2019 Black Book

SolidWorks Electrical 2017 Black Book
SolidWorks Electrical 2018 Black Book
SolidWorks Electrical 2019 Black Book

SolidWorks Flow Simulation 2019 Black Book

Mastercam X7 for SolidWorks 2014 Black Book
Mastercam 2017 for SolidWorks Black Book

Creo Parametric 5.0 Black Book
Creo Parametric 6.0 Black Book

Creo Manufacturing 4.0 Black Book

Basics of Autodesk Nastran In-CAD 2018

ETABS 2016 Black Book

Autodesk Revit 2020 Black Book

Autodesk CFD 2018 Black Book

Made in the USA
Monee, IL
03 January 2020